Opening Standards

The Information Society Series
Laura DeNardis and Michael Zimmer, Series Editors

Jonathan Band and Masanobu Katoh
Interfaces on Trial 2.0

Laura DeNardis, editor
Opening Standards: The Global Politics of Interoperability

Opening Standards

The Global Politics of Interoperability

Laura DeNardis, editor

The MIT Press
Cambridge, Massachusetts
London, England

For information about special quantity discounts, please email special_sales@mitpress.mit.edu

This book was set in Stone Sans and Stone Serif by Toppan Best-set Premedia Limited. Printed and bound in the United States of America.

Library of Congress Cataloging-in-Publication Data

Opening standards : the global politics of interoperability / edited by Laura DeNardis.
    p. cm.—(The information society series)
Includes bibliographical references and index.
ISBN 978-0-262-01602-5 (alk. paper)
1. Computer networks—Standards—Government policy. 2. Computer networks—Standards—Political aspects. 3. Computer networks—Standards—Economic aspects. 4. Internetworking (Telecommunication)—Technological innovations.
I. DeNardis, Laura, 1966–
TK5105.55.O65   2011
004.6′2—dc22
                          2011001928

10 9 8 7 6 5 4 3 2 1

Contents

Introduction: Global Controversies over Open Standards

Laura DeNardis

The candlelight vigil in front of the town hall in Bangalore, India, brought together young engineering students and information technology professionals along with an eclectic collection of Bangalore residents. One protester was reportedly a Bangalore scrap dealer whose business relied on a computer center in a local slum.[1] The purpose of the vigil, organized by a free software users group in India, was to protest the passage of a technical standard—OOXML, or Open Office eXtensible Markup Language—by the International Organization for Standardization (ISO). The protesters hoped to pressure the Indian government into filing an appeal over the passage of this standard. The controversy involved document file formats, or the standards underlying word processing documents, spreadsheets, and presentations. These standards establish common rules for structuring information contained within documents so they can be created and exchanged by any application adhering to the standards.

Politically charged controversies over document standards date back to at least 2004, when the Commonwealth of Massachusetts in the United States included a standard called Open Document Format (ODF) in a list of that state's required technical standards for new government information technology procurements. ODF was an openly published standard that could be implemented in products on a royalty-free basis. This open approach was consistent with the traditional openness of the Internet's underlying protocols but was a departure from the historically dominant approach to office applications—such as the Microsoft Office applications then based on closed specifications for text, spreadsheet, and presentation documents. These formatting structures have traditionally been proprietary unpublished specifications that are not available for other companies to use to create competing and interoperable products. One of the cited rationales for the initial Massachusetts standards policy was the concern about public documents stored in a format dependent upon a single corporation.

In one memorable statement, a public official stressed that it was a basic democratic imperative for public documents to not be locked into proprietary formats that might be inaccessible or unreadable in the future or subject to licenses that restrict access to public information. At the time, Microsoft was in the process of introducing a new version of its Office suite, OOXML, based on an XML document standard rather than proprietary binary formats. There have been many controversies since the introduction of OOXML and ODF including the question of what constitutes an open standard, what procedures are necessary to develop an open standard, what the appropriate role of governments should be in promoting open standards through procurement and other policies, as well as a host of other questions.[2]

Global controversies over document standards typify some characteristics of standards debates. Standards design and selection issues are sometimes as much about competitive battles among dominant information technology companies (e.g., Microsoft, Google, IBM, Oracle) and about social values (e.g., public access to government documents) as they are about questions of technical efficiency and interoperability. The document-standards debate also demonstrates how the question "What counts as an open standard?" can be so controversial and what is at stake in the answer to this question.

OOXML and ODF are only two standards. Countless standards enable interoperability among software and hardware products made by different manufacturers; they are blueprints for developing technologies that can communicate and exchange information with other technologies based on the same specifications. Routine Internet use involves direct engagement with hundreds of standards. Most Internet users are familiar with Bluetooth, Wi-Fi standards, an array of Voice over Internet Protocol (VoIP) standards, the MP3 format for encoding and compressing audio files, and HTTP, which enables the standard exchange of information between Web browsers and Web servers. These are just a few examples of the underlying standards that are arguably the most critical component of the Internet's technical and legal architecture.

An underlying theme of this book is that technical standards not only provide technological interoperability but also produce significant political and economic externalities. Battles over standards are sometimes market conflicts between technology companies, which obviously stand to benefit if the standards they use in products gain market traction. More broadly, the degree of openness of a standard can have a direct bearing on the competitive openness and pace of innovation in the information and communication technology (ICT) industry. On one hand, standards that are openly published can contribute to innovation by creating competitive markets for technology products. Any company or entrepreneur can access an openly published standard and develop products based on this standard. Internet standards such as TCP/IP (Transmission Control Protocol/Internet Protocol) have historically been openly available, contributing to the rapid pace of Internet innovation. On the other hand, standards that are not published or have underlying intellectual property restrictions imposed on them can be used as barriers to trade in global markets.

As will be discussed in this book, standards are also political, making decisions about individual civil liberties online. For example, some of the decisions structuring the standards underlying electronic medical records will determine the extent of user privacy in emerging eHealth systems. A striking aspect of this form of policy making is that standards are established primarily by private institutions rather than elected representatives. This has raised many questions about legitimacy and the necessary degree of openness and transparency of the development process for standards that might have direct policy implications.

As will be evident throughout this book, questions about openness exist in four general areas. The first is the development process: who is permitted to participate in designing a standard or to access information about that standard's development and associated deliberations, minutes, and records? If standards development were purely a technical exercise with no political implications, then the nature of the development process would be irrelevant. If standards development sometimes involves battles among companies and decisions that have public interest implications, then the degree of procedural openness and transparency is a relevant concern.

The second area, implementation, raises questions about the degree of a standard's openness in its implementation, meaning whether the standard itself is published, whether the standard can be accessed for free or for some fee, and to what extent the standard has underlying intellectual property restrictions on its implementation in products.

The third area, standards use, considers how standards influence product competition and user choice of technologies. Are there multiple competing products based on a particular standard and do users have product choices? And the fourth area, concerning government involvement in standardization, raises a final set of questions about the appropriate role, if any, of governments in promoting open standards. A recent global phenomenon has been the emergence of government policies establishing technology procurement policies based on open standards to promote the overall economic innovation, interoperability, and user choice that can result from open standards.[3]

In the context of this political momentum and ongoing industry debates about what counts as an open standard, even the meaning of such terms like "openness" and "interoperability" are highly contentious. *Opening Standards* brings together scholars and practitioners from a variety of perspectives to explain the debates about openness and interoperability in standards, to identify emerging problems, and to make normative recommendations about open standards. *Opening Standards* takes an interdisciplinary approach to addressing subject matter directly pertinent to current questions and controversies in information and communication technology policy. The book is organized into fourteen chapters grouped into four parts: (1) The Politics of Interoperability; (2) Standards, Innovation, and Development Economics; (3) Standards-Based Intellectual Property Debates; and (4) Interoperability and Openness.

Part I addresses some of the political questions about open standards and interoperability. Questions posed to authors included the following. In what ways do the technical decisions made by standards-setting organizations establish public policy and to what extent is the openness of a standard relevant to this form of policy making? How can standards processes reflect the public interest ? What is the appropriate responsibility, if any, of national governments and international bodies toward promoting open standards through such means as procurement, regulatory intervention and oversight, or standards development?

In chapter 1, John Morris, the general counsel of the Center for Democracy & Technology (CDT) in Washington, D.C., provides concrete examples of how technical design choices have enduring implications for public policy and individual rights. His chapter, "Injecting the Public Interest into Internet Standards," provides specific examples of how private standards bodies operating outside of traditional structures of government and public accountability make policy choices. Morris then examines ways in which the public interest can realistically enter this process.

Another issue at the intersection of politics and technical standards is the role governments should play in influencing standards development or adoption. In chapter 2, "The Government at the Standards Bazaar," Stacy Baird questions the extent to which it is appropriate for governments to intervene by mandating information technology standards. Baird argues that governments should be extremely reluctant to intervene in standards market activity and should be cautious when considering any type of standards adoption mandates.

In contrast to Baird's account, D. Linda Garcia of Georgetown University challenges assumptions that responsibility for setting standards lies squarely with the private sector. In chapter 3, "Governments, the Public Interest, and Standards Setting," Garcia describes how, regarding standards, the market does not necessarily produce efficient results and describes reasons (e.g., national economic health, national security, property rights) governments might have an interest in standards, whether as a rule maker, an enforcer and adjudicator, an educator, a broker, a subsidizer, a regulator, a consumer, or a developer.

Chapter 4 offers a specific case study about the politics of a single Internet protocol (standard) known as DNS Security Extensions (DNSSEC). In "Securing the Root," Internet governance scholars Brenden Kuerbis and Milton Mueller address the global policy problem of managing the root zone file of the Domain Name System (DNS). The Internet's root must be coordinated in order for the Internet to provide global interoperability. The question of who should have authority over the root zone file has historically been a divisive issue concerning the global Internet. At the same time, most people agree that the Internet should be made more secure and the DNSSEC protocol was designed to do this. To implement this protocol, the DNS root zone had to be revised, providing an opportunity to rethink and revise U.S. government control over the root zone file. This chapter describes how, despite DNSSEC being an openly developed standard, the U.S. government used the implementation of this standard to further entrench its authority over the Internet's domain name system.

Chapter 5, "Open Document Standards for Government: The South African Experience," written by South African scholar Andrew Rens, recounts the challenges involved in framing South Africa's open standards policies. South Africa was one of a number of developing countries that introduced a national framework for adopting and preferring open standards within public sector technology infrastructures. Rens describes the South African standards policy, including the requirement to use ODF, as well as South Africa's experience of ISO's adoption of OOXML. Rens provides a critique of the ISO standards-setting process and raises questions about the difference between a standard labeled "open" by a standards body and the ability of that standard to actually meet a government's objectives for an open standard.

Part II, Standards, Innovation, and Development Economics, examines the issue of open standards through a lens of economic theory and international relations, addressing the intersection between standards, competition, innovation policy, and global trade. In chapter 6, "An Economic Basis for Open Standards," economist Rishab Ghosh argues that open standards can be defined by the beneficial economic effect of ensuring full competition among suppliers of a technology. These competing suppliers, argues Ghosh, should have the equal ability to implement the standard. Ghosh also makes the case that public procurement should support open standards to help promote competitive markets for software products; that these policies should exclude compatibility with proprietary technologies as a requirement; and that open standards should be mandatory in the case of electronic government services and preferred in other public software procurement.

In chapter 7, "Open Innovation and Interoperability," Nicos L. Tsilas, Microsoft's senior director of interoperability and intellectual property policy, stresses the importance of a balanced definition of open standards that encourages intellectual property rights holders and implementers to collaborate and innovate. Tsilas describes an industry shift from closed to open innovation models that rely on external ideas and collaboration. This model, Tsilas suggests, is actually enabled by strong intellectual property incentives and protection systems and should distinguish between "people interoperability" and "technical interoperability." Tsilas recommends a definition of open standards for standards organizations and governments, which he argues should adopt neutral procurement policies toward specific standards.

Chapter 8, "Standards, Trade, and Development," turns to the issue of standards and global trade. John S. Wilson, lead economist in the Development Economics Research Group of the World Bank, warns that increasing nontariff technical barriers to trade, such as government attempts to influence markets through technical standards, are threatening the ability of open markets and trade to reduce poverty and improve global welfare. Wilson recommends several trade measures to address the increasing problem of nontariff technical barriers to trade and suggests the formation of a "Global Standards Consortium" dedicated to addressing policy questions at the intersection of development economics, technology, and standards.

Part III, Standards-Based Intellectual Property Debates, shifts attention to the core legal question underlying technical standards. Intellectual property rights are at the heart of controversies and key decision criteria about what constitutes an open standard. The numerous organizations setting technical standards for information exchange have divergent policies about such questions as whether standards should be royalty-free or available based on so-called reasonable and nondiscriminatory (RAND) terms and whether members are compelled to disclose patents and other intellectual property rights relevant to the implementation of a standard. Part III examines questions such as whether standards organizations should be able to "own" standards; whether standards should be eligible for copyright protection; what the key issues and concerns are over whether standards are royalty-free or available on a RAND basis (and what exactly does RAND even mean?); whether it is necessary to have one approach to intellectual property rights in standards; and in what ways patents, including nondisclosed patents, inhibit rather than promote innovation and competition.

In chapter 9, "Questioning Copyright in Standards," Pamela Samuelson, professor of law and information management at the University of California at Berkeley, explains how copyright has become a prominent concern in intellectual property rights debates in standards. Standards-setting organizations increasingly charge fees to those wishing to access and use a standard, such as ISO's policy that would have mandated annual fees for developers or information providers using standard Web country codes. Samuelson lays out case law and policy considerations related to copyright protection and standards, assesses whether standards organizations need copyright as an incentive, and identifies concerns about allowing standards institutions to own standards, especially when the standard is legally required.

Chapter 10 provides a historical case study of the intellectual property questions that arise in standards-setting institutions. In "Constructing Legitimacy: The W3C's Patent Policy," historian of technology Andrew L. Russell provides an account of a controversial policy flashpoint in the history of the World Wide Web Consortium's (W3C) patent policy. Russell starts with the assumption that the "Web became world wide because its standards were open." He describes a 2001 W3C recommendation to incorporate patents into Web standards and provides an account of the ensuing controversy and grassroots alarm. The W3C ultimately adopted a royalty-free patent policy and Russell explores this decision within broader historical questions about the relationship between standards and institutional power and legitimacy and possibilities for democratic control over technology.

In chapter 11, "Common and Uncommon Knowledge: Reducing Conflict between Standards and Patents," standards expert Brian Kahin identifies current problems with patents and standards including patent thickets, lowered thresholds for patent grants, and undisclosed patents. Kahin explains the inherent tension in the melding of standards and patents in that the value of patents is in exclusivity and "uncommon" knowledge and the value of standards is in ubiquity and "common" knowledge.

As parts I, II, and III will illustrate, attempts to define "openness" in standards is a controversial and difficult exercise. While previous chapters examine openness in various contexts, part IV, Interoperability and Openness, shifts more specifically to the question of how to define an open standard. Part IV begins with a summary of the problems to which open standards could respond. In chapter 12, "ICT Standards Setting Today: A System under Stress," Andrew Updegrove explains how the standards development infrastructure, with its nineteenth-century roots, is incapable of meeting today's requirements for universal and fast-paced ICT standards. Updegrove summarizes these shortcomings, describes ensuing societal implications, and surveys some possible political interventions to alleviate these problems.

In chapter 13, "Software Standards, Openness, and Interoperability," Robert S. Sutor, IBM's vice president of open systems, proposes definitions of a standard and an open standard and explains how these relate to interoperability. Sutor does not view open standards as a binary complement of proprietary standards but instead acknowledges a spectrum from completely closed to completely open. Sutor suggests that the openness of a standard can be assessed based on criteria related to procedural transparency, community, democracy, costs, freedoms and permissions, and restrictions. Sutor describes how the word "interoperability" is often misused by market interests and proposes a framework for defining software interoperability.

The final chapter of *Opening Standards* is "Open Standards: Definition and Policy." In chapter 14, Ken Krechmer lays out a framework for understanding various perspectives on the definition of open standards. Definitions vary based on interest groups including standards-setting organizations, commercial implementers, end users, economists, and the legal profession. Krechmer chooses not to treat governments as independent interests but as representative of a mixture of other viewpoints. Within this framework, Krechmer suggests ten requirements for open standards: open meeting, consensus, due process, one world, open intellectual property rights, open change, open documents, open interface, open access, and ongoing support.

In bringing together such diverse and interdisciplinary views on standardization, *Opening Standards* lays out what is at stake in open standards policies and definitions and develops some important themes. First, technical standards carry significant political and economic implications as well as providing technical interoperability and should be viewed as an integral part of information policy. Second, conflicts over standards development and adoption fit into broader economic, cultural, legal, and political tensions within the context of international Internet governance debates and Internet globalization. Finally, *Opening Standards* makes clear that, despite the historical traditions of the Internet, openness is not a given but must be defined and promoted in an information society in which technical standards increasingly control the pace of innovation, the extent of freedom online, and access to knowledge.

Notes

1. For pictures and more information, see "Cutting Through the Digital Divide," *The Hindu*, online edition, April 15, 2008, <http://www.hindu.com/2008/04/16/stories/2008041650950200.htm>.

2. For an account of the OOXML and ODF evolution and controversy, see Andy Updegrove, "ODF vs. OOXML: War of the Words (an eBook in Process)," November 25, 2007, <http://www.consortiuminfo.org/standardsblog/article.php?story=20071125145159900>.

3. See Laura DeNardis, "E-Governance Policies for Interoperability and Open Standards," *Policy & Internet* 2, no. 3 (2010), <http://www.psocommons.org/policyandinternet/vol2/iss3/art6/>.

I The Politics of Interoperability

1 Injecting the Public Interest into Internet Standards

John B. Morris Jr.

It is said that on the Internet, "code is law."[1] Seemingly narrow technical choices can have broad and lasting impacts on public policy and individual rights. These technical decisions are primarily made in the private bodies that set the technical standards for the Internet—such as the Internet Engineering Task Force (IETF), the World Wide Web Consortium (W3C), and a growing number of smaller standards bodies and industry consortia. These key standards bodies operate largely outside of the public eye and with little input from public interest groups or public policy makers. How then can the public's interest in an open, decentralized, global Internet be represented in these venues of Internet design?

For information and communication technology (ICT) standards resulting from these private processes to meet any comprehensive definition of "openness," standards developers must consider and address public policy concerns raised by their work, and should reflect the effective and considered input of public policy experts. Even if a technical standard that impacts a public concern is made freely available to all technology designers, it cannot be considered to be "open" unless it was developed with an effective opportunity for public input. As more and more public policy decisions shift away from legislatures and regulatory agencies and to private standards bodies, the necessary public policy analysis must also shift into the standards processes.

This chapter looks at the need to ensure that public policy concerns are appropriately considered within the standards bodies. To ensure that the Internet continues to develop with positive public policy impacts, there must be greater public interest participation in the standards processes, and the standards bodies themselves must move toward new procedures to consider and address the public interest. Both government and industry leaders should actively support the development of tools for public policy impact assessment.

Standards and the Internet: Essential Foundation and Critical Impacts

The Internet itself is built upon common technical standards. At its most fundamental level, the very idea of the Internet is based on standards: that distant and disparate computers and computer networks can communicate with each other if they all use the same agreed-upon protocol with which to send messages. Following this idea, computers made by different manufacturers using different software and operating systems can exchange messages because they all follow the same set of rules for messages sent between computers or between networks. One of the core standards enabling such "inter-network" messages is the Internet Protocol (or IP).

Moreover, on top of the standardized protocols that allow computers to talk to other computers are standards that allow specific programs to exchange information with similar programs on other computers. Email is an easy example of such standards—email standards, for example, specify that the "To" and "From" email addresses must be placed in specific places within a message, and standards also specify where in a message the "Subject" and the content of the email will be placed. Almost all other common ways to communicate over the Internet—by instant messaging (IM), Voice over Internet Protocol (VoIP), or using the World Wide Web— are based on agreed upon technical standards.

Email also provides an example of how technical decisions about standards can directly impact public policy concerns and questions. When the email standards were first created, the designers decided to allow the content of the email to be sent in unencrypted form, so that anyone who intercepts a message can read its content. A different possible approach to email could have required that all email messages be encrypted, and had that path been taken, emails would be more secure than the average email is today. To be sure, there are significant *technical* pros and cons raised by the question of whether to encrypt all email, but equally to be sure this decision *also* raises significant *public policy* pros and cons. The point is not to argue that email "should" or "should not" be encrypted, but that the technical design decision about whether or not email should be encrypted by default has important public policy ramifications—and those ramifications should be considered in the design process.

Beyond the example of email, there are a variety of instances in which technical design decisions in standards had (or had the potential to have) concrete and harmful impacts on public policy concerns:

• *IPv6 and Privacy* The development by the IETF of Internet Protocol Version 6 (IPv6) shows the impact of design on policy, in this case with regard to the systems of numeric addressing that are used on the Internet. All Internet users have—while they are online—a numeric IP address. In 1998, an IETF standard describing IPv6, a new protocol for Internet addressing, set off a major controversy about user privacy and anonymity. Under IPv4, the predecessor to IPv6, Internet addressing allowed a reasonable amount of privacy and anonymity, because the numeric IP address (such as 206.112.85.61) was typically not tied to any particular machine or user. With IPv6, however, one characteristic of the standard provided that, in many cases, a user's IP address would be derived from a unique number embedded in that user's Ethernet network card. IPv6 would therefore enable greater monitoring of users' online behavior since their IP address would be tied to a unique physical identifier.[2] Thus, for example, a particular laptop computer would be widely identifiable and traceable when it communicated online, no matter where or how the computer was connected to the Internet. The privacy implications of the new IPv6 address scheme likely were not intended or even fully recognized by its original designers—the use of a unique hardware ID was a clever and efficient technical approach to generating unique IP addresses. But once the concerns were raised, significant debate ensued both in the public policy space and among technologists. The issue was ultimately resolved by the IETF with publication of an optional addressing scheme for IPv6 that added privacy-protecting alternatives to the original design.[3]

• *OPES and Censorship*   For more than a year starting in 2000, the leadership of the IETF grappled with whether to sanction a proposed working group on Open Pluggable Edge Services (OPES). The proposed OPES protocol would permit operators of cache and other servers in the "middle" of the Internet to modify content midstream from a server to a user. While OPES would facilitate a range of useful and appropriate services, the proposal also raised significant questions about data integrity and user privacy. In particular, the original OPES proposal would have allowed a government to censor content as it traveled from Web site to user, without either end node knowing that the content had been changed or deleted. After these concerns were raised within the IETF community and by policy advocates (including the author), the IETF leadership set requirements that any work on OPES include strong protections for data integrity and privacy, and that end users be informed about any transformations made in the middle of the network.[4]

• *DOCSIS and Data Capacity*   Internet service over cable television systems, using cable modems, relies on a standardized communications protocol called DOCSIS (Data Over Cable Service Interface Specification) as the standard for transmission of Internet data over cable television networks. DOCSIS was created with virtually no public input by CableLabs, an industry consortium controlled by the cable companies. As originally designed, DOCSIS allocated only a very limited amount of capacity to Internet data service, and that capacity was heavily weighted toward downstream traffic—that is, data from the Internet to a user's computer moved far faster than information transmitted from the user to the Internet. This design limitation severely limited the ability of users to utilize any Internet services that required significant upstream data transfers, including VoIP, videoconferencing, or the operation of personal servers, and it became a significant topic of contention in the "open access" policy debates in the late 1990s. Users pushed back against this aspect of DOCSIS, and eventually the cable companies moved to eliminate the downstream bias, first in DOCSIS 1.1 (which increased the upstream data rate fourfold), in DOCSIS 2.0 (which further tripled the upstream rate), and in DOCSIS 3.0 (which dramatically increased the capacity in both directions).[5]

If public policy concerns had been considered *early* in the technical design process of these protocols (instead of either "later" or "never"), the initial technology designers might have made different technical choices— choices that furthered (or at least did not harm) the public policy goals. In some cases, there may be no technical or engineering reason to prefer a hypothetical "Approach A" over "Approach B," but there may be *policy* reasons why one approach is far better than the other. In other cases, "A" may be technically better than "B," but the public policy benefits of "B" may be so great as to lead the designers to choose "B." But if policy is not considered in the design process at all, then this type of choice may never happen.

The Need to Inject the Public Interest into Standards Development Processes

Although the public policy implications of a proposed technical standard are sometimes wholly overlooked, at other times policy concerns do arise and are considered within standards processes—but they most often arise on an ad hoc basis. This ad hoc approach presents at least two major problems: a lack of systematic analysis of public policy issues, and a lack of "public" or other outside input into the analysis that does take place.

Although many technologists within the leading standards bodies are concerned about policy issues, few have explicit expertise in policy making or at interpreting the public interest. Standards organizations typically (and appropriately) have emphasized technical goals over broad societal ones, but in the Internet's early history there was a significant overlap between the two. Openness, accessibility, anonymity, and robustness were all technical features of the network that became public values as well.

Additionally, since the Internet in its early days was quite small, the pressure for explicit analysis of public policy concerns was minimal— policy impacts deriving from technical choices would affect just a few people in a fairly homogeneous (albeit worldwide) community. The Internet's population and diversity of uses have grown enormously since the early days of the network, and technical design decisions now directly affect the online experiences and options of hundreds of millions of users around the world. Although many past standards were consistent with the public's interest in a robust and flexible new mode of communication, there is no assurance that this consistency will continue.

Moreover, the risk of divergence has been significantly heightened by the commercialization of the Internet. The introduction in the early 1990s of commercial traffic to the Internet began an influx of private interests to a standards community that had been largely research oriented. The subsequent explosion in commercial use of the Internet prefigured a significant increase in privately motivated participants in the standards process. This in turn has subtly changed Internet standards making. While most private sector participants make high-quality contributions to standards, the extent to which participants can be expected to agree about the network's architecture is diminished because of diverging market interests. And because of these changes, there is a growing risk that the public interest in standards could fade into the background of discussion among private interests. There is thus a need to take steps to inject public policy considerations into standards development.

To be most effective, consideration of policy issues must happen *early* in the design process. Development of a standard often takes between eighteen and thirty-six months (or more), and marketplace deployment may be months later. If policy concerns are not raised until after a standard is finalized, or after products are deployed, the chance of constructive change is very low. Legislative or regulatory fiat cannot inject into a service or product technical capabilities that were not designed in the first place, and can often at best only restart a lengthy standards design process. In many cases, postdesign regulation is powerless to put a harmful technological genie back in the bottle. To avoid these results, early consideration of public policy concerns is essential.

Importantly, consideration within a standards body of public policy concerns should ideally involve public interest advocates or experts, rather than simply relying on the engineers and other technical contributors to the standards process. A number of factors call for input by those with policy experience:

• Public policy concerns can be subtle, and some concerns may be overlooked entirely without direct public policy consideration of a technical proposal.

• Even when a policy issue is identified by technical participants, its resolution may require an added level of experience with the issue to be able to evaluate the gravity of the policy threat and the sufficiency of proposed solutions.

• Increasingly, private and commercial agendas are being pursued within technical standards bodies (attempting, for example, to push a technology through quickly without addressing inconveniences such as privacy considerations), and public concerns will be overlooked or inadequately addressed without participants whose primary agenda is the public interest.

For these and other reasons, it is vital that public interest advocates be involved in the work of Internet technical standards-setting bodies.

Challenges and Successes in Raising Policy Concerns in Technical Standards Bodies

Although highly desirable, sustained participation by public policy advocates in standards development work is hard to achieve. To attempt to address this need, in 2001 the Center for Democracy & Technology ("CDT") started its Internet Standards, Technology & Policy Project. CDT focused its attention on the IETF and, to a lesser extent, the W3C. The Project has had significant success in working within the standards bodies, but its work has highlighted a number of the serious obstacles to sustained public interest involvement in standards development efforts. The challenges to such involvement include the following:

• The technical standards-setting bodies are a radically different type of venue from the traditional legislative and regulatory arena in which public interest advocates have historically worked, and the traditional approaches used by public interest advocates do not easily translate to the technical forums of the standards bodies.

• Ongoing and active participation in a standards working group requires a very significant commitment of time (often estimated to require a base-line of approximately 20 percent of an individual's time to participate in a single working group).

• Effective public advocacy within the technical standards bodies requires the right mix of technical knowledge (or ability to learn) with public policy experience, which somewhat limits the pool of possible advocates.

• The time horizons for standards development efforts is very long, and may be too long to garner the dedicated attention of many public interest organizations or their funders, both of which are often balancing scarce resources and immediate policy crises.

• Many standards bodies have an institutional or cultural resistance to addressing public policy issues, often based on past unproductive experiences with public policy advocates who failed to tailor their message to the forum.

• The sheer size, number, and diversity of technical standards-setting bodies means that public interest advocates will not be able to "cover the whole waterfront" of standards bodies—there simply are too many standards bodies, consortia, and working groups for the public interest community to cover.

Notwithstanding these obstacles to public policy participation, such efforts can be effective. In some cases, public policy input has been a part of a technical design effort from its inception. In 1997, the W3C undertook to develop the Platform for Privacy Preferences (P3P) as a specification that enables Web sites to express—in a machine-readable way—their practices with regard to users' personally identifiable information. Numerous members of the public advocacy community and Internet industry partici-pated actively in P3P's development, providing extensive input into the vocabulary P3P uses to describe all the various practices and implications for personally identifiable information. Public interest participation proved to be a critical element of the P3P development process.[6]

In other cases, public interest advocates have injected themselves into existing standards discussions to raise issues of public concern. In debates within the IETF concerning IPv6 and OPES discussed earlier in this chapter, the input of public policy advocates helped to crystallize the policy issues raised by the technical proposals, and made clear to the technical com-munity that these concerns were significant.[7]

In another interaction with the IETF, public policy advocates have played a major role in the development of a protocol for privacy protection in location-tracking and location-dependent services. Working within the "GeoPriv" working group, public policy advocates pushed the IETF to include strong protections for privacy in any transmission that sends location information. Although GeoPriv remains a "work in progress," the effort demonstrates the potential for cooperation between standards technologists and the privacy community.[8]

Standards Bodies Should Work to Develop Procedures to Identify Policy Concerns

From a public policy perspective, the key question is how to obtain an outcome in the standards design process that appropriately balances both technical/engineering considerations *and* public policy concerns. To be considered an open standard—taking a robust view of "openness"—a standard should have undergone a process in which public policy issues are first identified, and then addressed.

As discussed, the effort to obtain a desirable outcome may require the active participation of public policy advocates in the standards design process. But an even more difficult threshold question is how design efforts that might impact public policy can even be identified in the first place. Both the standards development and public interest communities should collaborate to ensure that policy concerns are identified at an early stage of the design process. Even the direct recognition of a potential policy impact alone is likely to improve the handling of the policy concern.

A system of "public policy impact assessments" could form the foundation of a strategy for standards bodies to identify and address public policy impacts. The core idea is fairly simple—that technical standards-setting bodies should develop a procedure for a relatively brief but focused assessment of new technology proposals to identify whether public policy concerns might be affected. Ideally, members within the standards community could execute the initial assessment, without necessarily involving a public policy expert or advocate. The key purpose of such a public policy impact assessment would be to identify policy concerns early in the design process, not to indicate how those concerns should be addressed.

To achieve these goals, the public policy impact assessment must be one that examines technical design issues from the perspective of the technology designer, not the public policy advocate. In other words, the assessment must be in terms that are well understood by the community of technologists in the standards body. For example, the process of assessing potential public policy impacts should not simply ask questions like "does this technology harm privacy?" Instead, the assessment process should break the technology down into components that are known to raise privacy risks. Questions that would be more appropriate and constructive include "does this technology expose information about an end user to a third party?" or "does this technology permit the retention of information about an end user?" To develop an effective system of public policy impact assessments, abstract public policy concerns must be broken into concrete and familiar technological elements that can be evaluated.

Because of the great diversity of standards bodies (in terms of their focus, structure, and procedures), a single one-size-fits-all (or even one-size-fits-most) public policy impact assessment process may not be effective. Different standards bodies deal with different types of technologies, and thus the public policy issues most likely to arise within each standards body will be different. Similarly, the structure and procedures of different standards bodies may suggest quite different procedural options for actually implementing a public policy impact assessment process.

Conclusion

In the complex and rapidly evolving world of ICT standards, technical decisions can have lasting public policy consequences, but are often made without full appreciation of those consequences. Significant social benefits can arise from consideration of those policy impacts early in the technical standards development process—and well before products are actually produced and are difficult or impossible to change.

Engagement by policy experts or public interest advocates is the critical first step toward identifying and addressing public policy concerns raised in standards processes. But, while such engagement is essential to address policy concerns, it does not scale well today across the large number of Internet and ICT standards efforts. Rather, more systemic approaches to raising awareness about policy implications are also needed. A public policy impact assessment process could be a useful tool for many Internet standards bodies, especially where public policy issues are not a central focus or where strong public interest involvement does not already take place. In many cases, routinely asking a set of critical policy impact questions could go a long way toward identifying and addressing potential policy consequences early in the technology development life cycle.

Ultimately, both greater public advocate involvement in standards development and evolution of the standards processes themselves can together ensure that issues of public policy concern are recognized and addressed as the Internet continues to evolve—and addressed without the need for governmental control of, or intervention into, the technical design processes. By ensuring that public policy concerns are appropriately considered, technologists and policy advocates can ensure that the Internet will continue to be the most democratically empowering mode of communication ever developed.

Using a robust definition of "open standards," the standards development process must be "open" to the identification and consideration of public policy concerns. Standards that are guided solely by technical merit to the exclusion of policy considerations cannot be considered to be open in their creation.

Notes

1. See Lawrence Lessig, *Code and Other Laws of Cyberspace, Version 2.0* (New York: Basic Books, 2006).

2. See Matt Crawford, "Transmission of IPv6 Packets over Ethernet Networks," RFC 2464, December 1998.

3. See Thomas Narten and Richard Draves, "Privacy Extensions for Stateless Address Autoconfiguration in IPv6," RFC 3041, January 2001.

4. See Sally Floyd and Leslie Daigle, "IAB Architectural and Policy Considerations for Open Pluggable Edge Services," RFC 3238, January 2002.

5. See Robert Fanfelle, "DOCSIS 2.0: Upping Upstream Performance in Cable Modem Designs," *EE Times*, June 17, 2002, <http://www.eetimes.com/electronics-news/4142445/DOCSIS-2-0-Upping-Upstream-Performance-in-Cable-Modem-Designs>; see also "CableLabs Issues DOCSIS 3.0 Specifications Enabling 160 Mbps," August 7, 2006, <http://www.cablelabs.com/news/pr/2006/06_pr_docsis30_080706.html>.

6. See Lorrie Cranor, "The Role of Privacy Advocates and Data Protection Authorities in the Design and Deployment of the Platform for Privacy Preferences," 2002, <http://www.cfp2002.org/proceedings/proceedings/cranor.pdf>.

7. See, e.g., "CDT Comments on OPES" submitted to the IETF OPES mailing list, August 9, 2001, <http://www.imc.org/ietf-openproxy/mail-archive/msg00827.html>.

8. See John B. Morris Jr. and Jon Peterson, "Who's Watching You Now?" *IEEE Security and Privacy Magazine* 5, no. 1 (January/February 2007), <http://www.cdt.org/publications/20070100ieee.pdf>.

2 The Government at the Standards Bazaar

Stacy Baird

In recent years, there has been heightened interest in having a state or national government intervene in the information technology standards-setting process to mandate a particular standard.[1] The information technologies industries are in an extremely competitive commercial environment, one that relies on interoperability among increasingly heterogeneous products and services. Simultaneously, the question of technical interoperability has vexed governments in undertaking some of their traditional responsibilities. The high demand for interoperability is in turn creating an environment wherein stakeholders are more likely to turn to government to intervene in the market to aid in achieving particular goals more rapidly than may occur in the natural course of market activity, or to accelerate the advancement of one technological solution, business model, or corporate venture over another.

Technical interoperability may be achieved in a number of ways, through intellectual property licensing and cross-licensing, relatively simple technical means (for instance, in information technologies and consumer electronics, converters and translators are commonplace in both software and hardware); through industry collaboration with companies working to facilitate interoperability among their products; through a company designing its product to interoperate with the products of other companies; and through consulting services that facilitate interoperability among otherwise noninteroperable technologies. Interoperability between modern technologies is often a far simpler task than during previous eras when inventors were limited by physical characteristics and mechanical interactions. This said, I will be focusing on standards and standards setting, as standards have been the focal point for government action and significantly, an integral part of some commercial competitive strategies. The question of whether the government should mandate a particular information technology standard has arisen in several contexts, including entertainment content protection (e.g., standardized copy protection measures such as the broadcast flag, digital rights management, etc.), access to government services (e.g., state government requirement of the open-standard or open-source code formats for all government documents), and efforts to achieve greater interoperability for data exchange in the areas of law enforcement, national security, and healthcare. This article describes substantial rationale for government to be reluctant to mandate an information technology standard.

Basis for Government Reluctance in Mandating Information Technology Standards

There are four key arguments that support the view that government should be reluctant to mandate an information technology standard. The first is that the information technology industries are generally sophisticated and well structured to develop standards. The second is that U.S. law and public policy guides government, particularly the U.S. federal government, to a preference for market-developed standards. Third, trade agreements and national goals for international trade and economic development argue against governments setting technology standards that may impact international trade. The fourth factor is that there is a high risk of government failure, or "non-market failure."

The Relevant Industries Are Well Structured to Develop Standards

One of the first set of factors for the government in analyzing an apparent market failure is to consider how sophisticated the market participants are and how well developed the market is. In the context of standards development, the questions to consider might be: is the industry mature; are the participants sophisticated in their ability to develop standards; are there well-developed institutional structures to facilitate standards development; and so on. Each of the industries, computing and software, entertainment, consumer electronics and so forth, has a long and successful history of standards setting. Indeed, these are sophisticated participants in mature industries, experienced in developing standards. As evidence of this, there are a number of approaches and institutions, well established and newly evolving, in which these industries develop standards. Further, there are many and varied types of standards used by these industries.

Many Avenues Exist for Standards Development There are numerous forums for the development of information technology standards. The traditional courses for standards development are voluntary consensus forums including formal standards development organizations such as the Institute of Electrical and Electronics Engineers (IEEE), International Electrotechnical Commission (IEC), International Telecommunication Union (ITU), industry- or sector-specific standards-setting organizations (e.g., InterNational Committee for Information Technology Standards (INCITS), Internet Engineering Task Force (IETF), Telecommunications Industry Association (TIA), Organization for the Advancement of Structured Information Standards (OASIS), European Computer Manufacturers Association (ECMA), Association of Computing Machinery (ACM), Audio Engineering Society (AES), and Society of Motion Picture and Television Engineers (SMPTE)), and trade associations (e.g., Consumer Electronics Association (CEA) and the National Association of Broadcasters (NAB)). These forums have produced an endless list of standards, including: IEEE 802.11 (popularly known as Wi-Fi); IEEE 1394 (also known as Sony iLink or Apple Firewire high-bandwidth digital interconnect), TCP/IP Internet communications protocol (IETF), and so on. At the most formal end of standards setting in the United States are standards development organizations accredited by ANSI, the American National Standards Institute. ANSI is the only accredited U.S. entity that is a member of the International Organization for Standardization (ISO) and the International Electrotechnical Commission (IEC).

There is also a robust ecosystem for informal standards development. A now common approach to standards setting involves relevant industries or businesses developing and supporting a standard by mutual agreement through a consortium. Consortia are organizations formed by companies interested in developing a standard to serve their mutual interests. Typically, because these organizations are formed to meet the specific standards needs of the interested companies, the process can be more efficient. Consortia come in many flavors, from very informal to very formal, even having very similar processes and characteristics as a traditional standards development organization. Among the many consortia-developed standards are video standards such as VGA and SXGA analog computer display standards (VESA); digital transmission standards such as digital subscriber line, or DSL; Internet-related developer standards such as HTML (W3C), XML (W3C and OASIS), SOAP (W3C), and Synchronized Multimedia Integration Language (SMIL, W3C); and the Advanced Access Content System

Licensing Administrator (AACS LA) digital rights management for high-definition video disc standards (adopted into both HD-DVD and Blu-ray standards).

Although consortia can be less transparent or open in their processes than traditional standards-development organizations, they have an important place in the standards arena. As Oliver Smoot, then chairman of the board of ANSI, testified before Congress:

> The information technology industry does have a special challenge because it uses every kind of standardization process imaginable, ranging from the most informal meeting possible to the very formal processes that result in an American National Standard. However these challenges do not impair their ability to compete domestically or internationally. Now, even within the subset of standards development, and it is this very flexibility that makes them useful. . . . Because they meet real needs, consortia-developed standards are fully acceptable to, and widely used by, industry and the U.S. Government to procure and use advanced technologies and, in fact, to procure and use technologies of all kinds.[2]

As Gerald Ritterbusch, the director of standards for Caterpillar, observed at that same hearing:

> The IT industry needs the right mix of standards that are developed in both the formal and those that can develop through the consortia process. The IT industry has a definite need for speediness in bringing standards to the market so they can be used. Consortia provide the speed while the formal standards system, through its openness and balance, takes a little longer, but I believe that there needs to be the right mix of using both the formal and the consortia and that needs to be chosen by the users of the standards and the players in the process.[3]

Some have expressed the concern that consortia are potentially at risk of capture by the largest of industry players. Standards expert and former director of standards for Sun Microsystems, Carl Cargill, in testifying before Congress, observed, "Very rarely do you get a captive consortia that is trying to prejudice the market in its own favor. Normally, consortia benefit the entire market. That is one of the requirements."[4] In regard to mitigating the risk of antitrust issues where a standards-setting organization may have such concerns, as the FTC's David Balto observed, "where the standard setting process is dominated by users or other vertically related firms, rather than rival producers, competitive injury is unlikely. The involvement of buyers in the design of standards may reduce competitive concerns."[5]

One mechanism that is used to address complex patent licensing issues surrounding standards in an efficient manner is the "patent pool." A patent pool is the sharing, or pooling, of patent ownership interests to benefit the market at large. There is a long history of the use of patent pools in connection with the development of standards, or the adoption of a proprietary technology into a standard; the broadcasting, consumer electronics, and information technology industries have long been part of that history. Often it is the pioneers in an industry or in technical achievements that take this approach. One early example in the information technology sphere was AT&T, General Electric, and Westinghouse working together to develop standards for radio parts, spectrum management, and television transmission standards.[6] Fast forward to 1998, when Sony, Philips, and Pioneer developed the DVD-Video and DVD-ROM standard specifications, and 1999, when Hitachi, Matsushita, Time-Warner, Toshiba, and others pooled patents for DVD-compliant products. Modern computing technology standards using patent pools include MPEG, MPEG-2 AAC audio codec, DVI, and USB. The U.S. Patent and Trademark Office has clearly stated its support for patent pools, as has the Federal Trade Commission and the Department of Justice, providing guidelines for antitrust enforcement in regard to such collective rights management.

The federal government has endorsed consortia, informal multicompany standards development activities (including those that implicate patent pools), and even single-enterprise standards-setting activities as on the same footing as formal standards-setting organizations in meeting federal government requirements for "voluntary consensus standards." The National Technology Transfer and Advancement Act (NTTAA) sets out the mandate that federal government agencies use commercially developed "voluntary consensus standards" unless doing so would be against the law or otherwise impractical.[7] The revised Office of Management and Budget Circular A-119, which provides detailed guidance to federal agencies regarding this statutory mandate, is clear that standards developed by any private sector standards-setting enterprise would meet the meaning of voluntary consensus standards for the purposes of the requirements of Circular A-119. Formal standards bodies such as ANSI and ISO acknowledge the importance of the use of the full range of standards-setting forums, as well.

Finally, a standard may arise where a technology is so widely adopted by consumers or users that it becomes a de facto standard. Examples of de facto information technology standards include the Secure Digital (SD) memory card, Adobe PDF file format, Hewlett-Packard's Printer Control Language (PCL), and Sun Microsystems' Java programming language, among numerous others.

Worth noting, there are circumstances in which consumers or industry leaders embrace multiple competing standards that then coexist in the market. Some examples of widely adopted, yet competing standards include high-speed communications standards such as IEEE 802.11, USB, IEEE 1394, and DVI; the competing digital video disc formats DVD+ and DVD-; and multiple format standards for digital video (i.e., progressive, interlaced formats in various resolutions: 480p, 480i, 720p, 720i, 1080p, 1080i). In a few notable cases competition between standards has resulted in consumer confusion and a delay in consumer adoption, include the competition between Betamax and VHS, SuperAudio CD and DVD-Audio, and Blu-ray and HD DVD. On the upside, however, such market behavior results in user choice. Competing standards that survive in the market may each meet users' differing needs even potentially at the expense of true interoperability. The result may be standards-agnostic platforms (devices) or multistandard platforms that are interoperable through conversion, translators, or gateway tools (more common in regard to software as compared to hardware).

Eventually, where there is a viable commercial market (the convergence of a mature technology or standard and the conditions in which consumers are truly interested in having the products made possible by the standard), either the market formally adopts a standard or multiple, coexistent standards, or a de facto choice evolves.

Well-Developed Differing Types of Standards Reflect a Sophisticated Standards-Setting Environment   As evidence of the sophistication of the information technology standards-setting marketplace, there are numerous and highly differentiated types of market-developed standards that can achieve interoperability: open standards developed through formal standards-setting organizations; proprietary standards developed by informal standards bodies, consortia, or by individual company or groups of companies; de facto standards; or technologies that may have initially been based on a proprietary or de facto standard yet are subsequently submitted to a formal standards-setting organization and become an open standard.

The two most prominent types of standards are "open standards" and "proprietary standards." There are many definitions for the term or concept of an "open standard." I will offer the following as a guideline for comparison. An open standard is a technical specification that has the following characteristics:

a. It is developed, maintained, approved, or affirmed by rough consensus, in a voluntary private-sector (i.e., nongovernmental) standards-setting organization that is transparent in its process and open to all interested and qualified participants.

b. It is published (i.e., made available openly to the public) including specifications and supporting material providing sufficient detail to enable a complete understanding of the scope and purpose of the standard.

c. The documentation of the standard is publicly available without cost or for a reasonable fee for adoption and implementation by any interested party.

d. Any patent rights necessary to implement the standard are made available by those developing the standard to all implementers on reasonable and nondiscriminatory (RAND) terms (either with or without payment of a reasonable royalty or fee).

Well-known and widely implemented open standards include TCP/IP, HTML, HTTP, 802.11, MPEG, XML, SNMP, and SMTP.

"Proprietary standards" are technical specifications developed and maintained by a single entity or by a private, small group of cooperating entities. Standards are, by their nature, intellectual property and, thus, are potentially subject to ownership protected by copyright or patent law. Since proprietary standards are created by a small group of private parties, often working ad hoc, they are typically not subject to the formalized rules of a traditional standards-setting organization; and thus, the owners of the underlying intellectual property may control implementation of such a standard more tightly through the licensing terms. The key reason proprietary standards are developed is that working in small groups without many of the procedural issues of an open standards-setting organization (particularly issues having to do with consensus among many and the openness of the process) is more efficient, and thus, interoperable products can be developed and brought to market more quickly.

The status of a proprietary standard may change over time. Commonly, proprietary standards are developed by groups of companies working in consortia, by less formal efforts with the use of "patent pools" or cross-licensing, or even by a single company, and emerge as de facto standards. Some of these proprietary standards are subsequently submitted to formal standards-setting organizations to become formal open standards to encourage yet wider adoption or are adopted in the marketplace quite widely and become de facto standards.

Many, if not most, information technology standards, including open standards, have patented components that are owned or controlled by one or a few companies. Whether open standards or proprietary standards are involved, it is well established that entities that develop standards and own the associated patents license the technology on RAND terms, either with or without a reasonable royalty, and therefore facilitate the wider adoption of the standard.[8]

Each Relevant Industry Has a Long and Well-Developed History of Standards Setting   Each industry within the broader information technology environment has unto itself a long history of success relying on these many avenues for standards setting in the commercial marketplace. That success continues to this day. The early radio and television industry standards were developed by only a few competing companies under the auspices of the Federal Communications Commission (FCC), and its predecessor the Federal Radio Commission for the purpose of enforcement. More recently, digital television standards have been developed by the private sector and ratified by the FCC. The movie and music industries share similar histories, but entertainment standards have generally been market-driven, de facto standards. Take, for instance, the Edison cylinder that competed with the Berliner phonograph disk and Columbia's patented 33 RPM LP that coexisted in the market with RCA's 45 RPM disk and the many film format standards (and now digital cinema standards) that have facilitated international film distribution over the years. The consumer electronics industry shares much of the history with the entertainment industry, but is also often subject to government mandates (e.g., TV and radio standards). The computer industries have, throughout the years, developed standards through formal and informal means, including audio and video compression specifications developed by the ISO-adopted Moving Picture Experts Group (MPEG), Apple's IEEE 1394 digital communication specification, and the Universal Serial Bus (USB, USB2 and USB3).

As the National Institute of Standards and Technology (NIST) acting director testified before Congress in 2005, there are over 450 U.S. standards-setting organizations and an additional 150 consortia standards-development activities ongoing. There are more than 13,000 private sector standards in use by the federal government. "Our decentralized, private sector, demand-driven U.S. standards system has many strengths. U.S. companies derive significant advantage from the system's flexibility and responsiveness. The government also derives great benefit from the system, both as a customer and user of standards."[9]

Thus, it is well established—through the long history and up-to-date practices of formal and informal standards-setting organizations, the vibrancy of ad hoc standards setting or adoption through consortia and the use of patent pools, and marketplace adoption of both open standards and proprietary standards—that the information technology industries are well suited to develop standards in the marketplace.

U.S. Federal Law and Policy Prefers that Standards Be Developed in the Marketplace

In the context of standards setting, there is a substantial early history of the government as the exclusive or predominant standards-setting entity, rooted in its British heritage dating back many hundreds of years. However, over the course of the last two centuries, U.S. government policy has reflected an appreciation that industry is typically the most efficient and informed sector, as well as the most capable of developing standards. As the U.S. system has evolved, federal government policy has come to reflect a strong preference for developing standards in the private sector with a concomitant aversion to government standards mandates.

U.S. Domestic Law and Policy In December 2005, ANSI published *The United States Standards Strategy* (USSS). The USSS was approved by the board of directors of ANSI and was endorsed by the U.S. Department of Commerce.[10] As the introduction to the USSS states, "Voluntary consensus standards are at the foundation of the U.S. economy. . . . The United States is a market-driven, highly diversified society, and its standards system encompasses and reflects this framework. . . . A standards system is strengthened whenever standards developers share a common vision for meeting stakeholders needs. . . . Standards are essential to a sound national economy and to the facilitation of global commerce."[11]

In the United States, Congress has expressed statutorily a strong preference for private sector-developed standards and restraint in government mandating standards. In enacting the National Technology Transfer and Advancement Act of 1995 (NTTAA), Congress formally adopted into law what had since 1980 been the policy of the Executive Branch and embodied in guidance to federal agencies issued by the Office of Management and Budget Circular A-119.[12] With the NTTAA, Congress required federal agencies to abide by a preference for voluntary standards over government-specific standards. The preference for market-developed standards is evident in the report language that accompanied the NTTAA. To assure absolute clarity, the House Committee Report stated: "It is . . . the intent of the Committee to make private sector-developed consensus standards the rule, rather than the exception."[13] The 1998 revision of OMB Circular A-119 emphasized that it had "not been the intent of the Circular to create the basis for discrimination among standards developed in the private sector, whether consensus-based or, alternatively, industry-based or company-based."[14] Thus, it is clear that the federal government preference is to rely not only on private sector-developed standards, but also those standards developed in the full range of private sector forums.

The results of the enactment of the NTTAA are noteworthy. During fiscal year 2004, federal agencies reported using 4,559 private sector standards developed by the private sector. In contrast, during the same year, they reported using only seventy-one government-unique standards. An example of the FCC's approach to market-developed information technology standards can be found in their management of the development of the standards to facilitate interoperability among digital cable devices: "We have emphasized our reliance on market forces to bring innovation, choice and better prices to consumers. It is the work of private entities and the economic incentives motivating the participants in the OpenCable process that provide the most immediate opportunity for a degree of standardization that will both create scale economies reducing the cost of equipment and developing interfaces allowing the equipment to be readily sold through retail outlets."[15] Similarly, HDTV standards were developed in a consortium standards-setting process and subsequently ratified by the FCC.

Another example of the impact of the OMB Circular A-119 and the NTTAA can be found in examining the Department of Defense (DoD) policies on standards. In 1994, Secretary of Defense William Perry issued a memorandum entitled "Specifications and Standards—A New Way of Doing Business" (often referred to as "MilSPEC Reform") which set out as a priority for the DoD the increase in use of commercial technologies and the use of performance standards and commercial specifications and standards in "in lieu of military specifications and standards, unless no practical alternative exists to meet the user's needs."[16] Thus, the DoD, with a long history of setting government-specific standards, shifted policy dramatically to participation in the free market development of standards and, in fact, more frequent adoption of off-the-shelf solutions.

Harmonious with the intent of Congress, the USSS, published in 2005, was intended to guide American standards policies and U.S. trade relations as they implicate standards. The USSS sets as its cornerstone the process of sector-specific, market-driven, private sector-led standards, not a top-down, one-size-fits-all approach as found in some other countries.[17] According to the USSS, as a matter of its strategic vision, the standards community is committed to the notion that "[g]overnments rely on voluntary consensus standards as much as possible in regulation and procurement rather than creating additional regulatory requirements."[18]

Based on these facts, it is clear that the federal government is generally opposed to government intervention into the standards marketplace and such an intervention would be contrary to both the spirit of the policy and, potentially, the law.

Market-Developed Standards Are Fundamental to Eliminating Technical Barriers to Trade and Facilitating Global Economic Development

The USSS articulates clearly that from the U.S. government perspective, standards are at the core of U.S. trade policy. Then-Secretary of Commerce Donald L. Evans prefaced the USSS by stating: "The international language of commerce is standards. . . . Without standards, it would be difficult to imagine the tremendous volume and complexity of international trade."[19] A goal of foreign trade policy is to unify the approach governments take to develop standards, encouraging foreign governments to adopt voluntary consensus-developed standards. Further, "the U.S. government should work with other WTO members to seek full implementation of the Technical Barriers to Trade (TBT) Agreement and annexes . . . [and to] identify and eliminate or minimize the effect of technical barriers to trade that result from technical standards and their application."[20]

As Dr. Hratch G. Semerjian, acting director of the National Institute of Standards and Technology, testified before Congress in 2005, "Both U.S. standards interests and policy objectives will be served when the governments of our most important export markets are convinced of the strengths of this approach versus alternatives that are less open and transparent, and more subjective."[21]

The U.S. government domestic policy preference for market-developed standards, and the success of this policy, is a critical argument in support of U.S. government opposition to the use of government-established standards by foreign governments. Correspondingly, government intervention in the U.S. market to establish or mandate a particular information technology standard undercuts the U.S. position in this context. An action by the U.S. government or a government in the United States to intervene in the market to mandate a standard would be perceived by foreign governments as, at a minimum, hypocritical of U.S. foreign policy, and more likely, support for similar behavior by the foreign government. Simply put, any country interested in IT development, outsourcing, insourcing, or technology exchange should participate in global standards-setting processes, and not isolate itself by developing standards unique to that country.

A national action to the contrary would conflict with the goal of achieving economic development through participation in the global economy. Thus, all governments should consider the implications to international trade before mandating an information technology standard.

Risk of "Government Failure" Should Give Government Cause to Pause
It is often observed that the market is more well informed, efficient, flexible, and capable than government in developing information technology standards. In general, this observation leads to a concern that one major consequence of government intervention to address a market failure is the high risk of "nonmarket failure," also called "government failure." A nonmarket failure can be defined as the unintended and undesirable consequences of government failure where it intervenes to address a market failure.[22] In setting information technology standards, the risk of getting it wrong is very high and the consequences may be great because technology that has broad economic and social impact advances rapidly. Standards development in the area of information technology requires eloquence in incorporating flexibility into a standard to accommodate technical advances and changes in the marketplace. The market itself generally has the most sophisticated expertise in establishing standards (technical knowledge, institutional knowledge, standards-setting bodies, etc.) and the ability to revise standards as appropriate.

Federal Reserve Bank of Chicago Senior Economist Victor Stango observed:

[Early literature examining the economics of standards reflects] that even in instances where the market would move too swiftly or slowly between standards, a policymaker will have difficulty improving upon the market. For instance, when there is uncertainty regarding the benefits that would accrue from adoption, or which standard will achieve adoption first, a policymaker can improve on the market outcome only if it possesses superior information. Moreover, little is known about the positive aspects of standard-setting. For example, a policymaker may resolve uncertainty more quickly than would be the case in a standards war but also might be more likely to choose the "wrong" standard.[23]

Justice Stephen Breyer, prior to his appointment to the U.S. Supreme Court, described "government failure" in his seminal book, *Regulation and its Reform*. Breyer posited that regulatory failure occurs because of "mismatches," that is, the failure "to correctly match the [regulatory] tool to the problem at hand."[24] Sidney Shapiro succinctly describes this situation: "A mismatch can occur because government can misdiagnose the problem that it is attempting to solve and apply the wrong regulatory approach as a result, or even if a problem is correctly identified, government chooses a regulatory tool that is less effective and more expensive than other options."[25] The U.S. federal policy toward encryption in the 1990s represented such a mismatch.

Government failure is most likely to occur when a market is new. As the FCC observed, it is a perilous time to regulate "when consumer demands, business plans, and technologies remain unknown, unformed or incomplete."[26] In information technologies, rapid innovation is driven by industrial creativity, a healthy economy, commercial and government need, and enthusiastic consumer appetite. Standards are central to this innovation. Although the several industries that constitute the evolving information technology sector are established and sophisticated, in some regards the sector is relatively young in that we are seeing a paradigm-changing convergence of these industries, the confluence of which is in progress and advancing swiftly. It is counterintuitive to inject the government into such a highly dynamic environment.

Stanley M. Besen and Leland L. Johnson, two prominent experts on technological standards, have long argued that when industry is in a period of high innovation and volatility, the likelihood that a government standard will result in inefficient or artificial technological decisions or both is particularly acute.[27] Thus, formal standards setting in rapidly changing industries should always be avoided. When the technology "settles down," the advantages of standards will present themselves, resulting in de facto standards being established by the market or industry bodies. As Besen and Johnson conclude, "The government should refrain from attempting to mandate or evaluate standards when the technologies themselves are subject to rapid change. A major reason for the Commission's difficulty in establishing the first color television standard was the fact that competing technologies were undergoing rapid change even during the Commission's deliberations. It is only after the technologies have "settled down" that government action is most likely to be fruitful."[28]

This perspective is reflected in the FCC's thinking in regard to regulatory intervention in telecommunications standards setting. For example, the FCC adopted this market-based approach in the licensing of the Personal Communications Service (PCS) spectrum, concluding that the rapid technological change in PCS development demanded a flexible regulatory approach to technical standards: "Most parties recognize that PCS is at a nascent stage in its development and that imposition of a rigid technical framework at this time may stifle the introduction of important new technology. We agree, and find that the flexible approach toward PCS standards that we are adopting is the most appropriate approach."[29]

The FCC recognized that telecommunications is currently in a highly dynamic period and, given the dynamic environment, it is both an opportune and a perilous time for government regulation. So the FCC described in regard to interoperability standards for video navigation devices: "The markets involved [for navigational devices] are in the early stages of becoming competitive, and the participants in these markets are on the precipice of a change from analog to digital communications. Because of these changes, this is both a particularly opportune and a particularly perilous time for the adoption of regulations. . . . It is perilous because regulations have the potential to stifle growth, innovation, and technical developments at a time when consumer demands, business plans, and technologies remain unknown, unformed or incomplete."[30]

However, it may be that the FCC's role in developing navigational devices will serve as evidence of the perils of government intervention. The FCC is adopting the work of CableLabs, a consortium of cable service providers and equipment manufacturers, and others, to develop interoperability standards for navigational devices. However, the FCC had to intervene to make possible greater participation by computer, software, and entertainment companies. It appears that the cable companies dominated the process early on to the exclusion of these other key market sectors. It is likely that FCC's selection of a single industry to lead this effort was shortsighted and made with insufficient attention to the dynamics of the market environment. The government is typically not as nimble, efficient, or informed as the private sector at developing and advancing technology standards. Indeed, government may behave more like a tourist than an experienced local would in the bazaar, failing to understand or even perceive the nuances of each potential transaction, or failing to distinguish a good deal from a bad one. It is not overstating the truth to say that even those within the industry are often surprised by market behavior. But faced with that surprise, a business or sector is more rapidly able to adapt and take advantage of the turn of events than is government.

By contrast, the process of creating or changing a government-mandated standard typically takes years to accomplish. If a government mandates a standard, it is difficult to replace dated technologies embodied in the standard. For example, it took the FCC over two years to amend its ISDN rules to accommodate new technology. Of course, such time frames are inconsistent with the current rapid pace of innovation in the digital media distribution marketplace. The FCC acknowledged that by imposing a standard it "could reduce the incentive to conduct the research and development that leads to innovation."[31]

In a notable example of "government failure," in the early 1980s, Japan established a government-mandated analog HD TV standard.[32] At the time, the FCC had been considering the need to develop a high-definition standard. But high-definition technology in the 1980s was immature and equipment was large, required a great deal of maintenance, and consumed enormous amounts of power. The U.S. industry and FCC recognized these facts. Ultimately, with advances in digital technology that would result in more efficient use of spectrum and a higher quality picture, the United States and other countries chose to pursue digital for their high-definition television standards. Very simply put, the Japanese government's standard was premature and essentially failed before it was launched.

A more recent situation in which some have questioned whether government intervention in standards setting is appropriate or instead the path to nonmarket failure is the case of France's parliament proposing legislation addressing standards in digital rights management (DRM). In March 2006, the French Assemblée Nationale passed legislation that required DRM interoperability to improve consumer choice in music and video entertainment devices. The legislation required disclosure of all technical documentation and programming interfaces necessary to facilitate interoperability. For example, market leader Apple would have had to provide enough information to competitors so they could make their music and video files play on an iPod, or make devices that would play songs downloaded from iTunes. The bill also provided that the publication of the source code and technical documentation of an interoperating independent software is permissible.

It appeared to critics that the bill undermined the functional protections of the subject DRM. As one observer noted when the bill was under consideration, "The problem is that the type of information necessary to achieve interoperability is also precisely the information necessary to render DRM useless: the encryption algorithms, keys, content metadata, and so on."[33] In May 2006, the Sénat, the upper house of the French Parliament, declined to pass the same legislation, passing instead a bill that establishes a government tribunal to adjudicate DRM interoperability issues. As further evidence of the difficulties at the intersection of technology and law, and the potential for government failure, in August 2006, the French Conseil Constitutionnel vacated as unconstitutional provisions of the new law that permitted circumvention of DRM to accomplish interoperability, concluding that the definition of "interoperability" was too vague. The situation in France exemplifies why government should be reluctant to intervene in information technology standards setting. At a minimum, the case supports the notion that such government intervention carries with it substantial risk of government mistakes.

Given the dynamic conditions in the markets impacted by information technology standards, the balance of expertise favoring commercial developers over the government, the ability of industry to be more nimble in reacting to market conditions, and the open acknowledgment of these factors by government in the information technology standards-setting context, it is critical to recognize that as a general matter, the risk of and potential harm from government failure, as compared to a market failure, is substantial.

The market has also had its failures in standards setting. Even a standard that becomes formalized by a standards-developing organization may not meet with market success. The information superhighway is littered with discarded standards. Businesses, like governments, often may try to anticipate the direction of the market and fail to do so. But when a company or industry fails with a particular standard, it can simply abandon it. When the government makes this type of mistake, it takes time to undo it through either legislative or regulatory action.

Conclusion

Government should be reluctant to intervene in the setting of information technology standards—in particular, to *mandate* an information technology standard—because (1) the relevant industries are sophisticated in regard to standards setting and have many well-developed types of standards, and forums in which to develop standards; (2) the U.S. government has a strong preference for market-developed information technology standards and promotes this preference as a matter of both domestic law and policy and foreign trade policy; (3) international trade agreements limit the degree to which participating governments can mandate standards; and (4) in contrast to the sophistication of the marketplace, government is rarely as informed, sophisticated in its understanding of the market, or nimble enough to respond to market conditions; therefore, the risk of government failure is significant, and indeed greatest where the market is young and dynamic, as is the case with regard to the current market affected by information technology standards.

25. Sidney A. Shapiro, "American Regulatory Policy: Have We Found the 'Third Way'?" *University of Kansas Law Review* 48 (2000): 689, 698.

26. In re Implementation of Section 304 of the Telecommunications Act of 1996, 13 F.C.C.R. 14,775, 14,781 ¶ 15 (June 24, 1998).

27. Stanley M. Besen and Leland L. Johnson, *Compatibility Standards, Competition, and Innovation in the Broadcasting Industry* (Santa Monica, CA: RAND Corporation, 1986).

28. Ibid., p. 135.

29. In re Amendment of the Commission's Rules to Establish New Personal Communications Services, 73 Rad. Reg. 2d (P & F) 1477, ¶ 137 (report and order Oct. 22, 1993).

30. In re the Matter of Implementation of Section 304 of the Telecommunications Act of 1996, 18 F.C.C.R. 14,775, 14,781 ¶ 15 (June 24, 1998).

31. In re Advanced Television Systems & Their Impact Upon the Existing Television Broadcast Service, 11 F.C.C.R. 6235, 6251 ¶ 42 (May 20, 1996).

32. Sony/NHK Hi-Vision, a 1125-line analog technology, was first used in broadcasting in 1991. See David E. Sanger, "Few See Japan Make TV History," *New York Times*, Nov. 26, 1991, at D6.

33. Bill Rosenblatt, "French Parliament Passes DRM Interoperability Legislation," *DRM Watch*, Mar. 23, 2006, <http://www.drmwatch.com/legal/article.php/3593841>.

3 Governments, the Public Interest, and Standards Setting

D. Linda Garcia

In the United States, much of the global discussion about standards setting has focused on the question "What is the appropriate division of labor between the public and private sectors in this arena?" Building upon our federalist tradition, standards setters in the United States have held to the notion that standards setting is a private affair (OTA 1992). In most other countries, especially those like France—with a strong statist tradition—the national government has taken the lead. The decision to assign the responsibility for standard setting to the private sector has been based on two basic assumptions. First, it is believed that private sector standards are highly attuned to market forces, so they provide the greatest economic value. Second, the U.S. government is understood to have no stake in the outcome of standards processes apart from its role as a "consumer of standards." Thus, by participating in the standards process as a user, the government—it is believed—can fully serve the public interest.

These assumptions are hardly self-evident. For one, in the case of standards, market forces do not necessarily lead to efficient outcomes. Because standards exhibit many characteristics of public goods, standards setting is subject to considerable market failures (Farrell and Saloner 1988; Berg 1989). Moreover, market failures are especially likely in the case of information technology standards, which give rise to externalities and other network effects. Equally problematic—as the 1992 Office of Technology Assessment report pointed out—even when voluntary standards organizations step in to facilitate standards setting, bureaucratic failures can delay the process, while conflicts of interest—related in part to standards sales—may serve to distort outcomes (OTA 1992).

The second assumption—that government has no "public interest" in standards setting—is equally difficult to justify. Standards constitute an infrastructure or platform that supports and sustains the U.S. economy. As such, standards help to determine the efficiency and effectiveness of the economy, the cost, quality, and availability of products and services, and the state of the nation's health, safety, and quality of life.

Not surprisingly, therefore, most governments have always taken an interest in standards setting. Thus, European monarchs established standard weights and measures as a matter of royal prerogative. As Solomon has noted: "According to *The Oxford English Dictionary*, the word standard is derived from an early concept of the flag or standard bearer, one might say, 'the King's standard'" (Solomon 1989, 1–2). Today, in the increasingly competitive global environment, many states now link their standardization efforts to their trade policies, employing national standards as marketing devices to attract and lock in customers worldwide.

Standards Setting in the United States

In the United States standards setting developed along a unique path that continues to influence the relationships between public- and private-sector roles in standards setting. Emerging within the private sector, standards communities developed a voluntary consensus-based approach to the standards-setting process. More than anywhere else, these organizations were able to act independently not only from the state, but also from one another (OTA 1992).

The emergence of standards setting in the United States is closely linked to the industrial revolution. With the division of labor and specialization, tasks became more interdependent, requiring greater coordination and exchange. Standards greatly facilitated these processes (Beniger 1986). One need only consider the role of standards in mass production that required interchangeable parts. As described by Harold Williamson: "Chief among the other elements in the patterns of mass production is the principle of standardization. Stemming from the rudimentary division of labor, standardization involved the continuous pursuit and progressive realization, of uniformity of the materials, operations, and products of industry, which made possible the future subdivision and mechanization of labor" (Williamson 1951, 722).

The relationship between standards and mass production was self-reinforcing. Further advances in precision manufacturing required the development of machine tools and precision gauges, which in turn further drove the need for standards and standardized measures.

Standards were also spurred on by the extension of markets across the American continent. As trade became more dispersed, standards were needed to assure that products manufactured in different locales could work together and be easily replicated, assembled, and repaired. Moreover, standards were required to facilitate trading itself. For example, when the railroads extended trade over vast regions, standardized procedures for billing and exchange—such as bills of lading—were required. Likewise, standardized business practices and procedures, as well as standardized timekeeping, were needed to coordinate the increasingly complex railroad operations (Kirkland 1961).

As the role of standards increased, so did the number of people who had a stake in the standards process. Producers, for example, employed standards as trademarks to differentiate their products from their competitors and to price products for different markets. For suppliers, standards specifications meant reduced production costs. Consumers likewise benefited from standards. They not only conveyed product information and provided greater quality control; standardized products were also cheaper. The general public also called for the development of standards to protect against the growing technological mishaps that were associated with industrialization.

As more and more stakeholders became involved in standards, it became increasingly necessary to specialize standards-setting operations, and to differentiate among these groups. Of prime importance was the relationship between the public and private sectors. Although the government had actively promoted standardization at the turn of the century, it gradually relinquished this responsibility to the private standards development organizations (OTA 1992)

This American preference for private, pluralist solutions is as old as the U.S. Constitution itself. From the outset of the new republic, Americans proved to have a penchant for joining actions and establishing associations, a fact that did not escape the notice of Alexis de Tocqueville when he visited America in the mid-1880s. As he described in *Democracy in America*, "Whenever at the head of some new undertaking you see the Government of France, or a man of rank in England, in the United States you will be sure to find an association" (Tocqueville 1963). This support for voluntary, private associations was reinforced by a general suspicion of the state and preferences for market-based solutions (Wuthrow 1991). Thus, whereas in many other countries government actively sponsored the growth and development of business, in the United States industrial development was managed, directed, and financed primarily by the private sector (Vogel 1987).

The first standards organizations were in keeping with this tradition. Emerging to deal with specific needs as they arose, they were established on an industry-by-industry basis and took a variety of forms. Although efforts were made to coordinate their activities through the American National Standards Institute (ANSI)—the internationally accepted body in the International Organization for Standardization and the International Electrotechnical Commission—they have continued to operate on a pluralistic basis, with many of them circumventing ANSI.

The emergence of consortia in the late 1980s, together with the changing parameters of the global economy, has served to reinforce this diversity and independence. Commenting on the rise in the number and types of independent forums in which standards are being adopted, Werle has noted:

In the last two decades standardization organizations (SOs) in telecommunication and information policy . . . have proliferated. Both the globalization of markets and the blurring of technical boundaries have induced an overlap of domains of international and regional SOs. At the same time, SOs at the national level are losing significance. Traditional organizations have been restructured and—assisted by government—new official SOs have been created at the official level. Most dramatic, however, has been the growth of private consortiums and forums. Thus, official standard setting is confronted with an informal sector, the evolution of which indicates some discontent with the traditional organizations and entails an inherent potential of jurisdictional conflict. (Werle 2001, 392)

Despite their independence, American standards organizations resemble one another in several ways. In particular, they all arrive at decisions through a process of consensus and provide some level of due process. In addition, they all have mechanisms for participation, comment, and appeal. Equally—if not more—important, almost all standards organizations are adamant proponents of the voluntary standards process: whatever their disagreements among themselves, they have consistently joined together to defend against any government encroachment on their autonomy.

Interacting along these lines, U.S. standards organizations have been highly successful in legitimating their right to govern themselves. The federal government has rarely intervened in private-sector standards activities; instead, it has focused on preventing anticompetitive outcomes as well as on assuring the "fairness" of the system.

Standards Setting as a Complex System

Given the strong opposition to the U.S. government's involvement in standards setting, what kinds of assurances do we have that the broader public interest will be incorporated into standards goals and outcomes? To appreciate how this public interest might be brought to bear, we need to view standards organizations as they exist in a broader institutional environment, where influences spread among actors along nonlinear and unpredictable paths.

With this in mind, we might view the standards universe as a complex, multilayered system comprised of three unique *organizational fields* of activity—industry actors, standards organizations, and government officials—each of which, although acting according to its own meaning systems, rules, and procedures, overlap and are influenced by one another (Kontopoulos 2003) (see figure 3.1). It is by virtue of the interactions among these layers that multiple interests and perspectives are embedded in standards.

In figure 3.1, geometric shapes depict organizational fields at each level. At level one are networks of firms that produce goods and services

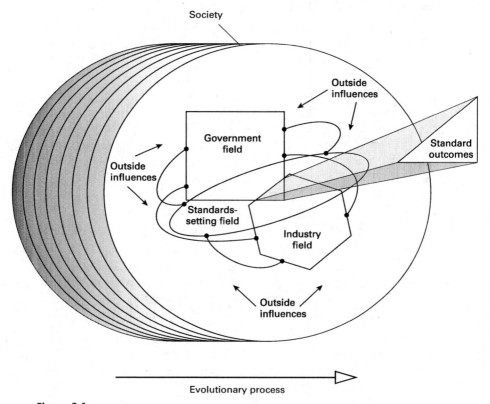

Figure 3.1
Standards setting as a complex adaptive process. Design courtesy of L. A. King.

requiring standards as well as those who consume these products. At level two is the network of standards development organizations that establish standards for these and other industries. Finally, at the third level—that of government—standards-related activities are governed by a set of rules specific to that level. However, because the system architecture is heterar-chical—that is to say, because the levels are not perfectly matched, but rather overlap—the choices made at any one level influence the operating rules and outcomes at other levels. In addition, external influences affect each level of the system. To appreciate the importance of these interactions across levels, one need only consider the dual role of corporations. On the one hand, they may be competitors in the market, each seeking to establish an industry standard, and thereby grasp the largest piece of the pie. On the other hand, they may extend their activities beyond the market, working together to establish a standard, thereby increasing the size of the pie.

In addition, one should also note the one-way arrow at the bottom of figure 3.1, which depicts standards setting as an evolutionary process. Accordingly, history matters, and there is no turning back. As a result, the system must be examined not only as it presently exists, but also in terms of how it has evolved, and how its past and present together might affect the future (Hodgson, Itao, and Yokokawa 2001).

Interactions and the spreading of ideas across organizational fields are likely to be greatest when actors operating in one level of the standards-setting process encounter some type of "failure." Equally important, there are multiple opportunities for such exchanges to take place, because fail-ures are common to each of the organizational fields.

At the level of *techno-economic field*, the market may make suboptimal choices or fail to achieve standards in a timely fashion or both. For example, in highly competitive markets, comprised of many firms, the transaction and coordination costs required to achieve standards may simply be too high. Alternatively, in oligopolistic markets, in which firms of relatively equal size can sustain proprietary solutions, the market may not "tip" in favor of a common standard. The public goods aspects of standards also give rise to market failures, insofar as public goods are typically underpro-duced. Equally important, for firms to choose efficient standards, they must have accurate and timely information. However, information about standards, like standards themselves, is a public good, which is typically underproduced (Berg 1989; Kindleberger 1983)

Faced with significant market failures, firms may decide to carry out their activities at the level of standards organizations. In this space, too, failures often occur. However, whereas in the techno-economic field we find market failures, in the standards organizational field we find social dilemmas—situations in which the dominant strategies pursued by individual actors lead to outcomes that are suboptimal for the collective as a whole (Heckathorn 1996; Kollock 1994; Miller 1998). Two sets of dilemmas are found in the standards-setting field. The first is the problem of collective action associated with the problem of who will bear the cost of organizing to set standards (Cornes and Sandler 1986). These costs include not only those entailed in bringing actors together and coordinating their activities, but also in setting up a governance structure and maintaining it over time (Litwak and Hylton 1962). Failures occur if there is no major player with an incentive to corral and coordinate individual actors, as well as pay the ongoing costs. The second dilemma—referred to as a "prisoners' dilemma"—relates to common pool problems entailed in allocating and appropriating benefits. Once standards organizations have been set up, the bargaining process takes over, and participants must agree to divide the benefits gained from cooperating in a way that serves not only each private actor's needs but also those of the group as a whole. However, given actors' interdependencies and asymmetric resources, some are unlikely to cooperate. In fact, those with the most autonomy have a strong incentive to act opportunistically (Nooteboom, Berger, and Noorderhaven 1997).

If, as has sometimes been the case, standards organizations are unable to resolve their own internal conflicts, government might be called upon to intervene. Dissenters within the standards field may look to government for support. Alternatively, dissatisfied with the field's disarray, lobbying for government involvement might come from private sector actors outside the field, or from interested policy makers within the government. In any case, when standards issues are raised to the level of government, the criteria for evaluating outcomes are typically cast far more broadly. It is at this point that the public interest is most likely to be promoted.

The government field is the realm of power and authority. Whereas in the private sector actors interact to achieve their own private ends, in the government field they cooperate and compete to achieve collective goals. Thus, the means of executing changes in this arena are participation and persuasion, while information, rhetoric, and the means of communication are critical resources (Knoke 1990; Stone 2002). Working together in groups and alliances, individuals employ information to shape attitudes and beliefs, in an effort to restructure the "rules of the game" in their favor. Policy outcomes take time to materialize, and are highly uncertain. Emerging in the course of a prolonged process of trial and error learning as well as intense struggles and negotiations for power and influence, they are rarely optimal (Campbell and Lindberg 1991; Kingdon 2002; Sabatier 1999). Equally problematic, the key decision-making criteria in this field—the public interest—are subject to change as actors define problems and frame debates according to their own policy agendas (Stone 2002). Thus, one of the major challenges at the governmental level is how to determine the public interest in standards setting and, having done so, how to keep government accountable while reconciling private- and public-sector goals.

Reconciling Public and Private Interest

Conceptually, there are three distinct ways of thinking about the public interest and the implications for government. For example, the term "public interest" can refer to private interests, such as property rights, which the government acts to ensure. The concept might also be used to describe specific goals that a government administration pursues through its policy initiatives. Alternatively, the term "public interest" might be used to specify that which is good for the polity as a whole—such as national defense, economic growth, and freedom of speech (Caporoso and Levine 2001; Stone 2002).

An argument can be made for government involvement in standards setting based on each of these grounds. For example, because standards constitute a form of property rights—insofar as they determine actors' abilities to appropriate or dispose of their resources or both as they see fit (Eggertsson 1996)—the government might be expected to establish policies that govern them. (Libecap 1989). Similarly, because standards constitute a set of performance criteria, all government policies have a standards component. Finally, because standards serve as a public infrastructure, the government must factor them into any efforts to assure national security as well as provide for the nation's political and economic welfare.

Pursuant to its standards goals, the government might play any number of roles. At a minimum, for example, the government acts as *rule maker*, establishing not only property rights in standards—and hence the obligations of and relationships among economic actors—but also the process by which these relationships can be legitimately negotiated within the standards-setting field. Moreover to ensure these rights, the government takes on the roles of *adjudicator* and *enforcer*. The government can also facilitate the standards-setting process, acting as an *educator* to reduce uncertainties; a *broker* to bring together players and aid in negotiations; or a *subsidizer* to provide critical resources. Acting more directly, the government plays the role of *regulator*, specifying and standardizing the characteristics or capability or both of a product, process, or technology. The government is also a user and *consumer* of standards. Moreover, when necessary, the government is a *developer* of standards through its own research and development efforts.

Although the government can help promote its standards goals, it is not an impartial or disinterested party. Government assumes the costs and benefits associated with engaging in the process, not solely out of its own goodwill, but also in exchange for the economic and political benefits that ensue. The way outcomes are structured will depend on the costs and benefits as the relevant decision makers assess them at any point in time. This problem of government accountability is compounded by a problem of bounded rationality. Assigning rights and responsibilities with respect to standards and standards setting, so as to maximize society's interests, while accommodating private sector needs, requires a degree of knowledge—both global as well as local. Decision makers are unlikely to have such knowledge under the best of circumstances, much less in the case of rapidly advancing technologies.

In the end, the quality of policy outcomes related to standards setting will depend on the quality of the decision-making process. As Campbell and Lindberg point out, government policy outcomes are not to be equated with the interests of individual actors, because these interests are both constituted through and constrained by actors' interactions with others in a variety of different contexts. Outcomes, then, are the product of collective "search processes" that entail learning by trial and error, compromise, and negotiation, as well as coercion and political struggle (Campbell and Lindberg 1991). The decisions that emerge as a result are more likely to approximate the public interest, and to be adaptive to changing circumstances, to the extent that channels of communication are open and actors are interconnected in complex and overlapping ways. Under such circumstances, not only will there be a greater variety of inputs into the process, but equally important, there will also be more adequate feedback mechanisms to continually sort out and select appropriate policies as circumstances and technologies change over time.

In the United States we typically think of assuring the public's interest by virtue of the balance of power between the three branches of government—the executive, legislature, and judiciary. Looking at the standards universe through the lens of complexity, however, we see that there are other forms of balance to be taken into account. It is through the nonlinear process by which standards are influenced and eventually evolve that multiple interests are negotiated according to diverse criteria, and eventually emerge in the form of a consensus-based standard.

References

Beniger, J. 1986. *The Control Revolution: Technology and the Economic Origins of the Information Society*. Cambridge, MA: Harvard University Press.

Berg, Sanford. 1989. Technical Standards for Public Goods: Demand Incentives for Cooperative Behavior. *Public Finance Quarterly* 17:377–396.

Campbell, J., and L. N. Lindberg. 1991. The Evolution of Governance Regimes. In *Governance of the American Economy*, ed. J. Campbell and J. R. Hollingsworth, 319–355. Cambridge, UK: Cambridge University Press.

Caporoso, J. A., and D. P. Levine. 2001. *Theories of Political Economy*. New York: Cambridge University Press.

Cornes, R., and T. Sandler. 1986. *The Theory of Externalities, Public Goods, and Club Goods*. Cambridge, UK, and New York: Cambridge University Press.

Eggertsson, Thrainn. 1996. A Note on Economic Institutions. In *Empirical Studies in Institutional Change*, ed. L. J. Alston, T. Eggertsson, and D. C. North, 6–24. New York: Cambridge University Press.

Farrell, Joseph, and Garth Saloner. 1988. Coordination through Committees and Markets. *Rand Journal of Economics* 19:235–252.

Heckathorn, D. D. 1996. The Dynamics and Dilemmas of Collective Action. *American Sociological Review* 61 (2): 250–277.

Hodgson, G. M., M. Itao, and N. Yokokawa. 2001. Introduction. In *Capitalism in Evolution: Global Contentions—East and West*, ed. G. M. Hodgson, M. Itao, and N. Yokokawa, 1–18. Cheltenham, UK, and Northampton, MA: E. Elgar.

Kindleberger, C. 1983. Standards as Public, Collective, and Private Goods. *Kylos* 36: 377–395.

Kingdon, J. W. 2002. *Agendas, Alternatives and Public Policies*. 2nd ed. New York: Longman.

Kirkland, Edward. 1961. *Industry Comes of Age: Business, Labor, and Public Policy*. New York: Rheinhard and Winston.

Knoke, D. 1990. *Political Networks: The Structural Perspective*. New York: Cambridge University Press.

Kollock, P. 1994. The Emergence of Exchange Structures: An Experimental Study of Uncertainty, Commitment, and Trust. *American Journal of Sociology* 100 (2): 313–345.

Kontopoulos, K. 2003. *The Logic of Social Structure*. New York: Cambridge University Press.

Libecap, G. D. 1989. *Contracting for Property Rights*. Cambridge, UK: Cambridge University Press.

Litwak, E., and L. Hylton. 1962. Interorganizational Analysis: A Hypothesis on Coordinating Agencies. *Administrative Science Quarterly* 6:395–420.

Miller, G. J. 1998. *Managerial Dilemmas: The Political Economy of Hierarchy*. Cambridge, UK: Cambridge University Press.

Nooteboom, B., H. Berger, and N. G. Noorderhaven. 1997. Effects of Trust and Governance on Relational Risk. *Academy of Management Journal* 40 (2): 308–338.

OTA (U.S. Congress Office of Technology Assessment). 1992. "Global Standards: Building Blocks for the Future." Washington, DC: U.S. Government Printing Office.

Sabatier, P. A. 1999. *Theories of the Policy Process*. Bolder, CO: Westview Press.

Solomon, Richard. 1989. *New Paradigms for Future Standards*. Cambridge, MA: MIT Media Lab .

Stone, D. 2002. *Policy Paradox: The Art of Political Decisions Making*. New York: W. W. Norton & Company.

Tocqueville, Alexis de. 1963. *Democracy in America*, ed. Richard D. Heffner. New York: Mentor Books.

Vogel, D. 1987. Government Industry Relations in the United States: An Overview. In *Comparative Government Industry Relations*, ed. Stephen Wilks and Maurice Wright, 113–140. Oxford: Clarendon Press.

Werle, R. 2001. Institutional Aspects of Standardization—Jurisdictional Conflicts and the Choice of Standards Organizations. *Journal of European Public Policy* 8 (3): 392–410.

Williamson, Harold, ed. 1951. *The Growth of the American Economy*. New York: Prentice Hall.

Wuthrow, R., ed. 1991. *Between States and Markets: The Voluntary Sector in Comparative Perspective*. Princeton, NJ: Princeton University Press.

4 Securing the Root

Brenden Kuerbis and Milton Mueller

Management of the Internet's Domain Name System (DNS) root zone file is a uniquely global policy problem. The DNS provides the semantically meaningful names that serve as unique identifiers for email or Web site addresses (e.g., www.example.com or user@example.com). The DNS name space is hierarchically structured but organizationally distributed. In essence, it is a global database that maps domain names to resource record data (e.g., an IP address). To remain globally interoperable there must be coordination at the top of the naming hierarchy, known as "the root." The root zone file is an 84 KB text file containing resource records defining the Internet's top-level domains (e.g., .com, .fr, .mil) and the IP addresses with which they are associated.[1]

Authority over the root zone file has been contentious and divisive at times.[2] Whoever controls the root of the DNS has control over a number of basic policies governing Internet identifiers, and some measure of indirect authority over Internet connectivity itself. However contentious the issue of control of the root may be, many agree that the Internet should be made more secure. The DNS Security Extensions (DNSSEC) protocol would make DNS resource record data more secure. In order to fully implement DNSSEC, however, the procedures for managing the DNS root zone had to be revised. This presented the world with an opportunity to diminish the impact of the legacy monopoly held by the U.S. government and to avoid another contentious debate over unilateral U.S. control. However, as this chapter describes, despite an ostensibly openly developed standard, and a relatively open institutional framework for putting into place the governance arrangements for implementing the standard, one actor—the U.S. government—held veto power in this case and was able to shape the implementation of DNSSEC at the root to maintain its authority over the DNS. This episode lends credence to principal-agent theorists in political science who show how ex ante and ex post measures can be used strategically by a governmental principal to monitor and control an ostensibly independent, nongovernmental agent.

What Is DNSSEC and How Does It Improve Internet Security?

The functioning of the DNS is dependent on the successful interaction between *resolvers* and *name servers*. Resolvers *query* name servers, sending a domain name and receiving a *response* with corresponding resource record information. DNSSEC is a proposed standard that modifies DNS resource records and protocols to provide security for query and response transactions made between name resolvers and name servers. By introducing public-key cryptographic signed data into the DNS using four new resource records, DNSSEC specifically provides the following:

• Source authentication: a resolver can determine that a response originated from a zone's authoritative name server.[3]
• Integrity verification: a resolver can determine that a response has not been tampered with in transit.
• Authenticated denial of existence: a resolver can verify that a particular query is unresolvable because no DNS resource record exists on the authoritative name server.

  DNSSEC is intended to protect against some DNS attacks, including spoofing attacks that use "man-in-the-middle" techniques like packet interception, transaction ID guessing and query prediction, and DNS cache poisoning techniques like name chaining and transaction ID prediction.[4] These attacks can be exploited to redirect resolver requests to bogus hosts, where other disruptive or criminal acts such as data phishing and malware infections can occur that threaten security.[5] While various types of DNS attacks have increased, there is no public data available that quantifies the risk and associated damage from attacks that could be prevented by DNSSEC, leaving many cost–benefit questions unanswered. Importantly, DNSSEC does not address other well-known DNS vulnerabilities like distributed denial of service (DDoS) attacks. Likewise, DNSSEC provides little defense against basic phishing attacks for which success is largely dependent on end-user behavior, or attacks that target the operational systems of DNS operators.[6]

Some Economics and Politics of DNSSEC

Despite widespread belief that remedying security vulnerabilities in the DNS would be beneficial, the development and deployment of the DNSSEC protocol has taken an extraordinarily long time. The specification was initially developed in the mid-1990s, several years after security vulnerabilities in the DNS became publicly known and discussed within the Internet Engineering Task Force (IETF). The protocol was first published as an RFC in 1997.[7] In 2001, substantial changes were proposed to the specification and it was rewritten between 2001 and 2005. Finally, in March 2005, the revised specification was approved by the Internet Engineering Steering Group (IESG) and published in three separate RFCs covering requirements, additional resources, and protocol modifications.[8] The delay in development is partially attributable to the technical and organizational complexity of the protocol, the economics associated with its implementation, and an expanding array of interests in a secure DNS.

By any measure, the DNS has been an incredibly reliable and effective globally distributed lookup directory, resolving billions of queries each day and facilitating substantial commercial activity. This success places a heavy burden of proof on any new proposals that add complexity by changing the underlying technology and processes. DNSSEC is not a simple protocol; it requires the development of upgraded or new software and imposes an additional computational burden on the resolver and name server infrastructure. The use of digital signatures introduces the need for methods and organizational security policies pertaining to key generation (e.g., algorithm, length), distribution, storage, and scheduled or emergency rollovers. These issues are particularly important for zones higher in an authentication chain. Additionally, the type and number of organizations affected by the changes DNSSEC requires have expanded. Originally, enterprises, universities, and government agencies were largely responsible for operating their own name servers. Today a whole industry sector has developed around managed DNS services.

DNSSEC also faces a classic chicken-and-egg adoption conundrum. On the one hand, without a critical mass of signed zones (and particularly .com and the root), there is no viable demand for the development of DNS security-aware applications. On the other hand, without such applications there is no demand for signed zones. However, there is recognition that other protocols and systems could leverage a security-enhanced DNS. For instance, Domain Keys Identified Mail (DKIM) proposes to use secure domains to authenticate the source or intermediary of an email message, as well as the contents of messages, in order to deal with email-based spam.[9] And identity management systems like OpenID, in which a user's identity is associated with a particular URL, could also leverage the widespread deployment of DNSSEC.[10] However, both of these are nascent technologies and certainly not "killer apps" that could spark DNSSEC adoption at this point. Faced with this uncertainty, many zone operators are still weighing the costs and benefits of DNSSEC.

Another possible benefit of DNSSEC is its ability to enable widespread encrypted communications, which has long been of concern to law enforcement and surveillance interests.[11] While the protocol itself specifically does not address confidentiality of data or communications, the adoption of DNSSEC could create a globally accessible, authenticable infrastructure for the secure distribution of other information. A secure DNS could help resolve long-standing problems associated with secure distribution of public keys and certificates and enable confidential communications, using DNSSEC in conjunction with popular systems. In fact, engineers working for the main U.S. government contractor on DNSSEC were cognizant of this benefit early on, viewing it as a potential "big driver behind DNS security."[12]

Given the associated hurdles and potential for DNSSEC, it is no surprise that there has been broad interest in the protocol's development and adoption. Early development came from specialized agencies within the U.S. Department of Defense (DoD) and its contractors, along with technical experts participating within the Security Area of the IETF. Interest in the protocol expanded greatly as the Internet developed into a widely used and critical piece of communications infrastructure. Beginning in 2001, development shifted to the IETF's Internet Area, and a range of technical experts from registries, DNS management and software providers, applications developers, U.S. government agencies, and individuals associated with government- and industry-supported research centers sought to influence DNSSEC. And as the protocol moved toward the deployment stage, Internet governance institutions like the Internet Corporation for Assigned Names and Numbers (ICANN) became increasingly involved.

The role of U.S. agencies in DNSSEC's evolution since 2001 has focused on both development and deployment activities. In addition to a general increase in funding of basic research on Internet security coinciding with the 2002 Cyber Security Research and Development Act,[13] the National Science Foundation has awarded grants to DNSSEC-specific projects and researchers directly involved in the standard's evolution. The DoD has continued its lengthy participation in applied DNSSEC research and the standard's development via private contractors. Individuals with these organizations have actively participated in the IETF process and continue efforts to promote DNSSEC within the Internet's technical community and ICANN.

The Department of Commerce's National Institute for Standards and Technology (NIST) was active in the revised protocol's development, participating extensively in the IETF's DNSEXT (DNS Extensions) Working Group since 2001, and leading IETF editorship of five core DNSSEC specifications. In part, these activities were driven by Title III of the E-Government Act of 2002 (i.e., the Federal Information Security Management Act (FISMA)), which required NIST to "develop standards and guidelines, including minimum requirements, for information systems used or operated by an agency or by a contractor of an agency or other organization on behalf of an agency, other than national security systems."[14] In addition, the Act required that NIST "consult with other agencies and offices and the private sector (including the Director of the Office of Management and Budget, the Departments of Defense and Energy, the National Security Agency, the General Accounting Office, and the Secretary of Homeland Security)."[15]

Beginning in 2003, the U.S. Department of Homeland Security's Directorate for Science and Technology became active through its Internet Infrastructure Security Program (IISP).[16] DHS involvement was in response to its role mandated as part of the 2002 Homeland Security Act, the *National Strategy to Secure Cyberspace*,[17] and the 2003 Homeland Security Presidential Directive 7, which positioned DHS to become the lead federal point of contact for the information technology and telecommunications industry sector. Working together to support compliance with Federal Information Processing Standards (FIPS) as required by FISMA, NIST drafted several documents pertaining to DNSSEC that were sponsored by DHS.

Special Publication 800–81, Secure Domain Name System (DNS) Deployment Guide was published in May 2006, providing implementation guidelines (e.g., key management policies) for government agencies running DNSSEC.[18] In October 2006, NIST together with two central defense contractors produced *Signing the Domain Name System Root Zone: Technical Specification*, which recommended changes in root zone file management that would enable implementation of DNSSEC.[19] And in December 2006, NIST announced the release of the revised *Special Publication 800–53, Recommended Security Controls for Federal Information Systems*, which provided guidance on the use of external information systems (like the DNS) and outlined plans for the staged deployment of DNSSEC technology within medium- and high-impact federal information technology systems.[20] It gave U.S. federal agencies one year after the document's final publication to comply with the new standard. OMB mandated that .gov second-level domains should be signed by December 2009.[21]

The Root of the Problem: Creating a Trust Anchor

DNSSEC implements a hierarchical model of trust. A DNS security-aware resolver's ability to validate name server responses is accomplished by establishing an authentication chain from a known trust anchor or anchors (i.e., a cryptographic public key[22]) to the zone that has provided the signed response. If a resolver is configured with a trust anchor (or more than one) that exists higher in the DNS tree, for instance, the root's public key,[23] it theoretically can verify any signed responses.[24] This is because a path can always be constructed from the root zone to lower zones, assuming every zone in the path is signed and carries a Delegation Signer (DS) resource record for child zones. This architectural design highlights the critical importance of parent zones maintaining and signing DS records, if widespread deployment of DNSSEC across the Internet is to be achieved.

However, what happens in a scenario in which portions of the DNS tree, and particularly the root, are not signed? An incomplete authentication hierarchy, where a parent zone does not support DNSSEC, created an "islands of trust" problem. For instance, the Swedish country code TLD—.se—was signed in 2006 yet its parent (the root) was not.[25] The .se zone was a secure island isolated from the rest of the DNS tree. Another example was the .gov TLD. DHS acknowledged in 2007 that it would be possible to deploy DNSSEC in zones the U.S. government was responsible for without securing the root.[26] And, in fact, in February 2009 the U.S. government's .gov zone was signed. In both cases, the absence of a signed root required the zone operator to maintain its own DNSSEC trust anchor that could be used by resolvers to validate resource records.

Alternatives to Signing the Root

In the absence of a signed root, interim solutions emerged for handing trust anchor material, including DNSSEC Look-aside Validation (DLV) and a Trust Anchor Repository (TAR).

DLV proposed to bypass the normal DNS hierarchy and allow resolvers to validate DNSSEC-signed data from zones whose ancestors either weren't signed (e.g., the root) or refused to publish DS records for their child zones. One specification suggested that the Internet Assigned Numbers Authority (IANA) maintain a DLV registry, although any party could maintain a registry of validated entry points to secure zones.[27] In fact, in March 2006, Internet Systems Consortium (ISC), developers of the widely used BIND resolver software, launched its own DLV registry, intending it as a bootstrapping measure until the root was signed.[28]

In April 2008, the ICANN board approved a TAR, authorizing IANA to create and maintain a registry of DNSSEC trust anchors for TLDs.[29] TLD operators could upload their trust anchor material to the TAR, where resolver operators could securely retrieve it. From an efficiency and political standpoint, the creation of a TAR by ICANN had many advantages, including that

• it provided TLD registries and resolver operators with a single repository for trust anchors to support DNSSEC deployment, operated by a nongovernmental, Internet community-trusted entity; and
• it avoided the USG political oversight of the root zone issue, since a TAR did not impact on the DNS root zone management process and the Department of Commerce would have no contractual oversight of how a TAR was implemented or operated.

While the DLV or TAR solutions removed the difficult hurdle associated with signing the root zone file, they also changed who absorbed the deployment and ongoing costs of DNSSEC. Such approaches risked eliminating the efficiencies gained by maintaining relatively few trust anchors for the secure, global DNS. Multiple organizations would have to deal with the same operational questions and expenses, namely key management. More importantly, having numerous trust anchors would increase the burden of security policy evaluation and key updating for resolver operators (i.e., to Internet service providers [ISPs] running caching resolvers, and perhaps ultimately, to security-aware stub resolvers used by end-user applications). Arguably, they presented situations that were simply not scalable across the entire Internet.

Determining Root Signing Authority

While evident that the best way to secure the DNS effectively, efficiently, and globally was to implement DNSSEC at the root, how that should be done remained unanswered. The existing root zone management process, controlled by the Department of Commerce through the "IANA functions" contract with ICANN and cooperative agreement with VeriSign, the root zone maintainer (RZM), required TLD registries to send change requests to ICANN (specifically IANA) for processing. Once it was determined that the changes met IANA's narrow technical requirements and the ICANN Board approved them, the request would be forwarded to the U.S. Department of Commerce for review and approval. If the Department of Commerce approved the changes, VeriSign would generate a revised root zone file and distribute it to a distribution master name server. From there, other root server operators (RSOs) located around the world could retrieve it. The development of a procedure to sign the DNS root zone file provided an opportunity to closely examine the management arrangement and potentially achieve shared responsibility for the Internet's root zone that took into account political, economic, and operational issues.

Awareness and Positioning Begins

A report prepared in late 2006 for the U.S. Department of Homeland Security proposed that a single organization be responsible for the key signing key (KSK) and zone signing key (ZSK) for the Internet's root zone.[30] Although the report did not explicitly say that the control of the keys would be held by DHS itself or even a U.S. government agency, the politically sensitive association between a U.S. national security organization and the root signing process triggered international concern.[31] This concern was first publicly expressed at an ICANN meeting in Lisbon by the president of the Canadian Internet Registration Authority (CIRA). It was followed by a flurry of stories questioning the motives of the U.S. government, and a public response by DHS over a month later in which the responsible program manager indicated a new specification would be released for public comment by late summer 2007.[32] Following this, numerous stakeholders publicly expressed opinions on the procedure for signing the root.

In March 2007, academics with expertise in Internet governance proposed that a limited number of nongovernmental organizations take responsibility for generating, using, and distributing root zone KSKs and ZSKs.[33] It also advocated removing completely the Department of Commerce's role in approving changes to the root zone, which served no technical purpose. Such a proposal distributed authority and provided increased resilience, and most importantly, eliminated the threat of political interference by any government. The authors also took issue with a proposal that suggested a restricted, multilateral "security council" model for governmental oversight of changes to the root, arguing that that approach simply compounded the political problem by thrusting more governments into a process where governments add no value in the first place.[34]

In June 2007, the European technical community represented by Réseaux IP Européens (RIPE) sent a letter to ICANN, urging the organization "to speed up and improve its efforts to get the root zone signed."[35] Shortly thereafter, in July 2007, IANA unveiled its root zone signing test bed. Importantly, IANA's test bed architecture had it assuming control for generating and using the KSK and ZSK to edit, sign, and publish the root zone, which would then be sent to VeriSign for distribution.[36] No doubt responding to this encroachment on its existing root zone management role, VeriSign announced in February 2008 at the ICANN-Dehli meeting that it would implement its own DNSSEC test bed for the root zone. The unexpected move raised questions from some ccTLD operators, who had indicated their support for ICANN/IANA to sign the root zone in a 2007 survey.[37]

ICANN and the Department of Commerce Tussle over Root Zone Authority
With more than a year of test bed operations under its belt, ICANN submitted its proposal for signing the root to the Department of Commerce's National Telecommunications and Information Administration (NTIA) on September 2, 2008.[38] It was clear from ICANN's correspondence that its proposal was based on the IANA test bed, modifying the current root zone management roles as indicated earlier and shown in figure 4.1.

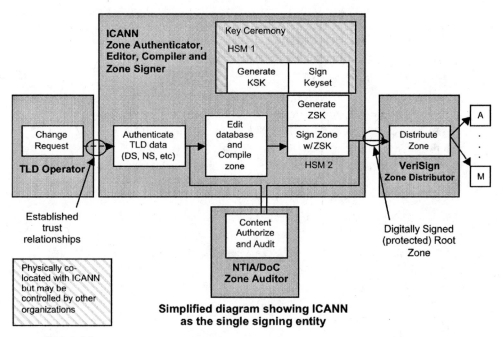

Figure 4.1
Reproduced from Internet Corporation for Assigned Names and Numbers (ICANN) DNSSEC Proposal (September 2, 2008), <http://www.ntia.doc.gov/DNS/ICANNDNS-SECProposal.pdf>.

Such an arrangement seemed consistent with prevailing Internet community sentiment, and it did not disturb the department's oversight role. It was also in line with the 2006 settlement agreement between ICANN and VeriSign over the .com registry contract, which included a Root Server Management Transition Completion Agreement that specified the parties move to "enable ICANN to edit, sign and publish the root zone."[39] Such a transition was, unsurprisingly, supported by ICANN's 2008 President's Strategy Committee (PSC) report titled *Improving Institutional Confidence*.[40]

Despite the convergence of expectations around ICANN to sign the root zone, NTIA had been consistently against such an idea. In response to the PSC report it stated:

The Department believes strongly that it is important to clarify that we are not in discussions with either party to change the respective roles of the Department, ICANN or VeriSign regarding the management of the authoritative root zone file, nor do we have any plans to undertake such discussions. Consistent with public statements made by the United States government starting in 2000 and reinforced by the 2005 U.S. Principles on the Internet's Domain Name and Addressing System, the Department, while open to operational efficiency measures that address governments' legitimate public policy and sovereignty concerns with respect to the management of their ccTLD, has no plans to transition management of the authoritative root zone file to ICANN as suggested in the PSC documents.[41]

Consistent with this position, NTIA responded quickly and unfavorably to ICANN's proposal, saying that it would be seeking public input in the matter and that it considered ICANN's proposal "to have been submitted as a proposed modification to the IANA functions contract."[42] And because the IANA proposal would "alter root system responsibilities contrary to the performance exclusions in the contract . . . the Department does not authorize ICANN to engage in public consultations on this proposal or the terms of the IANA functions contract." While the existing IANA functions contract clearly prevented ICANN from making any changes to the root zone management process without renegotiation, it was unclear under what authority the department could restrict a private public-benefit corporation from simply engaging in discussions on deployment of DNSSEC at the root.[43] Nonetheless, ICANN did not release its proposal for discussion at that time.

Soon after NTIA's response to ICANN, VeriSign released its own proposal for signing the root zone.[44] Importantly, it retained the existing root zone editing, authorizing, and publishing roles held by IANA, the Department of Commerce, and VeriSign, respectively. ICANN would receive registry key material (DS records) from TLD operators, similar to other resource record updates, for review and inclusion in the root zone upon approval from the Department of Commerce. The proposal recommended that VeriSign generate the ZSK, and sign and publish the root zone. And in an attempt to address the political sensitivities surrounding control of the KSK, VeriSign suggested distributing that activity to the root server operators.

The Internet Community Officially Weighs In

Now faced with competing and substantially different proposals, and having browbeaten ICANN for its attempts to take the initiative in defining a root signing process, the Department of Commerce took control of the process and issued a formal Notice of Inquiry (NOI). The NOI asked whether or not the root should be signed and offered six proposed process flows for comment, including ICANN's and VeriSign's proposals, as well one largely reflecting the existing management process.[45] Acknowledging the global interest and impact of signing the root, the Department of Commerce explicitly invited input from outside the United States. And to promote greater transparency, it required filing of ex parte communications.

Over fifty comments were received, mostly from organizations based in North America and Europe. It was clear there was strong support in general for signing the root zone. But other more nuanced positions emerged as well. First, several comments identified that the ZSK should remain under the control of whoever published the root zone. Second, it was argued that whatever process was chosen, it should not preclude the possibility of changing the process in the future.

However, it was less certain what specific process flow should be instituted. Some clearly stated ICANN should control any signing activity; others explicitly stated that VeriSign should not perform any signing activity, with one comment highlighting the potential competition policy issues of having the world's largest TLD operator also responsible for publishing the signed root. Global financial services company PayPal, one of the few non-Internet infrastructure-related companies to respond, argued it was not necessary to alter the current root zone management process in order to accommodate root signing, but that eventually the process should evolve to include a signing process distributed among several parties. The Internet Architecture Board made a similar statement, "that the implementation of DNSSEC at the root can and should align with the functions involved in root zone maintenance, generation, and audit.

The implementation of DNSSEC, however, need not today nor for the foreseeable future be cause to permanently fix the roles involved."

The Department of Commerce never published a formal summary and analysis of comments submitted, as is typically required of most agency proceedings. At the Sydney ICANN meeting in June 2009, NTIA presented its initial interpretation of the comments received. It stated that DNSSEC should be implemented at the root as soon as possible, and maintained "implementation should be aligned with functions of the [current] root zone management process."[46]

Determining Implementation Requirements for Root Signing

Having decided that the existing root zone management roles should be maintained, NTIA announced it was working with ICANN and VeriSign on an interim approach to deployment, by the end of 2009, of DNSSEC in the root zone.[47] An initial draft, developed largely internally by NIST with other U.S. government agency input, outlined technical requirements for implementation and proposed to "initially to overlay the deployment process on the existing root zone management process, thereby minimizing the introduction of new steps and changes of responsibilities among the involved parties." Additionally, it specified American-developed RSA cryptographic signing and hashing algorithms and key sizes to be implemented at the root zone, and recommended various NIST-authored FIPS documents as operational guidelines.

By early July 2009, NTIA had envisioned and initiated an ongoing informal consultation to evaluate the requirements. Instead of publishing the draft or forwarding it to the IETF's DNSEXT Working Group for public review, it circulated the draft among a limited number of individuals in the Internet's technical community, as well as ICANN and VeriSign, and "to the extent possible, input resulting from these consultations [was] reflected in the requirements."[48] The final document was formally released to the public at the end of October 2009. With requirements in hand, ICANN and VeriSign began the process of implementing DNSSEC at the root with an expected completion date of July 2010.

Principal-Agent Relationships and Control of the Secured Root

For principal-agent theorists in political science, the outcome surrounding securing the root is not surprising. How principals achieve their objectives through an agent without necessarily abdicating control has been explored in domestic and international contexts.[49] The main risk in principal-agent relationships is that the agent may deviate from the interests of the principal. Deviation is minimized when the principal is knowledgeable about the consequences of an agent's activities and when a principal and agent share common interests and desire the same outcomes.[50] The risk of deviation can be mitigated by principals through ex ante approaches like contractual obligations that constrain or guide agent behavior and the identification of optimal agents through screening and selection mechanisms; and ex post techniques such as the use of agent monitoring and reporting requirements, and designing institutional checks that ensure that no single agent can act unilaterally.[51]

The episode of securing the root illustrates these ex ante and ex post factors at work. In ICANN's transparent efforts to inform the Internet community of its plans for signing the root, it revealed its intentions to assume greater control in the root zone management process. NTIA relied on the obligations outlined in the IANA functions contract to slow down ICANN's momentum, allowing it time to institute a NOI process where NTIA could gather evidence to influence the process more directly.

The episode offers some valuable lessons. First, it is not enough to be concerned simply with pursuing the development of open standards. DNSSEC was developed in a setting (i.e., the IETF) that many consider an exemplar of open standards development. Second, there is a need to pay more attention to the governance arrangements in which open standards are implemented. The underlying relationships of institutions involved warrant closer examination, as they may be used strategically, even when relatively open and transparent processes are in place, to control outcomes.

Notes

1. Anyone can view the contents of the DNS root zone file; see <http://www.internic.net/zones/root.zone>.

2. For discussions of the World Summit on the Information Society and how U.S. control of the DNS root became a geopolitical controversy, see M. Mueller, *Networks and States: The Global Politics of Internet Governance* (Cambridge, MA: MIT Press, 2010); David Souter, "The View from the Summit: A Report on the Outcomes of the World Summit on the Information Society," *Info: The Journal of Policy, Regulation and Strategy for Telecommunications* 6, no. 1 (2004): 6–11.

3. A zone is an administratively determined section or "cut" of the domain name space. For example, .com, .edu, and .se are three top-level domain (TLD) zones; companyA.com is a second-level domain zone in the DNS. A zone is served by one

or more name servers, that is, a host machine that maintains DNS information for zero or more zones. In addition, for each zone, there exists a single authoritative DNS name server that hosts the original zone data, although this name server is typically mirrored in several locations. For TLD zones, the primary master server that hosts the root (".") zone file is authoritative. It is mirrored by root-server operators around the world.

4. For a detailed analysis of threats that DNSSEC addresses, see D. Atkins and R. Austein, "Threat Analysis of the Domain Name System (DNS)," RFC 3833 (August 2004), <http://www.ietf.org/rfc/rfc3833.txt> (accessed December 2006). For information on the different types of DNS spoofing attacks, see U. Steinhoff, A. Wiesmaier, and R. Araújo, "The State of the Art in DNS Spoofing," in 4th International Conference on Applied Cryptography and Network Security (ACNS'06); and S. Ariyapperuma and Chris J. Mitchell, Information Security Group, "Security Vulnerabilities in DNS and DNSSEC" (2007), <http://www.isg.rhul.ac.uk/cjm/svidad.pdf> (accessed January 2007).

5. For detail concerning a single episode of DNS poisoning that occurred in March 2005, see <http://isc.sans.org/presentations/dnspoisoning.html>.

6. In 2009, attacks against Twitter and Chinese search engine Baidu targeted their DNS registrars. In both cases, perpetrators allegedly compromised the registrars' security systems and were able to update DNS resource records and redirect domain names to defaced sites.

7. See D. E. Eastlake III and C. Kaufman, "Domain Name System Security Extensions," RFC 2065 (January 1997), <http://www.ietf.org/rfc/rfc2065.txt> (accessed March 15, 2005). This document became obsolete with the publication of D. Eastlake, "Domain Name System Security Extensions," RFC 2535 (March 1999), <http://www.ietf.org/rfc/rfc2535.txt>.

8. See R. Arends, R. Austein, M. Larson, D. Massey, and S. Rose, "DNS Security Introduction and Requirements," RFC 4033 (March 2005), <http://www.ietf.org/rfc/rfc4033.txt> (accessed March 15, 2005); R. Arends, R. Austein, M. Larson, D. Massey, and S. Rose RFC4034 "Resource Records for the DNS Security Extensions," RFC 4304 (2005), <http://www.ietf.org/rfc/rfc4304.txt> (accessed March 15, 2005); and R. Arends, R. Austein, M. Larson, D. Massey, and S. Rose, "Protocol Modifications for the DNS Security Extensions," RFC4035 (2005), <http://www.ietf.org/rfc/rfc4035.txt> (accessed March 2005).

9. See T. Hansen, D. Crocker, and P. Hallam-Baker, "DomainKeys Identified Mail (DKIM) Service Overview," RFC 5585 (July 2009), <http://datatracker.ietf.org/doc/rfc5585/>.

10. See D. Recordon and D. Reed, "OpenID 2.0: A Platform for User-centric Identity Management," in *Proceedings of the Second ACM Workshop on Digital Identity Management* (New York: Association of Computing Machinery, 2006), pp. 11–16.

11. In fact, early DNSSEC deployment efforts were tripped up by U.S. export controls, resulting in the temporary removal of BIND (i.e., the market-dominant DNS software) prototype source code from the Web. Originally classified in 1996 by the Bureau of Export Administration (BXA) as authentication software and therefore exempt from Export Administration Regulations, the software was reclassified as a controlled item almost a year later by BXA, making it subject to export restrictions. BXA concern centered on the inclusion of RSAREF, a collection of cryptographic routines source code that could be modified to provide data confidentiality. However, it was argued that BXA had questionable jurisdiction and its action was based upon an unwritten rule to reclassify the software. Eventually, with liberalization of export controls, the restriction was lifted. See Gilmore (2000), <http://www.chiark .greenend.org.uk/pipermail/ukcrypto/2000-February/047193.html> (accessed November 2008).

12. See presentation from Trusted Information Systems Labs at the May 2001 North American Networks Operators Group (NANOG) meeting, <http://www.nanog.org/ mtg-0105/ppt/lewis.ppt#280,13,Result: Value of Key Distribution>.

13. See United States Congress H.R. 3394, Cyber Security Research and Development Act (2001), <http://frwebgate.access.gpo.gov/cgi-bin/getdoc.cgi?dbname=107_cong _public_laws&docid=f:publ305.107>.

14. See E-Government Act of 2002, Pub. L. no. 107–347, 116 stat 2899 (2002) <http://frwebgate.access.gpo.gov/cgi-bin/getdoc.cgi?dbname=107_cong_public _laws&docid=f:publ347.107>.

15. The relationship between law enforcement and surveillance interests and technical agencies (like NIST) in the U.S. government, as it pertains to encryption use in communications systems in the United States, has been a source of controversy for two decades. See Whitfield Diffie and Susan Landau, *Privacy on the Line: The Politics of Wiretapping and Encryption* (Cambridge, MA: MIT Press, 1998) for the history of the National Security Agency's (NSA) role in encryption-related standards and the Computer Security Act of 1987, which moved official development of federal encryption standards (for unclassified material) to NIST from NSA. The importance of creating this separation still resonates with law makers; the current administration's proposal to move the NIST's Computer Security Division to the DHS (see Homeland Security Act of 2002 as introduced in the House) during its formation was met with strong resistance by Senator Maria Cantwell (WA) and others familiar with the "crypto-wars" of the early 1990s, and ultimately the proposal failed. See D. Carney, "DHS and NIST to Collaborate" (2003), <http:// www.techlawjournal.com/topstories/2003/20030522.asp> (accessed November 30, 2005).

16. See <http://www.us-cert.gov/press_room/050215cybersec.html> (accessed November 2008).

17. See <http://www.us-cert.gov/reading_room/cyberspace_strategy.pdf>.

18. See <http://csrc.nist.gov/publications/nistpubs/800-81/SP800-81.pdf> (accessed November 2008).

19. See <http://mail.shinkuro.com:8100/Lists/dnssec-deployment/Message/553-02-B/061031RootSignSpec.pdf> (accessed November 2008).

20. See <http://csrc.nist.gov/publications/nistpubs/800-53-Rev1/800-53-rev1-final-clean-sz.pdf> (accessed November 2008).

21. See OMB Memorandum M-08–23 (August 2008), <http://www.whitehouse.gov/omb/memoranda/fy2008/m08-23.pdf (accessed November 2008).

22. This key data are contained in the DNSKEY or a signed DS resource record.

23. To be precise, the key mentioned in note 22 is the key signing key (KSK) for the root zone. In fact, in most cases each zone will manage two types of key-pairs, KSKs and zone signing keys (ZSKs). The ZSK key-pair is used to sign and authenticate a particular zone's record sets, while the KSK key-pair can be used less frequently because it is used only to sign and authenticate a zone's ZSK.

24. R. Chandramouli and S. Rose, "Challenges in Securing the Domain Name System," *IEEE Security & Privacy* 4, no. 1 (2006): 84–87. This point is actually theoretical if the zones in which the majority of domain names exist (e.g., .com) do not implement DNSSEC.

25. Sweden's Internet Infrastructure Foundation announced commercial DNSSEC service in February 2006, with secure resolution being offered by Swedish ISP Telia-Sonera. See <http://www.iis.se/english/nyheter/news/2007-02-16?lang=en%20> (accessed November 2008).

26. <http://www.upi.com/Security_Terrorism/Analysis/2007/04/12/analysis_owning_the_keys_to_the_internet>.

27. See S. Weiler, "DNSSEC Lookaside Validation (DLV)," RFC 5074 (November 2007), <http://tools.ietf.org/html/rfc5074>.

28. See "ISC Launches DLV Registry to Kick off Worldwide DNSSEC Deployment," March 27, 2006, <https://www.isc.org/about/pr/2006032700>.

29. See ICANN Board approval at <http://www.icann.org/en/minutes/minutes-30apr08.htm>.

30. See "Signing the Domain Name System Root Zone: Technical Specification," <http://www.links.org/files/061031RootSignSpec.pdf> (accessed April 22, 2011).

31. See <http://www.heise.de/english/newsticker/news/87655/from/rss09>.

32. See <http://technews.acm.org/archives.cfm?fo=2007-04-apr/apr-16-2007.html&hdr=1>. The strong public reaction was perhaps reflective of the way in

which the DHS report was handled. The document was reviewed initially by other U.S. agencies and then distributed for comment in November 2006 to a limited group of technical experts in government, academia, and key Internet governance and infrastructure organizations from eight countries. Surprisingly, the document was marked "not for further distribution" yet posted to a publicly available listserv. An unknown number of comments on the report were received, but were not made available to the public.

33. See Brenden Kuerbis and Milton Mueller, "Securing the Root: A Proposal For Distributing Signing Authority," *Internet Governance Project*, paper IGP07-002, May 17, 2007, <http://internetgovernance.org/pdf/SecuringTheRoot.pdf>.

34. The Burr-Cade proposal was authored by Becky Burr (former NTIA official) and long-time Washington, DC, lobbyist Marilyn Cade. See <http://internetgovernance .org/pdf/burr-cade.pdf>.

35. See <http://www.ripe.net/ripe/wg/dns/icann-root-signing.pdf>.

36. See presentation by Richard Lamb, "IANA DNSSEC Systems Development," July 22, 2007, <http://www.potaroo.net/iepg/2007-07-ietf69/DNSSEC_at_IANA_IETF .pdf>.

37. See comments by Leslie Cowley during Dehli ccNSO meeting, transcript available at <https://delhi.icann.org/files/Delhi-ccNSO-12FEB08.txt>. Survey available at <http://ccnso.icann.org/surveys/dnssec-survey-report-2007.pdf>. The survey was repeated again in 2008 with results again indicating support for ICANN.

38. See <http://icann.org/correspondence/twomey-to-baker-02sep08.pdf>.

39. See the "Root Server Management Transition Completion Agreement," <http:// www.icann.org/en/topics/vrsn-settlement/revised-root-transition-agreement-clean -29jan06.pdf>.

40. See *Improving Institutional Confidence in ICANN* (2008), <http://icann.org/en/psc/ iic/improving-confidence-en.pdf>.

41. See "Public Comments: Improving Institutional Confidence in ICANN," <http:// www.ntia.doc.gov/comments/2008/ICANN_080730.html>.

42. See <http://icann.org/correspondence/baker-to-twomey-09sep08.pdf>.

43. See section C.4.2 of the contract, <http://www.ntia.doc.gov/ntiahome/ domainname/iana/ianacontract_081406.pdf>.

44. See   <http://dnssec-deployment.org/pipermail/dnssec-deployment/2008- September/002481.html>.

45. See <http://www.ntia.doc.gov/frnotices/2008/FR_DNSSEC_081009.pdf>.

46. See   <http://syd.icann.org/files/meetings/sydney2009/presentation-dnssec- workshop-heineman-24jun09-en.pdf>. The comments from RIPE and the IAB

are at <http://www.ntia.doc.gov/DNS/comments/comment026.pdf> and
<http://www.ntia.doc.gov/DNS/comments/comment017.pdf>, respectively.

47. See "Commerce Department to Work with ICANN and VeriSign to Enhance the
Security and Stability of the Internet's Domain Name and Addressing System," June
3, 2009, <http://www.ntia.doc.gov/press/2009/OIA_DNSSEC_090603.html>.

48. See *Testing and Implementation Requirements for the Initial Deployment of DNSSEC
in the Authoritative Root Zone*, October 29, 2009, <http://www.root-dnssec.org/
documentation>.

49. See, e.g., M. D. McCubbins, R. G. Noll, and B. R. Weingast, "Administrative
Procedures as Instruments of Political Control," *Journal of Law, Economics, and
Organization* 3, no. 2 (1987): 243–277; D. G. Hawkins, D. A. Lake, D. L. Nielson,
and M. J. Tierney, *Delegation and Agency in International Organizations* (New York:
Cambridge University Press, 2006).

50. See A. Lupia, "Delegation of Power: Agency Theory," in *International Encyclopedia
of the Social and Behavioral* Sciences, vol. 5 (Oxford, UK: Elsevier Science Limited,
2001), pp. 3375–3377.

51. See D. R. Kiewiet and M. D. McCubbins, *The Logic of Delegation* (Chicago:
University Of Chicago Press, 1991), p. 27; and McCubbins, Noll, and Weingast,
note 50.

5 Open Document Standards for Government: The South African Experience

Andrew Rens

During 2007 and 2008, South Africa was at the forefront of the growing global movement to promote the use of open standards in computer software both at home and on the international stage. This case study of the South African experience illustrates the growing importance of open standards to the state, in particular to the developmental state, and increasingly contested international standards-making processes.

Open Standards and the State

Modern states rely for their core functions on the processing of information through information and communication technologies. The technologies deployed by a state are therefore not incidental to its form but instead are powerful if often unrecognized influences on that form. As Sandra Braman states:

Because informational power has altered the materials, rules, institutions, ideas, and symbols that are the means by which other forms of power are exercised, a new type of system, the informational state, has emerged. Information policy is thus key both to understanding just how this change of state has come about and to analysing how the informational state exercises power domestically and around the world. Information policy is the proprioceptive organ of the nation-state, the means by which it senses itself and, therefore, the medium through which all other decision-making, public or private, takes place.[1]

One immediate consequence is that states have slowly come to pay attention to the effects of becoming dependent on proprietary software. The issues that software raises for states are both salient and unprecedented. It is trite to observe that information is essential for the operation of a state, but as Braman points out information and information processing are now constitutive of the very nature of the contemporary state. At the same time private actors that supply the state with software are wielding unprecedented monopoly power over the means of information processing through statutory grants of intellectual property.

Software and the State

The variety and range of concerns raised by the reliance by a state on proprietary closed source software can be illustrated by considering the concerns that have arisen around proprietary word processing software.

Some dominant software—such as the Microsoft Office suite, the dominant word processing software during the global shift from standalone mainframe computers to networked desktop computers—historically uses proprietary formats. At some point every proprietary format is no longer supported, either because the vendor has ceased to operate, or because the vendor no longer regards the format as important. As a consequence a state that has stored its records in that format can no longer access the information, such as birth and death records, that it needs to carry out its most elementary functions, namely issuing passports, raising taxes, and identifying individuals.

The problem of inaccessible archived public documents vividly illustrates the problem of dependence on any vendor. However, vendor dependence, known as "vendor lock-in" creates a number of other problems for the day-to-day business of governance. Reliance on a single vendor's proprietary format creates a single point of failure for government—if the software fails, then the government is reliant on the vendor's response for its core functions and very survival. The monopoly power that the vendor obtains over the government, including the high costs of switching to another format, enables the vendor to raise prices beyond market prices without the threat of competition. For developing countries the tendency of proprietary software vendors in developed countries to include code designed to report back alleged unauthorized copying of copyright works (so called Technical Protection Measures) is especially concerning since it amounts to the installation of spyware that reports to the corporate citizen of another sovereign in the government's core systems.

Problems raised for developing country governments by proprietary software are not only operational but economic. In developing countries, the state is often the largest purchaser of software, sometimes by orders of magnitude. In these circumstances, preference for a single proprietary format supported by a single vendor results in dominance in that market sector by the vendor. This raises competition regulation concerns: a market is subject to anticompetitive pressures because the state is subsidizing one vendor at the expense of others. Vendor lock-in enables a single firm to capture all the value. Since almost all proprietary software vendors are located in the global North, the use of proprietary software results in developing country taxpayers financing royalty payments to the global North, with negative consequences for the balance of payments and the tax base.

Overshadowing both operational and economic issues are the effects that state dependence on proprietary software formats have on access to knowledge by the people living in that state. People who need access to state-held knowledge are barred from doing so if they do not have the proprietary software needed; in other words, if they cannot pay the premium for the proprietary software used by the state. Propriety software dependence thus amounts to economic discrimination.

Problems arising from government use of proprietary software and associated vendor lock-in raise operational, economic, and democratic concerns. Operational issues are largely concerned with the internal operation of the state, while economic issues are concerned with the effects of the state's procurement of software on the economy, and democratic concerns with how the relationship of citizens and state is affected by the state's use of software.

However, when governments adopt open standards the harms are mitigated. Open standards enable the systems of different government entities to communicate and interoperate. When governments mandate the use of open standards then different organs of government need not all use the same software but simply standards-compliant software.

Open standards address the problem of vendor lock-in. When documents are stored in formats that comply with open standards, then a range of vendors and service providers are able to provide software and services, whether proprietary or free and open source software (FOSS). A government is no longer tied to a particular vendor but can easily switch between vendors, or procure products and services from a combination of vendors. If a demand arises for particular products or services and there are no existing suppliers, then market incentives can operate, and new players can enter the market without claims of infringement of intellectual property rights.

Open standards enable migration to FOSS. It is only through the adoption of FOSS as well as open standards that some problems caused by vendor lock-in can be addressed. FOSS code is open so that governments' own experts can address security issues, respond to known breaches, and eliminate spyware. The use of FOSS ensures that the code is always open so that it is always possible for anyone with sufficient technical skill to address malfunctioning code. Governments using FOSS pay for services rather than goods, changing the ways in which governments are able to procure and pay for information processing to their benefit. Open standards coupled with FOSS enable a government to spread its spending across an "ecosystem" of firms of different sizes, thereby enabling the range of small and large firms conducive to innovation.

Developing countries can increase efficiency and stimulate the growth of local information technology by adopting open standards. Through adopting standards that have FOSS implementations, government is able to address the issue of citizen access to government through information and communications technologies, since citizens will be able use FOSS to communicate with government without having to pay for a particular vendor's software.

South Africa's Adoption of Open Standards

On October 24, 2007, South African Minister of Public Administration Geraldine Fraser-Moleketi introduced version 4 of the Minimum Interoperability Standards for Information Systems in Government (MIOS): "The Minimum Information Interoperability Standards (MIOS) sets out the Government's technical principles and standards for achieving interoperability and information systems coherence across the public sector. The MIOS defines the essential pre-requisite for joined-up and web enabled Government. Next to security, it is an essential component in the overall e-Government strategy."[2]

The MIOS required the selection of open standards to the extent possible. It also set out the requirement for a standard to be regarded as open, which the MIOS states should meet all of the following criteria:

It should be maintained by a noncommercial organization.
Participation in the ongoing development work is based on decision-making processes that are open to all interested parties.
Open access: all may access committee documents, drafts and completed standards free of cost or for a negligible fee.
It must be possible for everyone to copy, distribute, and use the standard free of cost.
The intellectual rights required to implement the standard (e.g. essential patent claims) are irrevocably available, without any attached.
There are no reservations regarding reuse of the standard.
There are multiple implementations of the standard.[3]

Document Formats and International Standards Organizations

The MIOS requires the use of the Open Document Format (ODF). ODF was developed by a group of software developers, including proprietary software vendors and free software coders through the Organization for the Advancement of Structured Information Standards (OASIS). Software that uses ODF as its native format includes Open Office, Star Office, Google Docs, IBM Lotus Symphony, and NeoOffice.

The standard was submitted to the International Standards Organization (ISO) and International Electrotechnical Commission Joint Technical Committee 1 (JTC1). A specialist subcommittee of JTC1 known as SC34 considered the standard and unanimously approved it on May 3, 2006, when it became ISO/IEC 26300:2006.

ISO describes itself as a nongovernmental organization, "the world's largest developer and publisher of International Standards" and "a network of the national standards institutes of 162 countries, one member per country." ISO is not an intergovernmental organization, nor does it form part of the United Nations, although it is based in Geneva, where many UN organizations maintain their head offices. Although ISO is a global standards-setting body, its self-description as an NGO somewhat obscures its role and function. Members of ISO include many national standards organizations that are usually government bodies but also include other standards bodies, whose members are corporations. ISO's effective power in setting standards that often become law, either through treaties or national standards policies, makes it more powerful than most NGOs, and in practice, ISO acts as a consortium with strong links to governments but without the accountability required of multilateral intergovernmental organizations.

Although Microsoft had participated in OASIS and the development of the ODF standard, it also developed another document specification, based on its own proprietary format, called Office Open XML. Microsoft introduced OOXML to an organization known as Ecma International (ECMA), formerly the European Computer Manufacturers Association. ECMA describes itself as is "an industry association founded in 1961" for Information and Communication Technology (ICT) and Consumer Electronics (CE). ECMA is a member of ISO, and in turn submitted OOXML as a putative second document standard to ISO although ODF (which was already in use by a wide variety of software including within the open source community) had been adopted as the standard for open document formats by the ISO before the introduction of OOXML. ECMA used its knowledge of standards processes to place OOXML on the ISO fast-track process—a process that if successful would have led to the existence of two mutually incompatible standards documents. The ISO fast-track process required that members of SC34 vote to engage in ballots on adopting the standard on two separate occasions. Voting by an ISO member that is a national standards body is often informed by a national subcommittee formed as a mirror committee to the ISO subcommittee.

South Africa's Experience of ISO's Adoption of OOXML

At the behest of Microsoft, the South African Bureau of Standards convened a subcommittee to make a recommendation whether or not South Africa should vote for the aspirant second document standard. The subcommittee was SC71L. On July 18, 2007, SC71L was asked to make a technical assessment and recommendation on how South Africa should vote on the further progress of the proposed standard that would allow for the approval of OOXML.

The committee, made up of various stakeholders including representatives from civil society, voted overwhelmingly[4] to reject the proposal that OOXML become the standard. Stakeholders represented on SC71L included Freedom to Innovate South Africa and the African Commons Project, both nonprofit organizations, software vendors including IBM and Sun Microsystems, the South African government, and Microsoft and its allied vendors. This decision went on to inform the way South Africa voted at the subcommittee meeting in September 2007. The ISO fast-track processes requires that members of the subcommittee attempt to resolve any issues when a standard has been rejected with a view to amendment of the standard to enable its adoption. A second ballot on the standard is then held on adoption of the standard.

As a result, and although OOXML had been rejected in the first round of balloting, the ISO ballot resolution process required a second round. In the run up to the second ballot, there was a great deal of lobbying of members by both the FOSS movement and Microsoft. Many governments, civil society organizations, and software developers objected to the adoption of OOXML, pointing out that ODF, a universally compatible standard, had already been adopted in 2006. The South African government made its views on the matter clear: in a speech made just before the ISO vote, then Minister of Public Service and Administration Geraldine Fraser-Moleketi pointed out that software patents pose a threat to developing nations and that open standards are a critical factor in building interoperable systems that are important to governments:

The adoption of open standards by governments is a critical factor in building interoperable information systems which are open, accessible, fair and which reinforce democratic culture and good governance practices. . . . It is unfortunate that the leading vendor of office software, which enjoys considerable dominance in the market, chose not to participate and support ODF in its products, but rather to develop its own competing document standard which is now also awaiting judgment in the ISO process. If it is successful, it is difficult to see how consumers will benefit from these two overlapping ISO standards. I would like to appeal to vendors to listen to the demands of consumers as well as Free Software developers. Please work together to produce interoperable document standards. The proliferation of multiple standards in this space is confusing and costly.[5]

The ballot resolution meeting held in Geneva from February 25–29, 2008, was followed by the ballot process. South Africa along with other countries including Canada, Venezuela, New Zealand, and emerging economies China and India voted to reject the application. However, OOXML was approved with 86 percent of the votes. During and after the ballot procedure there were extensive claims that the process had been compromised, and Microsoft had intensely lobbied many countries that had traditionally not participated in ISO and stacked technical committees with Microsoft employees, solution providers, and resellers sympathetic to OOXML.

The fallout from the voting process was as extensive as it was dramatic. The head of the Norwegian delegation at ISO resigned from his position, claiming that, although the majority of the Norwegian technical team was opposed to approving OOXML as a standard, the bureaucracy at Standard Norway overruled them. Public protests were held in Norway and Minister Fraser-Moleketi's speech was quoted by the protesters. Ubuntu founder Mark Shuttleworth expressed his disappointment in the decision, telling interviewers it was is a "sad" day for ISO and the computing public.[6]

In May 2008, the South African Bureau of Standards appealed the ISO process. The ISO procedures do not admit an appeal of the actual results of such a ballot but rather they permit an appeal on the validity of the ballot resolution process that led to the vote. South Africa appealed and was soon joined by Brazil, India, and Venezuela, which also appealed on a variety of grounds not canvassed in the South African appeal. Appeals may be either technical or administrative in nature and raise questions of principle and whether the contents of a draft may be detrimental to the reputation of IEC or ISO.[7] The secretaries general make recommendations whether a conciliation panel should be formed. In July 2008, the directors general of ISO and IEC delivered a recommendation to the ISO technical management board (TMB) to reject appeals against the process to ratify Microsoft's OOXML as an international standard.[8] In other words the secretaries general did not consider it worthwhile to address the concerns about the integrity of the process raised by the emerging economies.

In September 2008 the lead information technology agencies of Brazil, Cuba, Ecuador, Paraguay, South Africa, and Venezuela agreed on the CONSEGI Declaration, a letter to ISO protesting a fast-track standards approval process for OOXML. The declaration states:

The issues which emerged over the past year have placed all of us at a difficult crossroads. Given the organization's inability to follow its own rules we are no longer confident that ISO/IEC will be capable of transforming itself into the open and vendor-neutral standards setting organization which is such an urgent requirement. What is now clear is that we will have to, albeit reluctantly, re-evaluate our assessment of ISO/IEC, particularly in its relevance to our various national government interoperability frameworks.

Conclusion

In the past, government decision makers have considered ISO certification as a short cut to evaluation of standards. After ISO's dismissal of the appeals by the emerging economies, government decision makers can no longer do so. Instead government decisions makers must evaluate whether standards are open themselves. In South Africa the MIOS sets out criteria to enable government decision makers to evaluate whether a standard is an open standard. The specialist subcommittee of the South African Bureau of Standards approved ODF as the national standard on April 22, 2008. The national standards bodies are not required to adopt all ISO standards as national standards, and OOXML has not been made a national standard in South Africa.

The dispute over document standards highlights how technical specifications are no longer the domain of technical experts, since they can limit or enable access to knowledge, affect mission-critical operations of government, and generate anticompetitive effects. The loss of confidence by South Africa and other emerging countries in the independence and integrity of ISO processes will require governments to evaluate standards critically for themselves. The inquiry is not whether a standard is labeled "open" by a standards body but whether it enables a government to achieve the objectives for which governments use open standards, such as vendor independence, interoperability, and access to knowledge. At the same time standards remain technically challenging, requiring domain-specific expertise. A possible solution obliquely suggested by the CONSEGI Declaration is that emerging countries such as South Africa and Brazil may create alternative structures to ISO.

Notes

This case study is based on Andrew Rens and Rebecca Kahn's "OOXML vs. ODF— Local and International Responses to the Use of Microsoft Formats as a Standard," in *Access to Knowledge in South Africa*, ed. Andrew Rens and Rebecca Kahn, Access to Knowledge Research Series (2009).

1. Sandra Braman, "An Introduction to Information Policy," in *Change of State: Information, Policy, and Power* (Cambridge, MA: MIT Press, 2006), p. 4.

2. MIOSV4.1 2007 at <http://www.sita.co.za/standard/MIOSv4.12007.pdf>.

3. Ibid., p. 10.

4. Specifically the votes amounted to 2 votes of yes, with comments; 2 votes of yes, without comments; and 13 votes of no, with comments.

5. Alastair Otter, "SA Minister Slams Software Patents," *Tectonic* (March 19, 2008), <http://www.tectonic.co.za/?p=2304>.

6. Paula Rooney, "Ubuntu's Shuttleworth Blames ISO for OOXML's Win," *ZDNet* (April 1, 2008), <http://www.zdnet.com/blog/open-source/ubuntus-shuttleworth -blames-iso-for-ooxmls-win/2222>.

7. In terms of Chapter 11 of ISO/IEC JTC 1 Directives 5th edition ISo/IEC N 8557 2007-04-05.

8. "ISO to TMB: Here Are the Appeals Against OOXML; They Should Be Denied," *Groklaw* (July 9, 2008), <http://www.groklaw.net/article.php?story =2008070907285710>.

II Standards, Innovation, and Development Economics

6 An Economic Basis for Open Standards

Rishab Ghosh

This chapter provides an overview of standards and standards-setting processes. It describes the economic effect of technology standards—de facto as well as de jure—and differentiates between the impact on competition and welfare that various levels of standards have. It argues that most of what is claimed for "open standards" in recent policy debates was already well encompassed by the term "standards"; a different term is needed only if it is defined clearly in order to provide a distinct economic effect.

This chapter argues that open standards, properly defined, can have the particular economic effect of allowing "natural" monopolies to form in a given technology, while ensuring full competition among suppliers of that technology. This is a distinct economic effect that deserves to be distinguished by the use of a separate term, hence "open" rather than "ordinary" standards—referred to as "semi-open" in this chapter.

The chapter explains why open standards must allow all possible competitors to operate on a basis of equal access to the ability to implement the standard, and why this means that the economic effect of open standards may require different conditions for different markets. In most *software* markets, where free/libre/open source software (FLOSS) provides significant competition, open standards can only be those that allow equal access to FLOSS producers.

A case is made for public procurement to support open standards, and empirical evidence provided from an analysis of actual tenders as well as from the FLOSSPOLS[1] survey of government authorities to demonstrate how procurement policies in practice impede competitive markets for software products. Finally, some guidelines are provided for effective policy in relation to open standards and interoperability:

1. Open standards should be defined in terms of a desired economic effect: supporting full competition in the market for suppliers of a technology

and related products and services, even when a natural monopoly arises
in the technology itself.

2. Open standards for software markets should be defined in order to be
compatible with FLOSS licenses, to achieve this economic effect.

3. Compatibility with proprietary technologies should be explicitly
excluded from public procurement criteria and replaced by interoperability
with products from multiple vendors.

4. Open standards should be mandatory for e-Government services and
preferred for all other public procurement of software and software
services.

An Economic Definition for Open Standards

Many applications of technology in today's information society are subject
to *network effects*: the benefits to a single user are significantly enhanced if
there are many other users of the same technology. The value to a user of
an email system, for instance, is limited unless the system can be used to
send emails to many others, and increases enormously with the number
of other users. This value, which is over and above the value of a single
copy of the technology, is the *network externality*, that is, the additional
value provided by the network effect.

Network effects can go hand in hand with entry barriers for new technologies. A new technology may be adopted if it provides recognized
benefits over a previous technology. However, since the value of a widely
used system is, due to network externalities, much higher than the value
inherent to a single user's copy of the technology, any new technology is
seriously hampered by its lack of an existing user base. A new email system
must be far superior to an old system in order for its inherent benefits to
outweigh the severe disadvantage caused by the lack of a preexisting
network. In applications highly susceptible to network effects, where the
network externalities account for a large share of the total value of the
system—such as email—this hurdle may be impossible to cross. Indeed,
the email system most widely used today has remained more or less
unchanged for over twenty years.[2]

The self-enhancing feedback loop caused by network effects together
with the barriers posed to alternative technologies results in the dominance of particular products in their application areas, as *natural monopolies*. Monopolies are not obviously good for consumers, but the presumption
of natural monopolies in many areas has often been thought to provide a
better value for overall welfare than, say, having various incompatible

systems leading to a balkanized network of groups of users unable to talk to each other. However, monopolies are in a position to capture (or internalize) the value of network externalities—although this value is by definition not an attribute of an individual user's product or service, a monopoly or dominant player is in a position to raise the price of an individual user's access beyond its inherent value, based on the external value of the network effect. An email system that allows one to communicate with millions of others may be priced higher than a more sophisticated system that was limited to only a few thousand others. Thus, while monopolies have long been tolerated in the telecommunications sector, they are usually subject to regulation to limit their natural tendency to work against consumer welfare.

Another approach to network effects, however, is to try to abstract the network externalities from specific products. This is achieved by identifying the feature of the technology that provides the network effect, and ensuring that its use is not limited to a specific product or service. Rather, products and services from different producers are made *interoperable* by agreeing on *standards* for the basic technology components that provide the network externalities. This way, in theory at least, a natural monopoly arises in terms of the technology, but competition can thrive in terms of actual products and services that interoperate.

The problem arises that the natural monopoly on the technology for interoperability may have rights associated with it, and these rights may be owned by one market player (or a consortium). Such rights may be exploited to generate monopoly rents, which may counteract the competition in interoperable products and services that are enabled through the use of the standard. For example, if the holder of rights to the standard seeks monopoly rents from all use of the standard, it has an anticompetitive advantage over other users of the standard.

Alternatively, rights holders can use their licensing policies to control the further development of the standard, and to influence the market of products and service around the standard. While such influence could be used to improve social welfare, it could also be used to anticompetitive ends, by selectively granting the rights to producers and service providers using the standard. Such selection need not be arbitrary, it can also be achieved through the setting of licensing conditions that favor or discriminate against specific groups of producers. If the holder of rights covering a standard is also a supplier of products and services based on the standard, it has strong incentives to set licensing conditions that disadvantage the strongest potential competing suppliers. Thus, the natural monopoly that the standard creates in terms of technology may come along with competition in the market for products and services, but this competition may be limited by the control by rights holders of the access to the standard technology.

Standards can be de facto, where natural monopoly arises from market conditions that are initially competitive among different technologies, with agreement among producers on the standard technology arriving without a formal process. Usually, such a standard emerges through market dominance of the technology, often hand in hand with market domination of the technology vendor. Rents from such de facto standards are among the most attractive available to IT firms.

Alternatively, standards can be de jure, whereby a natural monopoly on technology is agreed upon by a body that may be an association (perhaps, but not necessarily, with a public interest mandate) of some combination of technology users and suppliers. Bodies with some level of formal process for defining such standards include the International Telecommunication Union (ITU), the European Telecommunications Standards Institute (ETSI), the Institute of Electrical and Electronics Engineers (IEEE), the World Wide Web Consortium (W3C), and the Internet Engineering Task Force (IETF). While owners of rights over de facto standards clearly have the interest and ability to exploit their monopoly over the standard technology to control or dominate the market in products and services based on the standard, it is quite possible for owners of rights over de jure standards to do this as well. As Joel West writes, "attempts to create advantage and lock-in are far from limited to the sponsors of de facto standards. Sponsors of de jure and consortia standards also gain advantage from attracting adopters and creating lock-in, if such standards are encumbered by private patent claims, as are standards such as W-CDMA, MPEG-4 and DVD"[3]

Some standards bodies try to limit this control- and rent-seeking behavior by defining processes to allow input from a variety of players in the definition of the standard (which affects what technologies and thus what rights holders are involved in the chosen standard). Standards bodies also define policies on licensing rights covering the standard, with various degrees of limits placed on the rights holders' ability to control suppliers of products and services based on the standard. Common policies include the requirement that rights be licensed under RAND (reasonable and non-discriminatory) or royalty-free terms.

If technology licensing policies are adopted (whether by the fiat of standards bodies or voluntarily by the technology rights holders) allowing all potential suppliers of products and services based on the technology to use it, without providing a competitive advantage to the rights holders, the theoretical economic effect of interoperable standards may be achieved. Standards based on such licensing policies could be called "open standards," with natural monopolies in the technology itself but competition in the supply of products and services using the technology.

Economic Effects of Types of Standards

Much discussion around standards relates to the institutional processes of standard selection, and this has influenced the terminology surrounding standards: de facto, de jure, "open standards." This chapter focuses, however, on the economic effects of different frameworks for technologies, and suggests the use of terminology based on the economic effects rather than the institutional processes alone.

Based on the preceding discussion, one could define three broad classes of technology frameworks based on the three broad classes of economic effects that they achieve:

1. Proprietary technologies: a natural monopoly in a technology results in a natural monopoly in the market for services and products based on the technology. These often become de facto standards, in which case they are properly referred to as "proprietary standards." This occurs when the rights to the technology are available only to the rights holders, and results in a dominant position for the owner of the technology.

2. ("Semi-open") standards: a natural monopoly in a technology arises (de facto) or is defined and agreed upon (de jure), but *some* competition in the market for products and services based on the technology is provided for, although potentially dominated by rights holders of the technology. Unlike most of the literature, we distinguish such standards from the next category and therefore refer to them as "semi-open standards," encompassing most standards set by most industry and international standards bodies. This occurs when the rights to the standard are made available to economic actors other than the rights holders, possibly under terms that provide an advantage to the rights holders over other competing economic actors.

3. Open standards: a natural monopoly arises (de facto) or a monopoly is defined and agreed upon (de jure) in a technology, but the monopoly in the technology is accompanied by *full competition* in the market for products and services based on the technology, *with no a priori advantage based the ownership of the rights* for the rights holder. This occurs when access to the technology is available to *all* (potential) economic actors *on equal terms*

providing no advantages for the rights holders. In particular, rights to the standard are made available to economic actors other than the rights holders under terms that allow *all* potential competitors using *all* potential business models to compete with the same degree of access to the technology as the rights holders themselves. When *no* competitive advantage is held by some players solely by virtue of owning rights over a standard,[4] then a unique economic effect is achieved of separating the natural monopoly of the technology itself from any possible monopoly among suppliers of the technology.

It should be clear from this list that simple economic criteria are being used here to discriminate between different technology market models—the relationship between the natural monopoly of the technology and the extent of competition possible among suppliers of products and services based on that technology. Such criteria are meaningful for policy making, if policy is set in order to achieve a given economic effect. Clearly, a policy debate needs to distinguish between terms (such as "standard" and "open standard") on the basis of the differences in the effect of the concepts behind them, otherwise the terms are in themselves meaningless.

It should also be clear from the preceding definitions that there is a distinct difference in the economic effect between "proprietary technologies" (or "proprietary standards"), "standards," and "open standards," in a progression of increased market competition. For the sake of clarity, we will refer in this chapter to "standards" that are not "open standards" according to the preceding definition as *semi-open standards*. This is a progression of normative frameworks that overcome the natural monopolies in certain technologies arising from the network effects associated with them. To the extent that monopolies harm welfare, the ability to augment the natural monopolies in technologies with a competitive market in the supply of products and services based on these technologies is positive. Thus there is a basis for consumers in general and policy makers in particular to encourage these normative frameworks, and to attempt to drive suppliers and markets toward the "open standards" at the competitive end of this progression.

This list does not indicate the processes required in order to achieve its goals, or the specific licensing terms that may be required to differentiate between standards and open standards. Such details could differ between different technology domains and depend on the market conditions.

For instance, the effect of open standards may be achieved with licenses requiring significant licensing fees and restrictions on use in a market where only firms with deep pockets and strong legal support structures can implement the technology concerned—such as the market for GSM (Global System for Mobile communications) cell phones (see discussion in the next section). In such markets, where huge investments are required for product development, royalties may not pose additional entry barriers. Indeed, in such markets, licensing terms may be less important than the processes involved in determining a standard (i.e., choosing the monopoly technology), which is why discussion of open standards relating to hardware or telecommunications often focuses most on due process, participation in standards-setting, and the publication of specifications rather than pure competition effects.

Similarly, in markets based on unit sales, audit or "no-sublicensing" requirements may not pose additional entry barriers.

However, in a market in which competing products and services could be implemented by small firms or groups of individuals without significant funds or the ability to control or audit the use of the licensed technology (such as FLOSS developers publishing their work under reciprocal or "copyleft" licenses), the economic effect of open standards as described may only be achieved by licensing terms that are free of royalty and license-audit requirements.[5] Indeed, in some markets, not only are such producers potential providers of products, they also are the *main competitors* to suppliers that hold a dominant position. In markets where FLOSS developers provide the significant existing or potential competition, royalty, audit, or no-sublicensing conditions (among others) do pose barriers, and reduce competition greatly, preventing the open standard effect. Achieving under such market conditions the economic effect of full competition in the market for products and services based on open standards would thus require the rights to the standard being made available under terms compatible with the existing legal and technical methods of FLOSS development.

Open Standards: Different Terms in Different Markets

The preceding discussion indicates that to maximize social welfare through the achievement of full competition in the market for products, the same rules can lead to different results, and different rules can lead to the same results, from sector to sector and technology to technology based on the market conditions unique to each.

For example, the success of the GSM standard for mobile telephony has been cited by the European ICT Association (EICTA), in their response to the European Commission IDABC (Interoperable Delivery of European eGovernment Services to public Administrations, Businesses and Citizens) Programme's European Interoperability Framework (EIF).[6] EICTA and the Business Software Alliance (BSA), among others, use the example of GSM to argue in favor of standard adoption under licensing regimes that require royalty payments and other conditions. Indeed, such conditions have not necessarily reduced competition or overly advantaged some producers of GSM technologies over others. However, the requirements, in terms of financial, technical, and legal infrastructure, to produce GSM equipment are quite demanding. Compared to, say, the capital requirements for manufacturing telecommunications hardware, the licensing and royalty conditions of the GSM standard itself are relatively undemanding. For the moment, at least, the conditions to use the GSM standard do not pose a barrier to the entry of potential competitors. So the economic effects outlined under the "open standards" definition previously set forth may be achieved without having royalty-free licensing for use of the standard. (This may change in the future, as telecommunications protocols are increasingly implemented in software, if generic hardware could be adapted to various protocols by software producers requiring much lower capital; in such a scenario, the conditions to use the GSM standard may pose a more significant barrier to the entry of additional competitors and may lead to the GSM-like licensing conditions not qualifying for the economics-based definition of "open standard.")

These arguments supporting royalty or other restrictive licensing conditions have no connection, however, with most parts of the market for software, and it is software and data interchange formats that are the main focus of the IDABC EIF.[7]

We discuss for illustration the domain of desktop office productivity software such as word processors, where the market conditions are completely different from that of mobile telephony equipment manufacturing. There is clear market domination by one product, Microsoft Word, and the sole supplier of this product, Microsoft.

The most significant competitor in terms of current and potential usage is OpenOffice Writer, an application developed by FLOSS developers and distributed under the GNU Lesser General Public License (LGPL). Any technology that disadvantages OpenOffice developers clearly does not achieve the market effect of full competition. Any de facto or de jure standard that is not licensed under terms that are usable in the development of OpenOffice cannot achieve the market effect of full competition, as OpenOffice developers are among the most significant competitors to the dominant supplier (indeed, full competition would require allowing equal access to the technology not just to significant competitors but also to *all* potential competitors).

As mentioned, OpenOffice is licensed under the GNU LGPL, which has the following features (among others):

1. It requires that the software may be redistributed without charge or notice.
2. It does not allow distribution of the software to be monitored or audited.
3. It requires that derived works of the software may be built and redistributed without charge or notice to the original developer.
4. It is an irrevocable license, as long as its terms are met.

Arguably, these features are the basis for the success of OpenOffice as a competitive product with significant market share. Any technology proposed as a standard for word processing, therefore, that was not available to OpenOffice developers under conditions compatible with the features just noted, would not allow OpenOffice to use the proposed technology. The proposed technology would thus not have the economic effect that open standards should have, in the previously proposed definition, and would thus not be an open standard.

What licensing conditions for a given word processing technology *would* have the economic effect of an open standard? To be compatible (at least) with the features of potential competing producers such as OpenOffice, the licensing terms must have the following attributes:

1. They must not require royalty payments.
2. They must not require monitoring or auditing of the distribution of licensed products.
3. They must allow the automatic (sub-) licensing of the technology to works derived from the product developed under the first license, without royalty requirements, monitoring, or audit requirements for the creation or distribution of such derived works. A license that is limited strictly to implementation of the standard may prevent this, if the limitation is enforced.[8]
4. They must be irrevocable, with some possible exceptions compatible with FLOSS licensing terms (e.g., revoked in defense, if the licensee sues the licensor for patent infringement).

The OpenOffice document format itself meets these requirements and could reasonably be called an open standard in terms of its economic effect. Indeed, the OpenOffice format has, since being initially a de facto standard, been accepted as the basis for the OASIS ODF.

The economic effect of the OpenOffice format is seen by the existence of numerous products from independent producers, in addition to OpenOffice itself, that support the format.[9] Microsoft now supports this format and there was nothing in the licenses covering the format that would prevent Microsoft's support. The same could not be said historically for Microsoft's own formats for Microsoft Office, which have not met the present definition of open standards. Microsoft Office formats have previously been proprietary, and recent XML-based formats have been encumbered with licenses that, while royalty free, appear to have been designed to prevent implementation by Microsoft Office's main competitor, OpenOffice. A new irrevocable covenant not to enforce Microsoft's patents over Office 2003 XML against software products "conforming" to the format appears to make this format an open standard in terms of economic effect, as it appears this format could now be implemented by OpenOffice and other potential competitors.[10]

This discussion shows that while the economic effects of an open standard can be achieved in some telecommunications markets while charging significant royalties for access to the standard technology (as with GSM), in the market for word processing, *royalty-free licensing alone would be necessary but not sufficient to create an open standard.*

This is important in the context of some existing government definitions of open standards. For instance, the European Commission's IDABC EIF defines open standards as having the following minimum characteristics:

1. adopted and maintained by a nonprofit organization with a decision-making process open to all interested parties;
2. published specification document available at nominal or no charge;
3. patents irrevocably made available on a royalty-free basis; and
4. no constraints on the reuse of the standard.[11]

As argued by BSA and EICTA and referred to in the previous section, this definition, by requiring royalty-free patent licensing, may be too strict for mobile telephony. On the other hand, the definition is not strict or clear enough for the word-processing market, since it does not clearly prevent "no-sublicensing" or audit requirements necessary to ensure full competition.

The IDABC EIF may also be too strict in its requirement of irrevocable patent licensing. This does not allow for defensive suspension, which, if compatible with FLOSS licensing models, would also be compatible with open standards as defined on their basis of economic effect. Indeed, a number of FLOSS licenses themselves include defensive suspension clauses specifically in cases of rights holders being sued for patent infringement.

Similarly, other definitions of open standards that accept Adobe PDF as an open standard are inappropriate if the economic effect is used as a basis for measuring openness. Although some ISO standards are based on Adobe PDF, Adobe's PDF licensing terms are not irrevocable. In theory, Adobe could wait until naïve public bodies all use its format, then arbitrarily terminate the patent licenses allowing PDF readers from competing vendors, then charge for its own PDF Reader software.

Going beyond Word Processing

While this analysis has focused on the specific example of word processing and text documents, it should be noted that the leading competitors to dominant market players in several parts of the software market are produced by FLOSS developers, and FLOSS software provides increasingly viable (and certainly future potential) competition.

The preceding discussion suggests that for large parts of the software market FLOSS is closely linked to the effective implementation of open standards, for two reasons. First, if FLOSS provides an existing or potentially competitive solution for a given problem domain, an open standard would have to be compatible with the development and distribution of implementations under FLOSS licensing terms.

Second, for most software standards the formal specification is insufficient and the actual standard may differ across implementations. Thus, some bodies (such as the IETF) require multiple interoperating implementations before recognizing a standard. As West writes, "for complex digital systems standards, the formal specification is inherently incomplete and the actual standard is defined both through the written specification and through actual implementations . . . for any firm trying to implement a standard, knowledge of both the formal specification and existing implementations is valuable. Otherwise, the implementer faces an extended trial-and-error process as it seeks to discover how other firms have resolved specification ambiguities. So a typology of openness must consider the openness both of the specification and implementation."[12]

This suggests the need for a *reference implementation* to augment—if not, perhaps, replace—the formal specification of the standard. When such a reference implementation is available under a FLOSS license, it may achieve the economic effect of an open standard as already defined in this chapter, even without the institutional processes of standards setting, since the reference implementation may act as the formal specification (especially if sufficiently well documented) and be reproduced without economic restrictions by any potential vendor of the technology.[13]

Thus, in this regard the IDABC EIF definition of open standards is in one sense too restrictive in requiring a formal institutional process of standards setting. As shown in the previous section, formal institutional processes are neither sufficient, nor, as just discussed, even necessary to achieve the economic effects desired of open standards.

The previous discussion shows that although open standards and FLOSS are certainly not equivalent, they are closely related in terms of the economic effect they achieve, and the way in which they do this. The next section examines how this relates to public procurement policy.

Standards, Software, and Procurement

Beyond the general description of the economic effect of standards, there are several issues specifically related to the public procurement of software and the provision of e-Government services (government services for citizens and businesses) in particular.

Private consumers and firms may have some interest in furthering market competition so as not to lock themselves into technologies associated with continuous rent seeking from dominant players. This is rarely an obligation. Public sector consumers, however, have in many situations an obligation to support (and certainly not to harm) competition through their procurement practices, for a number of reasons:

1. They are obliged to avoid explicitly harming competition in the market of private consumers. Thus, public agencies should not require citizens to purchase systems from specific vendors in order to access public services, as this is equivalent to granting such vendors a state-sanctioned monopoly.
2. They are obliged to save costs—taxpayer money—over the very long term. This is equivalent to an obligation to further net welfare, which is harmed by rent-seeking behavior and weakened competition.

The first point implies that e-Government services should provide access based on open standards, as defined previously in this chapter on the basis of their *economic effect*: fostering a fully competitive market. In particular, the public sector should never require citizens to purchase systems from specific vendors in order to access public services: this is equivalent to granting such vendors a state-sanctioned monopoly. It is absurd to pursue vendors for anticompetitive practices, while at the same time entrenching the dominant market positions of vendors by requiring that citizens buy their software in order to access public services, or requiring that businesses buy their software in order to compete for public tenders. Examples abound, from the Dutch Tax Authority requiring the use of Windows for filing electronic tax returns,[14] or the U.S. Federal Emergency Management Agency initially requiring the use of Windows and Internet Explorer by New Orleans Hurricane Katrina victims filing claims for relief. While many such examples involve Microsoft, befitting its role as the dominant vendor in several end-user software markets, any government service based on proprietary or ("semi-open") standards furthers this anticompetitive effect.

The second point implies that for procurement of software *in general*, public authorities should preferentially implement software based on open standards, as defined by their economic effect of fostering a fully competitive market. Supporting "semi-open" standards alone without fostering a fully competitive market is harmful to competition and net welfare, and thus expensive by definition over the long term. While software based on open standards may not always be available, public agencies should encourage its development, and indicate their preference for open standards to vendors though preferential procurement of software based on open standards wherever it *is* available. Similarly, public agencies should use open standards wherever supported by the software they implement, in preference to any other technologies supported by such software.

Empirical evidence from the FLOSSPOLS survey of 955 public authorities across 13 EU countries shows that public authorities are not generally aware of the economic effect of their own procurement choices. In particular, while expressing support in general terms for open standards and interoperability, they are unclear about what these terms mean (or should mean, for any meaningful economic effect). This is best illustrated through the response public authorities give when asked to rank the importance to a procurement decision for new software on compatibility with software that they are already using, in comparison to interoperability with competing software.

The main advantage of an open standard is its capacity to be interoperable with other software systems. Thus, a software application based on open standards is fully interoperable with any other application using the same standards, and it is possible for any other application to use the same standard. As a result, software buyers often try to achieve "vendor independence," which is to retain the ability to change software products or producers in the future without loss of data or significant loss of functionality.

However, this goal can conflict with implicit or explicit criteria for software purchasing, in particular whether new software is compatible with previously purchased software. Buyers who use the latter criterion rather than a general requirement for open standards or vendor-independent interoperability in effect remain locked in to their previously purchased software. Thus, even if they see the benefits of open standards and believe in interoperability, buyers whose preference for new software is based instead on compatibility with previously installed software are not, in practice, supporting or benefiting from interoperability.

Public Procurement and Competition: Empirical Evidence

To examine the relationship between compatibility and interoperability, FLOSSPOLS survey respondents were asked whether they find it more important that new software they buy is compatible with other software from the same product family they already use ("compatibility," i.e., preferring previous suppliers) or that new software is compatible with software from other producers and product families ("interoperability," i.e., no anticompetitive preference in procurement). Fifty-nine percent of the respondents favored interoperability and 33 percent favored compatibility (8 percent said they did not know).[15] This shows that a significant share of public administrations in practice lock themselves into proprietary technologies. While this may have long-term costs for these public administrations, it also has long-term costs for net welfare.

Preferring "compatibility" may even violate public procurement principles, since a preference—explicit or implicit—for "compatibility with previously installed software" favors the single supplier of that software, if it is based on proprietary or semi-open standards. An explicit preference, instead, for interoperability with open standards as defined in this chapter does *not* favor a single supplier of technology and is therefore far more in keeping with public procurement principles. This may also be more consistent with public procurement *law*. The European Commission found[16] that public procurement requirements to supply hardware based on "Intel or equivalent" microprocessors, or even requiring clock rates specific to Intel processors without mentioning Intel was not compatible with EU law.[17] This did not result in formal legal action, because EU member states changed their procurement policies in response to the EC's warning and formal notices sent regarding their procurement policies. What applies to public procurement of hardware could reasonably be thought to apply to software procurement too, especially as the use of tenders with explicit requirements for compatibility with proprietary software standards appears to be quite common.

While this subject clearly needs empirical research beyond the scope of this analysis, a quick keyword search for tenders on TED, the EU's public procurement portal identified 149 recent tenders including the term "Microsoft." A study conducted by OpenForum Europe in 2008 found that "OFE's monitoring exercise shows that in 34 tender notices out of 136 (25 percent), trademarks were mentioned in procurement documents." A brief analysis below, of six calls for tender, identifies the strong anticompetitive effects of public procurement that favors "compatibility" with proprietary standards over "interoperability" with open standards.

1. The anticompetitive effect starts with the procurement process itself, which may require bidders to purchase software from specific vendors. For instance, a tender from Scottish Enterprise, 2005, state that "All expressions of interest shall be provided either on paper or both on paper and in electronic format (via floppy disk using Microsoft Office compatible products)."[18] While not as bad as requiring citizens to purchase software from a single vendor for access to essential government services, such procurement procedure requirements are clearly detrimental to competition in the market for software even among *private* consumers.

2. A typical case of explicit preference to bidders using technologies from favored providers is a tender from Fife Council, 2005, which is for additional services to be built around "an interactive site provisioned through the use of Macromedia Cold Fusion and Microsoft SQL."[19] Such anticompetitive preferences are quite common even when they are not explicitly stated—tenders for the provision of Web sites for the European Commission, for instance, may require compatibility with the europa.eu.int EU portal. As the Europa portal is based on proprietary technologies (including ColdFusion), a specific vendor preference is introduced into the market even without mentioning brand names. This perfectly illustrates vendor lock-in, and how the anticompetitive effect goes beyond the public sector alone when public bodies are locked in. The original procurement of technology for Europa may have indeed been truly competitive in nature. Since it obviously did not require the use of open standards, *all future procurement related to Europa* is anticompetitive in nature and favors the single vendor owning rights to the original technology chosen, directly (through purchase of the same vendors' software) and indirectly (through the

requirement that suppliers of additional Web sites compatible with Europa purchase these vendors' software).

3. An example of how past purchase of software based on proprietary technology ensures a preference for the same proprietary technology (and thus favoring its sole vendor directly, or bidders who are customers of that sole vendor) is in the tender from Eurojust, 2005, a European international organization, for a library automation system.[20] In this tender, the preference for compatibility with previously purchased proprietary technology is explicitly stated: "Eurojust employs Intel-based servers running Windows 2003 and workstations running Windows XP. The network protocol in use is TCP/IP. Any proposed software must be able to function efficiently in this environment. Eurojust has a strong preference for Microsoft SQL as the database to minimize the variety of software to be supported in-house. It must be possible to integrate the system with Microsoft's Active Directory for user information and access control." Clearly, Microsoft and its customers are favored in this tender. If the previously purchased software was based on open standards, the new system could have been required to be interoperable with those open standards, thus giving no preference to individual vendors.

4. Preference for individual vendors can get explicit: a tender from Consip, Ministry of Economy and Finance, Italy, 2005,[21] is representative of the several tenders found for "software licences." It requires "licenze d'uso di programmi software Microsoft Office" (i.e., usage licenses for Microsoft Office). It is supposedly a competitive tender, yet the only competition possible is among resellers of Microsoft.

5. Explicit preference for individual vendors can be extreme. In a procurement process that was "negotiated without a call for competition" (i.e., explicitly without competitive bidding but an offer invited from a single vendor), Hessische Zentrale für Datenverarbeitung, 2005,[22] signed a contract with Microsoft Ireland for "software licences" worth euro 2.69 million over three years. The justification provided for this negotiated procedure is a concise statement of the argument presented previously in this document: "The works/goods/services can be provided only by a particular tenderer for reasons that are: Connected with protection of exclusive rights." Clearly, if proprietary technology is specified as part of the requirements, as explained in above, only the rights holder can provide the technology, due to the "protection of exclusive rights" around the technology.

According to the European Commission, "Under European law on public procurement, a brand may be specified only if it is otherwise impossible to describe the product sufficiently precisely and intelligibly" [23] True, the only way to describe proprietary software products such as Microsoft Office or Macromedia ColdFusion is through their brand names. But specifying these products in public procurement, rather than product-independent technical requirements, is surely anticompetitive. Just as the EC argued that microprocessors can be selected on performance criteria rather than specific clock rates (which favor a single vendor), software and software services should be selected on the basis of technology rather than products.

In order to ensure that this is done continuously it is essential to avoid the progression described in the preceding examples, from one original purchase that was perhaps competitive, to implicitly or explicitly favoring the same vendor (or resellers) repeatedly in all further purchases. As the examples show, this leads eventually to favoring or even requiring private sector bidders to purchase software from the same preferred vendors, cementing their position in the market place beyond the public sector.

For the reasons presented, due to the lock-in effect of proprietary standards, and the effect of the relationship between public procurement and standards in the software market, the only way such sustained competitive public procurement can be achieved is through

1. defining procurement requirement by technology rather than individual (named) products,
2. explicitly excluding compatibility with proprietary technologies as a selection criterion,
3. requiring (or at least preferring) interoperability with open standards.

Empirical Evidence from the FLOSSPOLS Survey

In addition to the widespread prevalence of compatibility as a selection criterion above interoperability, the FLOSSPOLS survey also provides an empirical association between open standards and FLOSS. Local governments that consciously use FLOSS are much stronger supporters of interoperability (67 percent) compared to only 50 percent of nonusers. We see from the survey results that limitations to interoperability set by proprietary software vendors help to increase a demand for FLOSS in an organization. This is of course only when the IT department of that organization truly wants interoperability, and is aware of the conflict between interoperability and proprietary software applications that promote lock-in ("compatibility") with their own proprietary standards. In contrast, organizations that do not prefer interoperability with open standards in their purchasing decisions are more likely to remain locked in to proprietary vendors providing compatibility with previously purchased software.

The association among open standards, inter-vendor interoperability, FLOSS usage, and vendor lock-in is highlighted in two further findings from the FLOSSPOLS survey. First, FLOSS users—who, as mentioned, are likelier to favor open standards and interoperability—rely on more vendors on average than nonusers (who, as mentioned, are likelier to favor compatibility with previously purchased software and thus get locked in to past vendors). Forty-one percent of FLOSS users have one to four regular vendors for their IT software and services; 59 percent have more than four vendors. For nonusers of FLOSS this ratio is reversed—61 percent have one to four vendors and only 39 percent have more than four vendors. This indicates a higher degree of concentration and possibly lower competition among suppliers of nonusers of FLOSS in comparison to organizations with some FLOSS use. While the survey did not show a clear causal relationship between FLOSS use and number of vendors (which could be influenced by external factors), increasing competition is frequently cited by IT managers as a reasons to use FLOSS.[24]

Indeed, the survey showed a clear relationship between perceived overdependence on vendors and a desire to increase FLOSS use. Fifty-three percent of those who would like to increase their FLOSS use felt too dependent on vendors, compared to only 30 percent of those who do not want to increase FLOSS use. A closer look at *current* FLOSS nonusers clarifies the link between FLOSS use and vendor independence. We defined two subgroups of these nonusers: those who would value increased FLOSS use are "future adopters," and those who would not are "persistent non-users." Fifty-eight percent of the "future adopters" say they are too dependent on vendors, while only 32 percent of the "persistent non-users" feel too dependent. Similarly, only 39 percent of "future adopters," compared to 64 percent of "persistent non-users" feel *not* too dependent on vendors. These differences indicate that for even for those who do not already use FLOSS (consciously), vendor dependency is indeed a strong driving force toward FLOSS use in the future.

Policy Strategies for Public Procurement

Open standards are not the same as FLOSS, and public administrations generally support the principle of open standards even when they are reluctant to support any policy with regards to FLOSS. However, support for open standards is in practice not meaningful unless it is strong support—mandatory, where possible—and uses a clear definition of open standards based on an understanding of their effects. Empirical evidence[25] has shown that "most ICT managers do not know for sure which standards are open and which are closed," with surprisingly high shares of survey respondents presuming that standards they use (e.g., Microsoft Word DOC) must be open while others that they use rarely must be closed. The result is that a generally stated principle in favor of interoperability is often replaced in practice with policies that favor compatibility with the proprietary standards of previously purchased software. Not only does this result in vendor lock-in for buyers, it also reinforces the market position of dominant players, with broadly negative effects for competition. Moreover, public authorities that favor interoperability *in practice* seem to implicitly or explicitly encourage FLOSS use.

A recommendation for public policy for effective support for interoperability, therefore, must start with a mandatory requirement not to include compatibility with previously purchased software as a selection criterion for new software. Rather, interoperability with software from multiple vendors must be the sole compatibility criterion for new software.

Beyond this, similar effects with respect to interoperability may be achieved by the support of FLOSS, or the support of open standards. In the latter case, however, policy would need to be strong (if not mandatory) in order to be effective at all, with a clear definition of open standards following the framework provided previously in this chapter.

This may require that the definition of open standards be tailored to specific software domains, and perhaps the classification of individual standards as open or not. An indication of how this approach may work is provided by the Dutch CANOS classification table and the Government's OSOSS Programme, although the criteria used by them differ from ours, which are based on the economic effect of the standard.

For several software domains, FLOSS developers provide viable competitive products and therefore the definition of "open standards" must be compatible with FLOSS development and licensing models. As described earlier in this chapter, this typically means that licenses on rights over the standard must be made available to FLOSS developers on a royalty-free, audit-free, sublicensable and irrevocable basis.

Some commentators have pointed out that according to European law "only specifications that are issued by public standardization bodies are considered standards"[26] and only such standards can be specified in calls for tender. This is a result of European Directive 98/34/EC (EU 1998), which listing national standards bodies as well as recognized European standards bodies.[27] The Directive is designed to "create an environment that is conducive to the competitiveness of undertakings."[28] In practice, as in the example calls for tender, procurement processes are often anticompetitive. The argument set forth in this chapter has shown that the legalistic definition of standards used by the Directive (as approved by recognized public standards bodies, with no concern for their licensing methods) is no guarantor of competition in public procurement or in the economy at large.

Notes

This chapter is a result of the FLOSSPOLS project, funded under the European Union's Sixth Framework Research Programme, under the administration of the European Commission's Directorate General for Information Society eGovernment Unit, contract number FP6-IS-507524.

1. FLOSSPOLS was a project coordinated by MERIT, funded by the European Commission, that included a survey of about one thousand public administrations across Europe on open source, open standards, and procurement practices among other topics. See <http://flosspols.org/deliverables.php>.

2. The SMTP protocol, the basis for Internet email today, was defined in RFC #822, "Standard for the Format of ARPA Internet Text Messages" (1982), <http://www.ietf.org/rfc/rfc0822.txt>.

3. Joel West, "What Are Open Standards? Implications for Adoption, Competition and Policy," Standards and Public Policy Conference, Federal Reserve Bank of Chicago, May 11, 2004, Chicago, IL, <http://www.chicagofed.org/news_and_conferences/conferences_and_events/files/west.pdf> (accessed March 24, 2005).

4. It should be noted that controlling rights to technology is not the only way vendors can gain a competitive advantage. Developing or first implementing the technology can also provide competitive advantages. Some consideration may therefore be given to the governance of the development and maintenance process. However, the economic effects of an open standard are more likely to be influenced by the control of rights to a technology than clear governance mechanisms, e.g., of standards bodies. So with equal, sustained, and guaranteed access to the rights for all potential players, even de facto standards that do not have very clear governance mechanisms could be open standards in terms of the economic effect they achieve.

5. It may be noted here that licenses that prevent FLOSS implementations are indeed neither reasonable nor nondiscriminatory (i.e., not RAND).

6. European Commission, IDABC Programme, European Interoperability Framework (EIF), November 2004. This version (1.0) included a definition of "open standards" that requires that patents covering parts of the standard must be made

"irrevocably available on a royalty-free basis." Note that there are some later drafts of the EIF with evolving definitions; this text refers specifically to the definition in version 1.0.

7. Some other standards suggested by EICTA that have royalty requirements include other hardware standards such as IEEE 1394, and software standards such as MPEG that have in some cases proven to be impossible to implement due to royalty requirements.

8. Derived works could obviously include variations on the standard implementation. See, e.g., Richard M. Stallman, "Microsoft's New Monopoly," Newsforge, June 29, 2005, <http://software.newsforge.com/software/05/06/29/1418213.shtml?tid=1 50&tid=147&tid=1> (accessed December 6, 2005).

9. A list of software, including FLOSS applications as well as proprietary offerings from firms such as IBM, Sun Microsystems, and others—is available at <http:// en.wikipedia.org/wiki/OpenDocument#Current_support>.

10. Microsoft 2005. Commentators (e.g., Updegrove 2005) have raised questions regarding the wording of the covenant, and noted that it does not apply to future versions of the format. So, while Office 2003 XML appears now to be an open standard, one cannot say the same for future versions of the Microsoft Office format, such as Office 12 XML. The latter has been proposed to ECMA International, which approves a number of "semi-open" standards.

11. European Interoperability Framework; see note 6.

12. West, p. 24; see note 3.

13. Reference implementations that are not distributed under a FLOSS license clearly do not in themselves achieve the economic effect of open standards. Even with a FLOSS reference implementation, clear, documented specifications separate from the implementation are probably required to allow other implementations.

14. This was recently replaced by a Web-based system that appears to be open-standards compliant.

15. This and other responses from the survey are analyzed in detail in a separate report on the survey; see R. Glott and R. A. Ghosh, "Usage of and Attitudes towards Free/Libre and Open Source Software in European Governments," FLOSSPOLS Report Deliverable D03 (2005), <http://flosspols.org>. This chapter only draws conclusions specifically related to open standards and interoperability.

16. European Commission, "Public Procurement: Commission Examines Discriminatory Specifications in Supply Contracts for Computers in Four Member States," press release reference IP/04/1210, October 13, 2004, <http://europa.eu.int/rapid/ pressReleasesAction.do?reference=IP/04/1210&format=HTML&aged=0&language=E N&guiLanguage=en>.

17. Specifically, "Intel or equivalent" was found to be "a violation of Directive 93/36/EEC on public supply contracts, and specifying clock rates was found "contrary to Article 28 of the EC Treaty, which prohibits any barriers to intra-Community trade."

18. See <http://ted.publications.eu.int/udl?REQUEST=Seek-Deliver&LANGUAGE=EN&DOCID=189553-2005>.

19. See <http://ted.publications.eu.int/udl?REQUEST=Seek-Deliver&LANGUAGE=EN&DOCID=189364-2005>.

20. See <http://ted.publications.eu.int/udl?REQUEST=Seek-Deliver&LANGUAGE=EN&DOCID=59337-2005>.

21. See <http://ted.publications.eu.int/udl?REQUEST=Seek-Deliver&LANGUAGE=IT&DOCID=181643-2005>.

22. See <http://ted.publications.eu.int/udl?REQUEST=Seek-Deliver&LANGUAGE=EN&DOCID=172383-2005>.

23. European Commission; see note 16.

24. "According to Mauro Solari, Deputy President of the Province of Genova . . . 'it important not to have only one supplier.'. . . Reduced vendor dependence is expected to lead to increased market competition and weakening existing monopolies of certain proprietary software vendors." See R. A. Ghosh, "OpenOffice trials in the Province of Genova," European Commission IDABC Open Source Observatory Case Study, August 2005, <http://europa.eu.int/idabc/en/document/4563/470>.

25. Glott and Ghosh; see note 15.

26. For example: IDABC's Barbara Held, quoted by ZDNet UK News at <http://news.zdnet.co.uk/software/applications/0,39020384,39231581,00.htm>.

27. International bodies include the ISO; European bodies listed by the Directive include ETSI, which maintains the GSM mobile telephony standard, but not ECMA, to which Microsoft's document format has been submitted for approval.

28. EU 1998, Preamble clause 7.

7 Open Innovation and Interoperability

Nicos L. Tsilas

The information technology (IT) industry is driving an unprecedented level of interoperability and innovation, giving customers increased choice and innovative products. This chapter briefly addresses a few key issues facing the IT industry today, including (1) the transition of the IT industry (along with other industries) from a "Closed Innovation" model to an "Open Innovation" model; (2) the various types of interoperability and the optimal roles of industry and government in achieving interoperability; and (3) the importance of a balanced definition of "open standards" to ensure that intellectual property (IP) holders and implementers have the proper incentives to work together to develop and implement innovative technology solutions. The fourth section of this chapter offers some recommendations and issues for governments and policy makers to consider when adopting policies that touch on these important areas.

A common theme throughout the four sections of this chapter is that IP is a key enabler of greater innovation and enhanced interoperability in the IT marketplace. For this reason, it is essential that governments establish strong yet flexible IP incentive systems and IP protection frameworks, which are necessary to encourage greater innovation and expand interoperability efforts among market participants, both within and outside of the standards-setting process. Different companies may pursue diverse business models that emphasize and rely on different aspects of IP (e.g., hardware or software patents, business process patents, copyright restrictions governing the use of open source software, etc.), but these are value- and opportunity-driven distinctions. The reality is that IP is the new coin of the realm. In the new world of Open Innovation, IP's legal power to exclude is increasingly being replaced by its real-world ability to serve as a *bridge to collaboration*—as the currency or the "glue" of literally dozens of new business and financial models in which friends and foes alike are successfully finding new and exciting ways to *share* their IP and *collaborate* in order to achieve greater benefits for all. It is equally important that decision makers and industries recognize that a definition of open standards that embraces the inclusion of, and reasonable licensing for, patented technology actually *enhances* the open standards process and the resulting technological solutions. Any failure to preserve the very protections and incentives that bring partners *and* competitors to the same table, under a common purpose of innovation, will only serve to deter key IP holders from participating in and contributing to the standards development process and ultimately to stall the pro-consumer trends of interoperability- and innovation-enhancing collaborations that are increasingly taking hold in the IT marketplace.

Open Innovation

Innovation is the primary driving force in the IT industry today. The technology companies that thrive are the ones that generate innovative technologies responding to customer needs on an ongoing, sustainable basis. This innovation imperative is neither new nor unique to the IT industry, and this marketplace dynamic is unlikely to change any time soon. What *has* changed, however, are the strategies and business models companies use to develop and deliver products and services that users find compelling, and to generate a financial return on their innovations.

Shift from Closed Innovation to Open Innovation

As recently as the 1980s, it was commonplace for companies to pursue innovations almost exclusively through *in-house* research and development (R&D). In fact, a strong internal R&D program was often regarded as a strategic asset. It is no surprise that the resulting IP was guarded jealously and not shared. Companies (and particularly competitors) rarely collaborated or shared ideas, and innovation, by default, occurred in silos. An unfortunate consequence of this inward-focused approach was that unless an innovation or idea was considered potentially profitable in the near term *to the company that discovered it,* it often lay fallow. History has since revealed that the benefits of multitudes of innovative technologies, developed by some of the world's most advanced research labs, were lost as a result.

IT companies now use both internal *and external* sources of ideas to promote innovation in their own products and across the industry. The closed approach is inefficient and a potential disadvantage in the current marketplace in which businesses increasingly cooperate and collaborate with each other to gain efficiencies and better meet customer needs. Professor Henry Chesbrough has aptly described this new paradigm as "Open Innovation."[1]

Simply put, Open Innovation may be defined as the sharing of knowledge (including human and organizational capital, and know-how) and intellectual property innovations to both foster economic growth and meet customers' needs. In this paradigm, which recognizes that no one company has all the answers, and that all companies to some extent are "standing on the shoulders of giants," companies are increasingly motivated to collaborate with other companies in order to deliver innovative products. As more and more innovations emerge outside the corporate firewall, companies are realizing that they simply *must* collaborate with others if they want to survive and prosper in the global economy.

Companies are also increasingly recognizing the critical role that business models play in commercializing innovations. As a result, there has been an expansion in diverse and creative business models and associated business practices for the delivery of IT products and services. For example, business models in the IT sector include

• generating revenue primarily through advertising (e.g., Google);
• generating revenue primarily through the licensing of software products (e.g., Microsoft);
• generating revenue primarily through the sale of hardware products (e.g., Apple, and IBM's Mainframe Division);
• generating revenue primarily through consulting, integration, maintenance, and/or training services (this may involve the giving away or promotion of free or low-cost software as a loss leader for these revenue-generating services) (e.g., IBM's Consulting Services Division, Red Hat);
• generating revenue primarily through the delivery of software as a service (e.g., Salesforce.com); and
• generating revenue through any combination of the aforementioned (e.g., IBM).

Because business models are always evolving, and because policy positions are often advanced based on business model type, it is critical that governments and procurement officials understand the key business models of industry players when assessing technology solutions. For example, calls for mandates or preferences for particular types of technology approaches (such as patent-free standards or open source software) may often seem benign or customer focused on the surface. However, decision makers must recognize that such regulatory proposals are often part of a strategy to privilege the proponent's own business model. In such a highly dynamic marketplace in which diverse business models and practices are pursued and constantly changing and where innovation is rampant and important, decision makers are best served embracing a policy of *choice* that avoids mandating particular technology solutions or approaches and instead enables flexibility for government to choose from a variety of solutions, and industry to pursue various comparable technology innovations and alternatives.

Specific Examples of Open Innovation in Action

Microsoft, like many other IT companies, is committed to, and spends *billions* of dollars on, Open Innovation efforts with other firms:

• Microsoft spends over $1.4 billion on *licensing* the intellectual property of other firms. Microsoft also has numerous cross-licensing agreements with other firms in order to gain greater freedom to innovate, mitigate potential legal conflicts, and address customers' needs.

• Microsoft has been licensing its IP (including source code, schemas, protocols, and documentation, as well as associated copyrights, trademarks, patents, and trade secrets) under commercially reasonable terms to third parties since December 2003.

• In the last several years, Microsoft has entered into collaborations that promote interoperability with key competitors and partners, including (1) Hewlett-Packard, Accenture, and Avanade (cloud computing); (2) Cisco (interoperable security and VoIP solutions); (3) Oracle (database interoperability); (4) Apple, Google, Research in Motion, palmOne, Motorola, and Symbian (email, contacts, and calendar interoperability); (5) Sun Microsystems (Windows Client, Windows Server, and Java-.NET interoperability); (6) Unisys (European border control and visa management interoperability); (7) Nokia (digital music interoperability across diverse wireless devices); (8) Vodafone (PC-mobile interoperability); (9) IBM, SAP, and BEA (Web services standards and interoperability); (10) JBoss (open source and Windows server interoperability); (11) SugarCRM (open source CRM interoperability with Windows server); (12) RealNetworks (digital media— music and games—interoperability); (13) Siemens (real-time collaboration and enterprise communications); (14) Texas Instrument (portable media center interoperability); (15) France Telecom (platform interoperability); (16) Novell (Windows-Linux interoperability); and Xandros (systems management and server interoperability and document compatibility).

• After working with the open source software (OSS) community to develop the right approach, Microsoft launched its Open Specification Promise

(OSP) in 2006 to facilitate easier and more efficient access by all developers no matter their development model to Microsoft technologies and IP. The OSP provides royalty-free patent access across proprietary and OSS platforms to implement a constantly increasing number of technical specifications that support interoperability, including thirty-eight Web services specifications, virtual hard drive formats, anti-spam technologies, and OpenXML.

• Microsoft participates in more than four hundred standards activities and patent pools worldwide, in which it commits to offer either royalty-bearing or royalty-free licenses, depending on the type of standard and rules of the standards-setting organization.

• Microsoft's IP Ventures group works with Microsoft Research to identify key early-stage, cutting-edge technologies for licensing to small businesses and startups, partnering with government development agencies around the world, and in some instances making IP-for-equity investments in the nascent ventures.

• Recognizing the important responsibility that it bears by virtue of the mission-critical use of its "high-volume" products around the world, and the increased importance of interoperability and data portability to customers, Microsoft established a set of Interoperability Principles in 2008. These Interoperability Principles include commitments to designing its high-volume products and running its business in the areas of open connections, support for standards, data portability, and open industry engagement for Microsoft's six high-volume products (Windows 7 including the .NET Framework, Windows Server 2008, SQL Server 2008, Office 2007, Exchange 2007, and Office SharePoint Server 2007, as well as future versions of these products).

In short, Microsoft works with more than 750,000 companies around the world and is an active and enthusiastic participant in Open Innovation. IDC studies have found that, for every dollar that Microsoft generates in revenue, between nine and seventeen additional dollars are generated for Microsoft's local partners and the IT ecosystem. Microsoft depends heavily on alliances with partners and competitors alike (local, global, multilaterals, and third-party entities, including, for example, its November 2006 patent cooperation agreement with Novell, a leading provider of Linux and other open source software), as well as with government and academia.

Other leading technology companies have also embraced Open Innovation principles and transformed the ways in which they develop, manage, and monetize their IP. IBM, for example, has gradually moved beyond the "not-invented-here" mentality and now focuses intently on working with other companies to help shape externally developed technologies (commonly in the open source arena), which are then incorporated into IBM's own products. IBM's Consulting Services Division also builds on this strategy by using open source software and helping other companies integrate and maintain these externally developed solutions. At the same time, IBM no longer seeks to deploy all of its innovations exclusively within its own products and services. In making its technologies available on the open market, IBM earns a significant portion of its revenue (more than $1 billion annually) through licensing its IP externally to partners and competitors alike.[2]

As part of its innovation strategy, Intel relies more heavily on external R&D than perhaps any other company in its respective primary market. Through a combination of generous research grants to universities and independent labs, and considerable venture capital investment in startup firms, Intel gains valuable insight into future technology opportunities and uses that information to direct complementary and concurrent internal R&D projects. This open approach to innovation inherently helps to broaden Intel's social and technical resources within and between businesses, and support in the marketplace.[3]

Microsoft and these companies pursue these collaborations and investments not simply out of altruism, but also because Open Innovation is the key to competitiveness, profitability, and responsiveness to customers' needs. Today, Open Innovation is simply smart business; tomorrow it will be a matter of life or death.

Healthy IP Incentive Systems, Strong IP Protection, and Broad IP Licensing Are Essential to Open Innovation Regardless of the Business Model

The open and collaborative approach to innovation has been spurred, more than anything else, by a strong IP incentive and protection framework that flexibly applies to diverse business environments. Under the Open Innovation model, intellectual property's power to exclude is increasingly being replaced by its ability to serve as a bridge to collaboration—as the currency or the "secret sauce" of literally dozens of new business and financial models and ways of partnering with friends and foes alike. Importantly, history has shown that—"open" or not—innovation only flourishes where the proper incentives are in place. Economists have found that, worldwide, it is not capital resources but the strength of a country's intellectual property system that is the more potent spur to technology development and economic growth. As one study from the National Bureau of

Economic Research noted, in the absence of IP incentive systems and strong intellectual property rights, "the leading places have insufficient incentive to invent and the follower places have excessive incentive to copy" rather than invent for themselves.[4]

Equally important is IP licensing among companies. Indeed, to compete effectively within the Open Innovation paradigm, IT companies must think creatively and strategically about how best to use IP to build technology bridges—not only with their customers and partners, but also with their competitors. This is most commonly done through IP licensing. IP licensing promotes competition and consumer interests in several ways. First, licensing gives both inventors and users of new technologies strong incentives to work together to make the most efficient use of their respective resources. Second, licensing promotes the broad dissemination of technology innovations, which benefit consumers in the form of new, competing products and lower prices. Finally, licensing may provide innovative firms with funds to reinvest in research and development, leading to further advances in technology. Thus, it is no surprise that a survey by *The Economist* found that 68 percent of senior executives in Europe say that "their top strategy for accelerating innovation over the next two years" is to increase patent licensing and other IP-enabled collaboration with outside firms.[5]

Regardless of the particular business models and business practices pursued, all IT companies are incentivized by, and believe in, the value and opportunities IP creates. Of course, these IP policy positions will vary based on respective business models. For example, a hardware company has greater incentives to build and strengthen robust patents, an ad-based revenue generating company in diluting copyrights and bolstering trade secrets, and a consulting services-oriented company in diluting software patents and bolstering copyright protection. But across the board, all use and see IP as the cornerstone and foundation for Open Innovation, and as an enabler of their business model.

Interoperability

Technical Interoperability and People Interoperability Distinguished
Private and public sector customers have identified interoperability as a necessary feature of IT products and services, ranking it with security and reliability. Interoperability is a feature of products and services that allows the connection of people, data, and diverse systems. Interoperability can be divided into two general categories: (1) technical interoperability and

(2) people interoperability. The distinctions between the two are important, particularly regarding the proper roles of industry and government in advancing interoperability goals.

1. Technical Interoperability. This category encompasses the ability of heterogeneous IT networks, applications, or components to exchange and use information, that is, to "talk to and understand" each other.[6] It deals with the technical issues of linking IT products and services together and covers areas such as data integration, virtualization, interfaces, and accessibility.

a. Four Methods of Accomplishing Technical Interoperability. There is no single solution pursued by IT companies for achieving technical interoperability. Rather, the IT industry has achieved interoperability through four complementary and time-tested methods:

• *Products*:   The explicit design of products to be interoperable with other products and services "*out of the box*" with little need for customization or integration services;

• *Community*:   Working with the IT community, including partners, customers, and competitors alike to develop interoperable products and solutions;

• *Access*:   Providing and gaining access to technology through the licensing of patents, copyrights, trademarks, and other IP rights; and

• *Standards*:   Developing and implementing industry standards (including both "open standards" and broadly accessible "proprietary standards"[7]) and incorporating them into products and services.

b. The Importance of Choice and Flexibility in Regulatory Approaches. All vendors accomplish interoperability via these four methods. But depending on a company's specific business model, it may emphasize or rely on one or more approaches. For example, although Microsoft uses all four methods in different situations, it focuses primarily on accomplishing interoperability through the explicit design of interoperable products that work with others right out of the box, working with partners, customers, and competitors, and the licensing of IP. A product like Windows 7 incorporates all four methods: It has many new features designed by Microsoft developers to specifically meet customer interoperability needs (e.g., better integration of digital content, and plug and play of peripherals, improved application interoperability, etc.); it includes features that were codeveloped with partners and competitors; Microsoft licenses in IP and technology to enable various Windows 7 features; and Windows 7 implements hundreds of industry standards (e.g., Wi-Fi, Bluetooth, USB, IrDA). Back in

June 2006, Microsoft announced the "Windows Principles," a set of voluntary tenets that guide the development of the Windows desktop operating system. The Windows Principles promote greater choice for computer manufacturers and customers, opportunities for developers, and interoperability for users. For example, under one of the Windows Principles, Microsoft commits to design Windows and to license it so as to make it easy to install non-Microsoft programs, and to configure Windows-based PCs to use non-Microsoft programs, instead of, or in addition to, native Windows features.

Other companies have a core business model that focuses more on the generation of revenue through IT consulting, integration, training, and maintenance services (e.g., IBM, Red Hat). Because such companies make money by stitching together various hardware and software products, they are not as interested in pursuing or endorsing products that are interoperable right out of the box. Instead, they support new standards and new software models in order to replace or supplement existing interoperable solutions and thereby create a greater need for their services. Such companies often promote open source software, patent-free and royalty-free open standards, and compulsory IP licensing as a way of commoditizing and displacing competitors' proprietary software, thereby reducing their own costs and affording them the opportunity to give away free or low-cost software as a loss leader in order to gain higher margins for their core consulting and services businesses.

As previously noted, governments and procurement officials would be well served to understand the key business models of industry players when assessing what technology solutions to embrace. Policies of *choice* will avoid advantaging or disadvantaging companies based on their business or licensing models and instead allow flexibility for industry to pursue various comparable technology alternatives and business models to best meet customer and marketplace needs.

2. People Interoperability. This category of interoperability encompasses the less tangible and often more complex issues of organizational, semantic, and policy interoperability. Interoperability is further influenced by various cultural, political, economic, and similar "environmental" factors as described below.

a. Organizational Interoperability. This aspect of interoperability addresses business goals, modeling business processes and ensuring the collaboration of organizations such as ministries, bureaus, departments of state, and national governments that wish to exchange information but may have different internal structures and processes. Organizational interoperability entails defining and focusing on the project objective regardless of ownership, location, make, version, or design of the IT systems being used.

b. Semantic Interoperability. This aspect ensures that the precise meaning of exchanged information is understandable by applications not initially developed for this purpose. It involves the definition of a common language and vocabularies so that two or more organizations and computer systems can exchange information and ensure consistency in how such information is represented and understood. For example, if a document contains a field called "last name," it is important that the various organizations and computer systems that wish to read and properly process this document have a common understanding beforehand that this field is intended to include just the last name of the person, not the entire name.

c. Policy Interoperability. This refers to the legal or business policies that need to be in place between organizations, states, and/or countries to ensure the accurate, reliable, and meaningful exchange of information. Common policies that are often a focus for governments deploying e-government systems and looking to improve interoperability include accessibility, privacy, security, data retention, and multilingualism.

d. Overarching "Environmental" Factors in Interoperability. To solve interoperability issues, organizations need to be aware of how the environment impacts their approaches and decisions, and work appropriately to maintain a balance. All of the following environmental factors impact interoperability and are interrelated.

• *Cultural/Social Factors*: These factors, which include personal belief systems, morals, values, and prejudices (e.g., views on discrimination, the work force, the natural environment, and privacy), impact how we interpret the world and affect our decisions ranging from the ownership and sharing of processes and data, competitive forces and security, and the effect of automation on work forces.

• *Political Factors*: The decision to make resources more widely available has political implications for the organizations concerned (where this may be a loss of control or ownership; an assignment of governing rights to a distant government that is perceived as less capable or in tune with the local citizens), their staff (who may not possess the skills required to support more complex systems and a newly dispersed user community), and the end users (who may not accept a perceived loss of control for their own reasons).

• *Economic Factors*:   The decision to improve interoperability may create certain efficiencies, cost savings, and opportunities for the governing decision maker, but may result in a loss of revenue for a specific part of that decision maker's government (either through direct loss of revenue or through the loss of jobs) or the introduction of new costs related to process change, extensive staff and user training, and so on, which must be taken into account.

Consider the following example demonstrating how the two types of interoperability interact: From a *technical* interoperability perspective, it would seem straightforward for IT companies to develop a national interoperable database of drivers' licenses that integrate the various existing state and local records; but from a *people* interoperability perspective, achieving this objective may be difficult because most local jurisdictions are very reluctant to cede control of such issues to the federal government. Other organizational, legal, political, cultural, or economic barriers may also stand in the way.

The various factors identified previously have a direct impact on how decision makers approach interoperability. Governments and procurement officials sometimes focus too heavily on the *technical* interoperability issues (such as whether to mandate or prefer the OpenDocument (ODF) file format over Open XML or open source solutions over proprietary software solutions), which the IT industry is already well equipped to address, when they should really be focusing instead on the more difficult *people* interoperability issues they are better equipped to resolve.

Interoperability Is a Key Feature, but Its Relative Importance May Vary Based on Customer Demands and Other Factors

Interoperability is just one of many features of IT products and services. Other important features include security, ease of use, accessibility, reliability, and privacy. Enhancing one of these features, however, can often result in certain tradeoffs with respect to other features. Thus, in certain contexts, such as document file formats, interoperability may be deemed by the user to be as important as security, reliability, or any other feature. In other contexts, interoperability can be of relatively little value to customers, as evidenced, for example, by the success and significant market share of Apple's iPod products, which offer few, if any, interoperability benefits. Microsoft, in contrast, focused intently on interoperability in the nascent digital content space through its "PlaysForSure" initiative. Customers, however, found the interoperable devices to be complicated, not as reliable, and with a clunky user interface; thus they did not embrace them in the marketplace despite their high level of interoperability.

In summary, optimal levels of interoperability will vary based on (1) customer needs and desires; (2) the nature of the product or service at issue (hardware or software); (3) the maturity of the technology available; (4) industry externalities such as competitor, partner, and regulatory issues; and (5) the business models employed by industry participants.

Putting "Open Standards" in Perspective, and the Importance of a Balanced Definition

As noted earlier, one of the four ways that IT vendors accomplish interoperability is through the development and implementation of open standards and broadly accessible proprietary standards in products and services. While most agree on the value of open standards for interoperability, there is debate about how best to define the term. Unfortunately, certain recent attempts to do this in Europe and elsewhere are inconsistent with well-established industry norms and would impede technological innovation and interoperability going forward.

Before addressing actual definitions, it is important to put this debate in perspective. Standards can be used to achieve interoperability, to commoditize competitors' products, or both. A firm's business model will dictate how much emphasis is put on standards from a strategic business perspective and how they will be used. It is common, for example, for companies that generate revenue from consulting and integration services to promote standards as the only way of accomplishing interoperability, to create standards initiatives that target a competitor's existing product in an effort to commoditize it, and then to lobby governments to mandate that newly developed standard. By standardizing competitors' products and creating multiple standards whose IP is often licensed on royalty-free terms, and which are implemented in open source software, the consulting business model is heavily favored, that is, new value is provided to the customer (and revenue to the company) not through the software itself but through the services that are needed to install, integrate, maintain, and educate users about the new system.

At the heart of these debates are the business models and strategic policies of firms, all set in the context of vigorous competition. Ultimately, the market should and does decide which business models, products, and services will succeed. Policy makers should take approaches that acknowledge and further enable the Open Innovation paradigm and the high level of interoperability and competition in the IT industry, and that promote *choice* in business and licensing models and in meeting customer interoperability needs.

Case Study: IDA Definition of "Open Standards"

There has been a prolonged discussion in the European Union (EU) about the definition of open standards in the context of e-government services. It resulted in a 2004 statement by an agency called the Interchange of Data between Administrations (IDA).[8] IDA stated that the following are the minimal characteristics of an open standard:

1. The standard is adopted and will be maintained by a not-for-profit organization, and its ongoing development occurs on the basis of an open decision-making procedure available to all interested parties (consensus or majority decision etc.).

2. The standard has been published and the standard specification document is available either freely or at a nominal charge. It must be permissible to all to copy, distribute, and use it for no fee or at a nominal fee.

3. *The intellectual property—i.e., patents possibly present—of (parts of) the standard is made irrevocably available on a royalty-free basis* (emphasis added).

4. *There are no constraints on the reuse of the standard* (emphasis added).

This definition (and the one suggested to the FTC, discussion of which follows) is rooted in a misguided notion that intellectual property and open standards are mutually exclusive concepts. This view may be driven in part by proponents of open source software, such as the Free Software Foundation (FSF), which seek to remove patents, royalties, and licensing restrictions from standards, or at least from some artificially designated subset of standards, such as "software" or "Internet" standards.[9] By doing this, they seek to avoid any tension between reasonable and nondiscriminatory (RAND) patent licensing (with or without a royalty component) and certain OSS licenses.[10] For example, because certain OSS licenses, such as the General Public License (GPL), prohibit royalties, field-of-use restrictions, or sublicensing restrictions, FSF supports attempts by IDA and others to redefine open standards to fit within these OSS restrictions.

But such an attempt to equate open standards with patent-free standards is squarely at odds with the approach taken by the world's leading standards development organizations. For example, contrary to the IDA definition, the intellectual property rights (IPR) policies of ETSI, IEEE, IETF, ISO/IEC, ITU, OMA, ANSI, ECMA, and other leading standards organizations do not mandate patent-free standards or even royalty-free patent licensing; they support the patent holder's rights to seek reasonable licensing terms in exchange for agreeing to share innovative technology with all implementers of the standard. Rather, these leading standards organizations have long recognized the need to *balance* the rights of patent owners with the needs of implementers who wish to create products that incorporate the standard. This healthy, cooperative relationship between innovators that contribute to a standard and implementers that make use of the standard engenders technical advancement and spurs industry uptake of the technology, thereby enhancing interoperability. These standards bodies strike this balance between the interests of implementers and patent holders by allowing patent holders who are participating in the standardization process to commit to license their essential patents covering a standard to all implementers of the standard on RAND terms.

For example, several of the world's leading standards organizations—including ITU, ETSI, ATIS, TIA, TSACC (Canada), TTA (Korea), TTC (Japan), ARIB (Japan), CCSA (China), and ACIF (Australia)—, acting as part of the "Global Standards Collaboration,"[11] resolved to strongly support the adoption of effective intellectual property rights that are transparent, widely accepted, and encourage broad-based participation and the contribution of valuable technical solutions by respecting intellectual property rights, including the right of the intellectual property holder to receive reasonable and adequate compensation for the shared use of its technology.

Such RAND policies seek to provide a level of assurance to implementers with respect to the availability of essential patents that may be held by participants in the standards process. RAND also ensures that the licensing terms will be reasonable. In this way, RAND licensing promotes the rapid adoption of standards and new technologies, and encourages entry by the greatest number of new producers. As history has shown, this results in comprehensive standards, better products, and lower prices for consumers.

ANSI Rebuts a Similar Definition of "Open Standards"

A similarly misguided attempt to define open standards occurred in the context of a 2004 summit at the U.S. Federal Trade Commission (FTC). A commenter submitted the following set of principles to define an open standard:

1. Everyone is free to copy and distribute the official specification for an open standard under an open source license.

2. Everyone is free to make or use embodiments of an open standard under unconditional licenses to patent claims necessary to practice that standard.

3. Everyone is free to distribute externally, sell, offer for sale, have made or import embodiments of an open standard under patent licenses that may be *conditioned only on reciprocal licenses to any of licensees' patent claims necessary to practice that standard* (emphasis added).

4. A patent license for an open standard may be terminated as to any licensee who sues the licensor or any other licensee for infringement of patent claims necessary to practice that standard.

5. *All patent licenses necessary to practice an open standard are worldwide, royalty free, nonexclusive, perpetual, and sublicensable* (emphasis added).[12]

Principle 2's reference to "unconditional licenses" and principle 5's requirement for mandatory royalty-free and sublicensable patent licenses echo the fourth and third criteria in the proposed IDA definition. ANSI submitted a responsive letter to the FTC pointing out the key shortcomings of this proposed definition. Among other things, ANSI observed the following:

Contrary to the implication of these "principles," ANSI does not understand the term "open standard" to refer to a standard that is unconditionally and freely available to those who wish to practice such standard. A holder of an essential patent typically has the right to require that implementers execute licenses containing reasonable and non-discriminatory terms and conditions. This is true even if the standards body's patent policy is based on a "royalty-free" licensing commitment or the patent holder itself has agreed to offer its essential patents to implementers for free.

Indeed, we are not aware of any standards body that mandates that all essential patents be subject to "unconditional licenses" or that must be "sublicensable." The standards bodies that often are cited as examples of well-recognized, "open standards" developers (such as those accredited by ANSI, OASIS, W3C, ISO, IEC, and ITU) would not meet the "principles" set forth above, as none of them require holders of essential patents to waive all of their rights in connection with those patents. Instead, most standards bodies adopt a patent policy that seeks to balance (a) the legitimate ownership rights of participants who are willing to contribute their innovative technology to a standards development effort with (b) the needs of those seeking to implement the standard so they have sufficient access to that technology on a reasonable and open basis.[13]

Whether a standard qualifies as "open" has nothing to do with the type of software used to implement that standard. It is equally feasible for an open standard to be implemented in proprietary software as in OSS. In fact, ANSI and others, including the U.S. State Department, have criticized attempts to conflate OSS and open standards. As ANSI commented: "'Open source' software refers to software that is distributed under a certain specified software distribution license. It has nothing to do with the process by which a technical standard or specification is formulated and embedded technology is licensed."[14]

In short, there are significant problems with the preceding proposed definitions of open standards. First, as noted, they are inconsistent with the approach taken in the IPR policies of leading open standards organizations worldwide, which expressly acknowledge the right of patent holders to charge reasonable royalties, and to place reasonable restrictions—such as field-of-use restrictions, reciprocity requirements, and restrictions on sublicensing—on the licensing of their essential technology covering an open standard. Even the W3C patent policy, while seeking commitments from participants to license their necessary patent claims royalty-free, permit these other reasonable terms and conditions.[15]

The IDA and similar definitions would unravel the delicate balance that has been achieved by these RAND-based IPR policies. More specifically, by mandating royalty-free licensing and unfettered sublicensing and by prohibiting other reasonable licensing terms, such definitions would likely deter key patent holders from participating in and contributing to the standards development process. This, in turn, would deprive such standards of the best technical solutions. It would also allow the key patent holders (who would not be subject to the organization's IPR policies) either to refuse to license their essential technology or to impose unreasonable terms and conditions on implementers of the standard. In short, attempts to ensure patent-free or royalty-free standards through an inflexible and anti-RAND definition of open standards could backfire. It could result in blocking patents or usurious licensing fees. In either case, the unfortunate result would be a breakdown of the innovation cycle, so that important new standards and products might never see the light of day.

Second, many successful and widely deployed open standards are covered by such RAND licenses. For example, licensing for the following open standards, among countless others, involves field-of-use restrictions and reciprocity requirements: Session Initiation Protocol (SIP), Dynamic Host Configuration Protocol (DHCP), WLAN protocol, XML Configuration Access Protocol (XCAP), Internet Key Exchange (IKE), and GSM. Likewise, well-known and commonly used standards, such as MPEG, GSM, 3GPP, and IEEE 1394, all involve IP licensing that is not royalty-free. Thus, if the IDA or similar definition of "open standards" were accepted, hundreds of international standards that have been developed and widely deployed by these and other such leading standards developers would not qualify as open standards. As a result, the universe of "open" standards available to governments in their procurement decisions would shrink considerably, which would hamper technological innovation and interoperability going forward.

More recently even greater consensus is emerging regarding a more balanced approach toward defining open standards as evidenced from statements from the Global Standards Collaboration (GSC), the ITU-T, ANSI, and the Telecommunications Industry Association.[16] And the European Interoperability Framework is expected to be announcing a revised IDA definition of "open standards."

Toward a Proper Definition of "Open Standards"

Based on the foregoing, the author respectfully proposes that the following be considered and embraced by standards organizations and governments alike as a proper definition of an "open standard":

An "open standard" is a technical specification (i.e., a set of technical functionality requirements) that has the following characteristics:

1. It is developed or approved/affirmed and maintained by consensus, in a voluntary, market-driven standards setting organization that is open to all interested and qualified participants.
2. It is published without restriction (in electronic or tangible form) in sufficient detail to enable a complete understanding of the standard's scope and purpose (e.g., potential implementers are not restricted from accessing the standard).
3. It is publicly available without cost or for a reasonable fee for adoption and implementation by any interested party.
4. Any patent rights necessary to implement the standard are made available by those developing the standard to all implementers on RAND terms (either with or without payment of a reasonable royalty or fee).

Various well-established standards organizations and industry organizations have recently adopted definitions of "open standards" that are very similar to the definition just set forth.[17] This definition of "open standards" preserves the necessary balance described above that leading standards organizations seek to achieve between IP holders and implementer. It is also flexible enough to accommodate an open standards effort that seeks royalty-free licensing commitments from patent holders in a given situation. The best way to avoid the pitfalls and deleterious effects described earlier is to use this more balanced, time-tested, and flexible definition.

Doing so will continue to foster the significant levels of innovation, competition, and interoperability being driven by current standards development processes.

Key Recommendations/Issues for Consideration by Governments and Policy Makers

1. The unprecedented level of technical interoperability in the IT industry today has been achieved by a number of time-tested and complementary means (i.e., the four pillars of interoperability: products, community, access, and standards). Standards (both open and proprietary) are only one way to achieve technical interoperability, particularly in the world of modern electronics where translators/converters are often an effective means.
2. Technical interoperability is an important and desired product/service feature, but its relative importance to customers may vary in different circumstances as compared to other key features such as security and ease of use.
3. The IT industry is best suited and situated to achieve technical interoperability. Government should allow industry to lead in this area, and its role in achieving technical interoperability should be extremely limited.
4. Governments are often best suited and situated to promote people interoperability, and can help the interoperability ecosystem by improving areas where they have direct (and perhaps exclusive) influence, such as in the less tangible and often more complex areas of organizational, semantic, and policy interoperability.
5. Governments should not mandate or extend preferences to specific technology solutions, platforms, or business/licensing models, or mandate particular means of achieving interoperability to the exclusion of others. Such mandates/preferences chill innovation and competition, and impede public sector customers from deploying the best technical solutions available for their e-government systems to meet citizen needs.
6. Rather, governments should develop procurement policies that are neutral with respect to specific technologies or platforms and that are based on reasonable, objective criteria, such as (1) interoperability/reliance on industry standards, (2) total cost of ownership/value for money, (3) reliability, (4) vendor support, (5) ease of use, (6) security, and (7) availability of warranties and indemnities for intellectual property claims.
7. More broadly speaking, governments should embrace a policy that allows for "choice" by their software procurement and other divisions

seeking interoperability solutions—choice as to which one of the four pillars, or combination of them, is the best means to achieve interoperability in a given situation; choice regarding which open standard(s) and/or proprietary standard(s) on which to rely under the circumstances; and choice between open source software and proprietary software in the procurement process. This flexible approach predicated on choice is particularly appropriate in the rapidly converging IT world, in which customers and governments increasingly rely on a combination of proprietary and open source software, as well as open standards and proprietary standards, to develop an ideal interoperability strategy.

8. In the current era of Open Innovation, the IT industry is highly competitive and very dynamic, with companies employing numerous business models to best meet customer, marketplace, and their own revenue-generation needs. It is important for governments to understand these business models and their competitive nature, as well as the motivations and strategies of companies when they discuss interoperability and propose government regulation. In particular, it is essential that decision makers recognize that a company's regulatory proposals (e.g., to favor open source software or open standards to the exclusion of other alternatives) are often part of a strategy to bolster the proponent's own business plan, which may be focused on other elements to enhance its bottom line.

9. If collaborating companies do not have clear and transparent property rights through which they can demarcate the boundaries of their collaboration, they quite likely would anticipate too much risk in sharing ideas. Therefore, governments should adopt and enforce strong yet flexible IP protections for industry as a key to facilitating greater innovation, collaboration, interoperability, and local economic growth.

10. Adoption of a definition of "open standards" that recognizes and appropriately balances the interests of both IP holders and implementers is important to sustain and enhance the significant levels of interoperability, innovation, competition, and consumer choice that have characterized the IT industry to date.

Notes

1. "Open Innovation is a paradigm that assumes that firms can and should use external ideas as well as internal ideas, and internal and external paths to market, as the firm looks to advance their technology" (Henry W. Chesbrough, *Open Innovation: The New Imperative for Creating and Profiting from Technology* [Cambridge, MA: Harvard Business School Press, 2006], p. xxiv).

2. Ibid., pp. 93–112.

3. Ibid., pp. 113–133.

4. Robert J. Barro and Xavier Sala-I-Martin, *Technology Diffusion, Convergence, and Growth*, Working Paper 5151 (Cambridge, MA: National Bureau of Economic Research, 1995). Reprinted in *Journal of Economic Growth* 23, no. 2 (1997).

5. "The Value of Knowledge: European Firms and the Intellectual Property Challenge," an Economist Intelligence Unit white paper sponsored by Qualcomm, *The Economist*, January 2007, at p. 13.

6. Harry Newton, *Newton's Telecom Dictionary: The Official Dictionary of Telecommunications Networking and Internet,* 17th ed. (San Francisco: CMP Books, 2001), defining "interoperability" as "the ability to operate software and exchange information in a heterogeneous network, i.e., one large network made up of several different local area networks."

7. See this chapter's third section (Putting "Open Standards" in Perspective, and the Importance of a Balanced Definition) for a discussion of open standards. "Proprietary standards" are technical specifications developed and maintained by a single entity or by a private, small group of cooperating entities. Proprietary is a legal term and does not mean "closed" or the opposite of interoperability; it simply indicates that a different—often smaller and quicker—process was used to develop the standard at issue. Some examples of proprietary standards include Adobe's Portable Document Format (PDF), HP's Printer Command Language (PCL), IBM's Video Graphics Array (VGA), Sun's Java, Hayes's AT modem command set, Microsoft's Rich Text Format (RTF), Intel's x86 architecture, and the Universal Service Bus (USB).

8. IDA's definition of an "open standard" is included on page 9 of its European Interoperability Framework for pan-European eGovernment Services (see <http://ec.europa.eu/idabc/servlets/Docd552.pdf?id=19529>).

9. See James V. DeLong, "Opening up an Open-source Roadblock," cnet news (Feb. 21, 2007), <http://news.com.com/2010-7344_3-6160824.html> (noting that the Free Software Foundation ("FSF"), for example, "regards proprietary software as immoral, patents as the work of the devil . . . and markets for intellectual creations as undesirable or irrelevant").

10. See <http://www.opensource.org> listing more than fifty licenses governing the distribution of OSS, some of which are extremely permissive, such as the Berkeley Software Distribution (BSD) license—which is a simple software license whose only

requirements are copyright attribution and license reproduction—but others of which are very restrictive, such as the GNU General Public License (GPL), which presents challenges to business models that rely on direct commercialization of the software itself and requires that any work that includes GPL code, if distributed at all, be distributed under the terms of the GPL.

11. Information about the Global Standards Collaboration is available at <http://www.gsc.etsi.org/>.

12. Lawrence E. Rosen, "E-Mail Authentication Summit—Comments," memorandum to FCC Secretary (Sept. 29, 2004), at 4, <http://www.ftc.gov/os/comments/emailauthentication/512447-0038.pdf>.

13. Comments of ANSI to FTC on E-Mail Authentication Summit (Oct. 27, 2004) (ANSI's comments to the FTC are available from ANSI upon email request to Patty Griffin, vice president and general counsel, ANSI-PGriffin@ansi.org). It is also important to note that "open standards" and "open source software" are entirely distinct concepts. Open standards are technical *specifications* developed through an open, market-driven, consensus-based process (see proposed definition that follows), whereas OSS is software that is licensed in a particular way (i.e., under the terms of one of the more than fifty OSS licenses) and may be used to *implement* an open standard in a particular product or service.

14. See ANSI FTC Letter, note 13.

15. See the W3C patent policy of February 5, 2004, at <http://www.w3.org/Consortium/Patent-Policy-20040205/>.

16. See Resolution GSC-10/04: (Joint Session) Open Standards, <http://www.itu.int/ITU-T/gsc/gsc10/index.html>; International Telecommunication Union (ITU), TSB Director's Ad Hoc IPR Group, "Definition of 'Open Standards,'" <http://www.itu.int/ITU-T/othergroups/ipr-adhoc/openstandards.html>; American National Standards Institute (ANSI), <http://publicaa.ansi.org/sites/apdl/Documents/Standards%20Activities/Critical%20Issues%20Papers/Griffin%20-%20Open%20Standards%20-%2005-05.doc> (accessed December 2005); Telecommunications Industry Association (TIA), <http://www.tiaonline.org/standards/about/documents/TIA-IPR_20080620-003_TIA_OPEN_STANDARDS-CLEAN_R4.pdf>.

17. See, e.g., ITU's "Definition of 'Open Standards,' note 16; ANSI, "Introduction to ANSI: Overview of the U.S. Standardization System," <http://www.ansi.org/about_ansi/introduction/introduction.aspx?menuid=1>; Business Software Alliance (BSA), "BSA Statement on Technology Standards," <http://www.bsa.org/usa/policy/loader.cfm?url=/commonspot/security/getfile.cfm&pageid=22407&hitboxdone=yes> (accessed December 2005).

8 Standards, Trade, and Development

John S. Wilson

The expansion of global trade over the past fifty years has contributed to economic welfare, poverty reduction, and human development in important ways. Despite the downturn in trade due to the global economic crisis, the World Bank forecast that global trade volumes would grow by 4.3 percent in 2010 and by 6.2 percent in 2011 (World Bank 2010). Poverty is an immediate global problem, with more than one billion people living in extreme poverty. Although trade is not the only mechanism to reduce poverty, it can contribute to economic growth and help to lift people out of poverty. The removal of policies that distort production of new technologies, prevent effective diffusion of innovation, and block private sector participation in world markets is also part of reaching these overall goals. It is within this broad context that standards and technical regulations should be viewed. There is both empirical and case study evidence to support this view.[1]

Private sector-led standards, and increasingly open information and communication technology (ICT) standards, represent a strong platform for continued innovation and economic advancement. It is not fundamentally a question of how private standards are developed, but rather once they are produced, how or whether a regulatory intervention develops. If regulation is required, balanced against the need for intellectual property protection, consumer welfare, benefits of public interconnectivity and other concerns, it must be based on nondiscrimination, transparency, and other well-established economic principles.

As such, the rise of nontariff technical barriers to trade, including government attempts to shape technology markets, is a threat to global welfare and the poverty reduction that open markets and trade promote. This is not simply a question of barriers in developed countries; it also concerns the barriers (both at and behind the border) that developing countries maintain. Concerning the information technology and communications sector, several steps could be considered in a trade context to address challenges and threats to economic growth posed by the expansion of nontariff technical barriers to trade.

The World Trade Organization (WTO) Information Technology Agreement (ITA), negotiated in 1996, made significant progress in eliminating tariffs on information and telecommunications products. Extension of the ITA to nontariff measures, including standards, testing, certification, and other issues, makes a good deal of sense in light of the increasing government use of technical standards to influence the ICT sector. Progress toward a conclusion to the Doha negotiations is extremely important, but talks under the ITA can move ahead under their own mandate. It is quite unlikely, however, that the WTO Technical Barriers to Trade Agreement will be amended to address sector-specific concerns, including principles on standards development in information technology, given the apparent lack of support and interest in reopening the agreement. What would clearly help, in an overall context, is a new and serious multinational effort (public and private) to develop empirical data and evidence on standards. This is a clear and evident need and is critically important to sound public policy decisions. There are consortia for standards development, so why not a "Global Standards Consortium" devoted to the study of policy-relevant questions on standards, technology, and economic development?

Introduction

Technical regulations, such as product certification requirements, performance mandates, testing procedures, conformity assessments, and labeling standards, exist to ensure consumer safety, network reliability, interoperability, and other goals. In principle, product standards[2] play a variety of roles in overcoming market failures. For example, emission standards for cars motivate firms to internalize the costs of promoting environmental quality. Food safety standards help to ensure that consumers are protected from health risks and deceptive practices, information about which would not ordinarily be available in private markets. By the same token, standards in the ICT sector can ensure interoperability of systems and networks.

For consumers, efficient and nondiscriminatory standards allow comparison of products on a common basis in terms of regulatory characteristics, permitting enhanced competition. From the producers' perspective, production of goods subject to recognized and open international standards can achieve economies of scale and reduce overall costs. Because standards themselves embody information about technical knowledge, conformity to efficient standards encourages firms to improve the quality and reliability of their products.

Standards may also reduce transaction costs in business by increasing the transparency of product information and compatibility of products and components (David and Greenstein 1990).[3] This is possible as technical regulations can increase the flow of information between producers and consumers regarding the inherent characteristics and quality of products. Jones and Hudson (1996), using a model with a variance reduction approach, argued that standardization reduces the costs of uncertainty associated with assessing product quality. Cost savings are reflected in the reduction of time and effort that consumers spend on product searches.

Despite the potential to expand competition and trade, standards may be set to achieve the opposite outcomes. In general, standards can act to raise the compliance costs of some firms (e.g., new entrants) relative to other firms (e.g., incumbents), thereby restricting competition. Fischer and Serra (2000) examine the behavior of a country that imposes a minimum standard on a good produced by a domestic firm and a foreign competitor. In their model, costs rise with the standard, and there is a fixed setup cost of producing at two standard levels. Depending on the size of the foreign market and the fixed setup cost, they showed that the domestic firm will lobby for the lowest minimum standard that excludes the foreign firm or for no standard at all.

Indeed, there has been a rising use of technical regulations and standards as instruments of commercial policy in the unilateral, regional, and global trade settings (Maskus and Wilson 2001). The use of information and communication technology standards as a trade policy instrument has become more attractive partly because "traditional" barriers to trade, such as tariffs and quotas, are diminishing in importance, and partly because standards are critical to the growing ICT sector. This is especially true for governments that are determined to support their domestic technology and communications sectors as part of a wider industrial strategy. These nontariff barriers have become of particular concern and are a threat to continued benefits of open trade to both *developed* and *developing* nations.

The costs associated with foreign standards and technical regulations may be borne publicly and privately. But developing countries typically have neither the public resources required to provide national laboratories for testing and certification nor the capability for collective action to raise their standards. As a result, a significant portion of meeting the costs of standards may be borne by individual firms. There is growing empirical evidence that a proliferation of new standards in this area could have a significant and detrimental effect on ICT exports from developing countries (Portugal, Reyes, and Wilson 2009).

Given this context, standards and technical regulations are an increasingly prominent part of international trade policy debate. This is particularly true in regard to how standards affect exporters and the costs and benefits for global trade in adopting consensus international standards and removing discriminatory technical barriers. Unfortunately, there have been few empirical studies that examine the impacts of standards imposed within the framework of tradeoffs of setting standards at international levels, unilaterally, via consortia, or other methods. This includes sector studies in the information technology and communications sector, as well.

There have been several studies completed recently, however, based on the World Bank's Technical Barriers to Trade (TBT) Survey database to inform questions regarding standards, technical regulations, and developing countries. The database provides firm-level data on production and export activities, cost structures, impediments to domestic sales and exports, and compliance with standards and technical regulations.

Summary Results from Selected Studies

The World Bank Standards and Trade Survey (World Bank 2004) produced firm data on the impact of technical requirements and standards on developing country exports. The intent of the survey was to solicit input from agricultural, manufacturing, and trade firms in various emerging market countries regarding technical barriers encountered that impact the firms' ability to successfully export products. The data provides financial information for each firm and describes the effect of domestic and foreign technical regulations on exports, international standards, and other various impediments to business and export.

The data collected covers 689 firms in 24 industries in 17 developing countries. The use of a uniform methodology across countries and industries enables comparison of standards and regulations, and their impacts on firms' production and conformance activities between countries and industries. Information on technical regulations specific to five major export markets also enables a comparison of the stringency and importance of technical regulations by export market. The five export markets are the United States, the European Union, Japan, Canada, and Australia.

An overview of the results and descriptive statistics results from data for the seventeen countries in the World Bank Standards and Trade Survey is provided in Otsuki and Wilson (2004). The major findings include those related to general factors that affect businesses in these developing countries and their export success. Among the major barriers are limited access to credit and low demand for both exporting and nonexporting firms. Product quality is also reported to be a major factor affecting export success. For firms that are willing but unable to export, low demand and costs of transporting goods are major impediments to exports.

Part of the new research agenda on product standards examines how standards affect two types of costs on firms: fixed and variable. The former can determine the entry decisions for firms seeking to access foreign markets, while the latter can determine the propensity to export once entry decision was taken. Chen, Otsuki, and Wilson (2006) examine how meeting foreign standards affects firms' export performance, reflected in export propensity and market diversification. Results suggest that technical regulations can adversely affect firms' propensity to export in developing countries. In particular, testing procedures and lengthy inspection procedures reduce exports by 9 percent and 3 percent, respectively.

Furthermore, in the model deployed in this analysis, the difference in standards across foreign countries causes diseconomy of scale for firms and affects decisions about whether to enter export markets. The results suggest that standards, under certain conditions, can impede exporters' market entry, reducing the likelihood of exporting to more than three markets by as much as 7 percent. In addition, firms that outsource components are more challenged by compliance with multiple standards.

The costs of compliance to standards involve payments for additional inputs, such as capital and labor. The issue is analyzed, in the context of a production function, in Maskus, Otsuki, and Wilson (2005). The authors develop econometric models to provide the first estimates of the incremental production costs for firms in developing nations in conforming to standards imposed by major importing countries. Results indicate that standards do increase short-run production costs by requiring additional inputs of labor and capital. A 1 percent increase in investment to meet compliance costs in importing countries raises variable production costs by between 0.06 and 0.13 percent. Among other findings are that the fixed costs of compliance are nontrivial: approximately $425,000 per firm or about 4.7 percent of value added on average.

The results in Maskus, Otsuki, and Wilson (2005) may be interpreted as one indication of the extent to which standards and technical regulations can constitute barriers to trade. While the relative impact on costs of compliance is relatively small, these costs can be decisive factors driving export success for companies. Shepherd (2007), for example, uses a World Bank database on EU standards in the textile, clothing, and footwear sectors to present evidence that increases in standards is associated with a significant decrease in export product variety from trading partner countries; more specifically, he finds that a 10 percent increase in the total number of standards is associated with a nearly 6 percent decrease in product variety, and that this effect is 50 percent stronger for low-income trading partner countries. In this context, there is scope for considering that the costs associated with more limited exports to countries with import regulations may not conform to WTO rules encouraging harmonization of regulations to international standards, for example. Policy solutions then might be sought by identifying the extent to which subsidies or public support programs are needed to offset the cost disadvantage that arises from non-harmonized technical regulations.

The issue of harmonized standards and their impact on trade is examined in Chen, Suzuki, and Wilson (2006). The paper focuses on the effect of Mutual Recognition Agreements (MRAs) on exports from developing countries. Negotiations involving standards raise issues that are both politically and analytically challenging. Unlike tariffs, standards cannot be simply negotiated away. The primary purpose of standards should center on the enhancement of welfare by remedying market failure—arising, perhaps, from safety attributes of products, negative environmental externalities, or product incompatibility due to the producers' failure to coordinate. With these objectives in mind, Mayeda (2004) asserts that, from a development perspective, harmonization is largely ineffective, as it often fails to recognize the need for countries to adapt laws and legal institutions to their own particular domestic circumstances. Agreements on standards must therefore secure the gains from integrated markets without unduly compromising the role of standards as remedies for market failure. Not only are the motives for standards ostensibly aimed at maximizing welfare, but also that they be applied in a nondiscriminatory manner on both foreign and domestic firms. However, in spite of the supposed symmetry of treatment, the impact on trade can be highly asymmetric because the costs of compliance can differ across countries.

There are in fact three main types of agreements dealing with technical barriers to trade. The simplest and potentially most powerful is the mutual recognition of existing standards, whereby a country grants unrestricted access of its market to products that meet any participating country's standards. This was the approach taken in principle by the European Union, with the spur of the 1979 Cassis de Dijon judgment of the European Court of Justice. MRAs are, however, not likely to be an option if there are significant differences among the initial standards of the countries, as became evident in the context of the EU.

In such cases, a certain degree of harmonization is a precondition for countries to allow products of other countries to access their markets. The most important example of such harmonization is the New Approach of the European Union, which resulted in a set of directives from the European Commission setting out essential health and safety requirements for most regulated products.

In other cases, neither mutual recognition nor harmonization of substantive standards may be deemed feasible or desirable. Countries may nevertheless choose at least to mutually recognize each other's conformity assessment requirements, that is, country A trusts country B to certify that the products made by country B conform to country A's standards. In this case, producers from country B may still face different standards in different markets, as opposed to in a mutual-recognition case. Conformity assessment could be done locally resulting in lower costs of compliance.

Examples of the MRA approach include the intra-EU mutual recognition system in sectors where there are no EU harmonized directives as well as the EU's agreements with a number of other countries. A key element of these agreements is the rule of origin. The MRAs between the EU and USA and the EU and Canada specify that conformity assessment done in one of the MRA countries, in which products are manufactured or through which they are imported, is accepted throughout the entire agreement region. Other agreements, such as the MRAs concluded by the EU with Australia and New Zealand, impose restrictive rules of origin that require that third country products continue to meet the conformity assessment of each country in the region.

This chapter addresses the question of how MRAs on conformity assessment between two trading partners affect firms' export decisions in developing countries. Specifically, it examines two distinct aspects of export behavior of firms, namely, *whether to export* and *how much to export*. It also compares such effects with those of the traditional Preferential Trade Agreements, which have been focused on reducing tariffs.

Preliminary findings indicate that MRAs do affect firms' decisions about whether to export while they have little effect on their decisions about how much to export. MRAs appear to reduce such fixed costs to enter export markets. Specifically, preliminary results show that the probability of firms in developing countries to export is approximately 52 percent higher if trading partner countries have such agreements. The effect is more pronounced in the agricultural sector; the probability of agricultural firms to export is approximately 75 percent higher with MRAs in place. This may also suggest that it is considerably more difficult for agricultural firms in developing countries to enter new export markets without MRAs.

Standards and Information Technology: A Quick Review

As noted, standards can be an important engine driving trade and economic growth. The ICT sector in particular is dependent on an efficient standards-setting environment in which diffusion of technology, interoperability, and competition is facilitated. Open standards, in this sense, have indeed helped innovation and the diffusion of new technologies. This has benefited the global economy and the IT sector in particular, which has grown rapidly over the past several decades. One study concludes that 13 percent of the British increase in productivity post–World War II can be contributed to standards, and that the implementation of standards in the ICT field was the single most important contributor to this increase (Temple et al. 2005). Other studies have focused on the effects of technology standards in particular areas, and found that they have had a positive impact on overall growth.

This dynamic progress is expected to continue. For example, the number of cellular subscribers in the world increased from nearly 1.8 billion in 2004 to 4 billion by 2009. During the same period, the number of Internet users worldwide increased by more than 100 percent—with almost a quarter of the world's 6.7 billion people using the Internet by the end of 2008. This explosive development in the demand for information and communication technologies is not limited to rich countries. According to the International Telecommunication Union, growth rates for mobile phone use averaged 32 percent in Africa for 2006–2007, higher than any other region. Developing countries, therefore, have a direct stake in ensuring open, transparent, and private sector-led voluntary standards to facilitate continued access to these products.

Information and communications technologies have helped to reshape countries' trade patterns and economic structure. In the case of the United States, for instance, the information and communication sector contributes to less than 10 percent of GDP, but almost as much as one fifth of U.S. exports are in the ICT sectors (United Nations Comtrade 2007; United States Bureau of Economic Analysis 2007). Middle-income developing countries, such as India, and others are also making progress in expanding trade in these products.

These developments not only bring great potential for economic development and poverty reduction, but also provide significant market opportunities for individual firms and countries. Standards, as noted, can provide important positive externalities if they are adopted in a transparent and open manner. But as standards also are an important factor in the technology diffusion process, which in turn is important for firms' competitiveness in the information and communication industry, they give rise to incentives for governments and policy makers to try and influence how voluntary standards are set. These incentives have become much stronger as the industry has grown. In this regard, the question of how standards are developed—and where necessary mandated in technical regulations—is increasingly relevant to international trade and development.

During the past few years several countries have developed national strategies for standards. The objective to support economic interests is evident, although there are multiple underlying factors underpinning these policies. Countries that have implemented or are developing such strategies, often rather general in scope and objectives, include the United States, Japan, Germany, and France. It is reasonable to think that more countries will join in and develop national strategies of their own, or move to develop these in regional settings.

Nevertheless, the existence of a comprehensive plan on standards is not the only platform through which countries can act to support the domestic information and communication industries, or to help specific firms involved in that sector. The debate over China's role in standards and its increasingly important role as producer of new innovation and technologies has converged to offer one example of government-standards policy seeking to affect technology markets. China continues to develop a long-term strategy on standards (Breidne and Hektor 2006), but the Chinese government reportedly views the use of national standards as a viable tool for achieving its industrial policy goals.

One example of this approach was the Chinese government's decision in 2003 which declared that WAPI (WLAN Authentication and Privacy Infrastructure—China's own standard for wireless local area network) had to be supported by all wireless devices sold on the Chinese market. WAPI was incompatible with the standard for wireless local network used internationally. Moreover, as the WAPI standard was only disclosed to a few Chinese firms, this policy implicitly forced foreign firms to team up with the Chinese firms in order for them to continue to produce for the market.

After significant debate, the WAPI standard was rejected in 2006 by the International Organization for Standardization (Clendenin 2006).

Standards in certain instances can lead to segmented markets, less competition, and higher prices. The use of standards for protectionist purposes, therefore, is detrimental from a development perspective. There are three aspects that need to be taken into account when considering standards and their use in technology-intensive sectors. First, higher prices on information and communication technologies induced by market failures can limit consumers in poor countries from purchasing these goods and services. Second, the economic effects from different national standards implemented to support domestic interests impedes international trade and there are direct compliance costs borne by exporters to produce in accordance with a specific standard

As in the case of the WAPI standard, firms that are not provided with relevant information underlying the standard face an additional opportunity cost—in terms of intellectual property—if they are forced to partner up with firms that have the relevant information. They confront the tradeoff of sharing intellectual property or not producing for the market at all. Finally, there is a longer-term dynamic process at play here from a development perspective in regard to consequences induced by government direction of standards in the ICT sector. This involves problems associated with restricting information over the long term and seeking to protect through highly inefficient industrial policies infant industries. The United Nations' 2001 final report on the Digital Opportunity Initiative asserts that ICT can have positive impacts on development that go beyond the direct economic effects. ICT can be a powerful tool for development because it has inherent and unique characteristics that "dramatically improve communication and the exchange of information to strengthen and create new economic and social networks." (United Nations 2001). I would suggest that these benefits can only be reached with private sector-led standards systems and transfer of information on standards procedures to all relevant actors in the market.

Conclusion and Suggestions for Further Research

The review of selected studies outlined here indicates several general conclusions about standards as they relate to trade and development prospects. First, there is increasing empirical evidence that standards affect international trade, including the ability of developing country firms to expand export opportunities. In addition, as noted in the studies that draw on the

Technical Barriers to Trade database, the cost of compliance with multiple technical regulations can be estimated and these costs can be significant. Moreover, national standards and international standards continue to diverge, which has consequences in regard to trade flows. Setting standards at more stringent levels than international standards can have an important impact on trade prospects for developing country exporters. Systematic differences between types of standards and differences across sectors need to be further explored and may be possible with data such as that available in the TBT database.

What about directions for future research? Research to date on standards relies primarily on cross-sectional variations at a point in time. In order to obtain more robust and precise results regarding the impact of standards on trade, new research with panel data and dynamic models is needed. The World Bank is currently considering, for example, extending the TBT database into a panel dataset. Moreover, new dynamic models should take into account both short-run and long-run costs and benefits from meeting foreign standards. This framework could also be applied to questions associated with open standards and the information technology sector, for example.

Limited numbers of reliable datasets, which allow for quantifying the impact of technical standards on international trade, are an important impediment for future studies. The difficulty in collecting data is a result of heterogeneity of nontechnical barriers to trade among different countries. Also, the collection of the firm-level data that will allow for cost analysis of technical product standards is a prerequisite for future research in this area. This should therefore be a priority for research organizations engaged in economic research and trade.

Notes

This chapter draws on John S. Wilson, "Standards and Developing Country Exports: A Quick Review of Selected Studies and Suggestions for New Research," a paper prepared for the Summer Symposium of the International Agricultural Trade Research Consortium (IATRC), May 2006, Bonn, Germany. The assistance of Andreas Hatzigeorgiou and Benjamin J. Taylor in preparation of this chapter is gratefully acknowledged. The findings, interpretations, and conclusions expressed here are entirely those of the author. They do not necessarily represent the view of the World Bank, its executive directors, or the countries they represent. Email: jswilson@world-bank.org.

1. In regard to regulation, see the data in the World Bank's Doing Business 2010 report on regulatory barriers to business and economic activity, <http://www.doingbusiness.org>.

2. The terms "standards" and "standards and technical regulations" are used inter-changeably throughout this paper. The WTO provides a clear distinction between standards and technical regulations; the former are voluntary and the latter are mandatory technical requirements. In many cases "standards" cover mandatory technical requirements.

3. This paper surveys the literature on standards-setting processes and their conse-quences for industry structure and economic welfare. David and Greenstein exam-ined four kinds of standardization processes: (1) market competition involving products embodying nonproprietary standards, (2) market competition among (pro-prietary) standards, (3) agreements within voluntary standards-writing organiza-tions, and (4) direct governmental promulgation.

References

Breidne, M., and A. Hektor. 2006. "Standarder slagfält i konkurrensen—IKT-strategier i Kina och Japan." Policy brief. Stersund, Sweden: Swedish Institute for Growth Policy Studies.

Chen, Maggie Xiaoyang, Tsunehiro Otsuki, and John S. Wilson. 2006. "Do Standards Matter for Export Success?" *World Bank Working Paper*, No. 3809. Washington, DC: The World Bank.

Chen, Maggie Xiaoyang, Ayako Suzuki, and John S. Wilson. 2006. "Do Mutual Recognition Agreements Expand Trade?" Mimeo. Washington, DC: The World Bank.

Clendenin, M. 2006. ISO Rejects China's WLAN Standard. *EETimes* (March 12). <http://www.eetimes.com/showArticle.jhtml?articleID=181502994> (accessed June 12, 2007).

David, Paul A., and Shane Greenstein. 1990. The Economics of Compatibility Stan-dards: An Introduction to Recent Research. *Economics of Innovation and New Technol-ogy* 1:3–41.

Fischer, Ronald, and Pablo Serra. 2000. Standards and Protection. *Journal of Interna-tional Economics* 52:377–400.

Jones, P., and J. Hudson. 1996. Standardization and the Costs of Assessing Quality. *European Journal of Political Economy* 12:355–361.

Kym, Anderson, Richard Damania, and Lee Ann Jackson. 2004. "Trade, Standards, and the Political Economy of Genetically Modified Food." *CIES Discussion Paper*, no. 0410. School of Economics, University of Adelaide, Australia.

Maskus, Keith, and John S. Wilson. 2001. A Review of Past Attempts and the New Policy Context. In *Quantifying the Impact of Technical Barriers to Trade: Can It Be*

Done? ed. Keith Maskus and John S. Wilson, 1–27. Ann Arbor: University of Michigan Press.

Maskus, Keith, Tsunehiro Otsuki, and John S. Wilson. 2005. "The Cost of Compliance with Product Standards for Firms in Developing Countries: An Econometric Study." *The World Bank Policy Research Working Paper Series*, no. 3590. Washington, DC: The World Bank.

Mayeda, Graham. 2004. Developing Disharmony? The SPS and TBT Agreements and the Impact of Harmonization on Developing Countries. *Journal of International Economic Law* 7 (4): 737–764.

Otsuki, Tsunehiro, and John S. Wilson. 2004. *Standards and Technical Regulations and Firm's Ability to Export: New Evidence from World Bank Standards and Trade Survey.* Washington, DC: The World Bank.

Portugal, Alberto, Jose-Daniel Reyes, and John S. Wilson. 2009. "Beyond the Information Technology Agreement: Harmonization of Standards and Trade in Electronics." *The World Bank Policy Research Working Paper Series*, no. 4916. Washington, DC: The World Bank.

Shepherd, Ben. 2007. "Product Standards, Harmonization, and Trade: Evidence from the Extensive Margin." *The World Bank Policy Research Working Paper Series*, no. 4390. Washington, DC: The World Bank.

Temple, P., R. Witt, C. Spencer, K. Blind, A. Jungmittag, and G. M. Swann. 2005. "The Empirical Economics of Standards." United Kingdom Department of Trade and Industry Economics Paper No. 12.

United Nations. 2001. Creating a Development Dynamic—Final Report of the Digital Opportunity Initiative. <http://www.opt-init.org/framework/> (accessed June 2007).

United Nations Comtrade. 2007. United Nations Commodity Trade Statistics Database. <http://comtrade.un.org> (accessed June 2007).

United States Bureau of Economic Analysis. 2007. Annual Industry Accounts. <http://www.bea.gov/industry/index.htm> (accessed June 2007).

World Bank. 2004. *The World Bank Technical Barriers to Trade Survey.* <http://www1.worldbank.org/wbiep/st-db/> (accessed October 20, 2006).

World Bank. 2010. *Global Economic Prospects 2009: Crisis, Finance, and Growth.* Washington, DC: The World Bank.

III Standards-Based Intellectual Property Debates

9   Questioning Copyright in Standards

Pamela Samuelson

Standards are essential to the operation of the Internet, the World Wide Web, and indeed, the modern information society, an integral part of the largely invisible infrastructure of the modern world that makes things work. Every time people send email, for example, more than two hundred formally adopted Internet standards are implicated.[1] With the rise of the information economy, copyright has become a new prominent factor in the longstanding debate over intellectual property rights in standards, as standards-setting organizations (SSOs) increasingly claim and charge substantial fees for access to and rights to use standards such as the International Organization for Standardization (ISO) country, currency, and language codes and medical and dental procedure codes promulgated by the American Medical Association (AMA) and the American Dental Association (ADA).

The high importance of claims of copyright in standards is illustrated by a "clarification" of its intellectual property policy that ISO published in July 2003. It would have required all software developers and commercial resellers of data who embedded data elements from ISO's standard country, language, and currency codes to pay an annual fee (or a one-time fee plus regular maintenance fees) for doing so.[2] Tim Berners-Lee, director of the World Wide Web Consortium (W3C), wrote a letter to ISO's president to object to this policy because of its negative impact on the evolution of the Web:

These and similar codes are widely used on the Web. In particular the language and country codes are of direct interest to W3C and the users of W3C Recommendations in the context of HTTP, HTML and XML and various other technologies. Language and country codes currently provide a single, standard way of identifying languages (and locales) throughout the Web. Multilingual Web sites and Web pages, as well as internationalization and localization features, would be particularly affected.

Any charges for the use of these standards are going to lead to fragmentation, delay in deployment, and in effect a lack of standardization. In particular, those users who depend upon multi-lingual or non-English language services will suffer. . . .

Given that this policy would have profound impact not only on ISO, but also on industry and users of the Web at large, we urge ISO to further consider this policy and its broader implications and consequences, and to reassure the community as quickly as possible that there will be no charges for the use of these standards.[3]

The ISO policy would also have devastating consequences for open source developers.[4] After several other organizations published statements of concern about the policy,[5] ISO tabled it—for now. But ISO did not commit itself to continuing to make these codes available without charge for software, Internet, and Web applications, and it continues to charge substantial fees for downloads of the standards and for reproductions of the full standards.

This chapter will consider whether standards such as these, especially those whose use is mandated by government rules, should be eligible for copyright protection as a matter of U.S. copyright law. The first section— Standards May Be Unprotectable Systems under Sec. 102(b)—reviews lawsuits that challenged copyrights in numbering systems devised to enable efficient communication. It argues that two decisions upholding copyrights in AMA and ADA codes were incorrectly decided in light of other case law, the statutory exclusion of systems from copyright, and various policy considerations. The second section, titled Standards May Be or Become Unprotectable by Copyright under the Scenes a Faire or Merger Doctrines, presents case law and policy considerations that have persuaded courts to exclude standards from the scope of copyright protection under the scenes a faire and merger of idea and expression doctrines. This section suggests that government mandates to use certain standards should affect the ability to claim copyright in standards. The third section, on Incentives and Competition Policy Concerns about Copyrights in Standards, considers whether SSOs need copyright incentives to develop and maintain industry standards they promulgate and whether arguments based on incentives should prevail over other considerations. It identifies competition and other public policy concerns that call into question allowing SSOs to own standards, particularly those whose use is required by law.

Standards May Be Unprotectable Systems under Sec. 102(b)

Copyright protection has sometimes been claimed in coding systems. They typically use numbers, abbreviations, or other symbols to represent certain data elements in accordance with rules or organizing principles. Sometimes such systems have been collectively drafted to serve as industry standards, although some systems drafted by one person or firm have become, or their drafters intended them to become, de facto standards in the market. This section argues that two United States appellate court decisions upholding copyrights in number-coding systems were wrongly decided in light of other case law, the statutory exclusion of systems from copyright protection under 17 U.S.C. sec. 102(b), longstanding precedents interpreting this exclusion, and copyright policies.

Case Law Upholding Copyright in Numbering Systems

The AMA has developed and refined a coding system for standard terminology for medical procedures over several decades, which it publishes in print form and online as the "Current Procedural Terminology" (CPT).[6] The stated purpose of the CPT is "to provide a uniform language that accurately describes medical, surgical, and diagnostic services, and thereby serves as an effective means for reliable nationwide communication among physicians, and other healthcare providers, patients, and third parties."[7] The CPT is widely used in "report[ing] medical procedures and services under public and private health insurance programs . . . [and] for administrative management purposes such as claims processing and developing guidelines for medical care review."[8] In the 1980s, the federal government's Health Care Financing Administration (HCFA) mandated use of the CPT when reporting services for Medicare and Medicaid reimbursement. The CPT has thus become a standard in two senses: the AMA promulgated it to be a standard coding system for physicians and other health professionals and services, and it has been mandated as a standard for doing a certain kind of business with the U.S. government.

The CPT classifies more than six thousand procedures into one of six groups: evaluation, anesthesiology, surgery, radiology, pathology and medicine. "Within each section, procedures are arranged to enable the user to locate the code number readily."[9] For example, within the surgery category, the CPT arranges subsections by body part. Within each body part subcategory is an organized list of different kinds of procedures pertinent to that body part. The CPT sets forth a standard name for each medical procedure and assigns a unique five-digit number to each procedure. Removing an implant from an elbow joint, for example, is designated by the number 24160.

Practice Management Information Corp. (PMIC) decided to publish the CPT in one of its medical practice books. After the AMA threatened legal action against this publication, PMIC sought a declaratory judgment that the AMA code had become uncopyrightable after HCFA mandated its use, or alternatively, that the AMA misused its copyright by an exclusive license that forbade the agency to use "any other system of procedure nomenclature . . . for reporting physicians' services."[10] A trial judge issued a preliminary injunction against PMIC's publication of the AMA code. The U.S. Ninth Circuit Court of Appeals affirmed in part and reversed in part.

PMIC's invalidity argument rested mainly on U.S. Supreme Court case law about the uncopyrightability of judicial opinions and statutes. In *Banks v. Manchester*, for example, the Supreme Court decided that judicial opinions could not be copyrighted. The Ninth Circuit distinguished *Banks* as involving government employees who didn't need copyright incentives to write judicial opinions. The AMA, by contrast, was a private entity that claimed copyright incentives were important to it. *Banks* also rejected copyright claims in judicial opinions on due process grounds (that is, on a theory that people should have unfettered access to the law). There was, however, "no evidence that anyone wishing to use the [AMA code] has any difficulty obtaining access to it" and the AMA has "no incentive to limit or forego publication" of the code.[11] PMIC was "not a potential user denied access to the [code] but a putative copier wishing to share in the AMA's statutory monopoly."[12] The court was wary of "terminat[ing]" the AMA's copyright based on the risk that the AMA would restrict access to CPT when other remedies, such as mandatory licensing at a reasonable royalty, were available to contend with misuse.

The court expressed concern that "invalidating [AMA's] copyright on the ground that the CPT entered the public domain when HCFA required its use would expose the copyrights on a wide range of privately authored model codes, standards, and reference works to invalidation."[13] Because the Supreme Court had never considered whether private actors could enforce copyrights in rules they had drafted after government adoption, and two other courts had, in its view, "declined to enjoin enforcement of private copyrights in these circumstances,"[14] the Ninth Circuit ruled against PMIC's challenge to the AMA's copyright.

Yet the Ninth Circuit lifted the preliminary injunction because it agreed with PMIC that the AMA had misused its copyright by entering into an exclusive licensing deal with HCFA.[15] This misuse limited the AMA's right to enforce the copyright until the misuse had been "purged."[16]

On appeal, PMIC belatedly argued that the AMA code had become uncopyrightable because the HCFA mandate had caused the CPT to become an unprotectable "idea" under section 102(b) of the U.S. Copyright Act, the merger doctrine, and *Sega Ent. Ltd. v. Accolade, Inc.*[17] The court's articulation of PMIC's 102(b)/merger theory is too cryptic to be decoded, but the court distinguished *Sega* as having involved an effort to suppress creativity: "The AMA's copyright does not stifle independent creative expression in the medical coding industry. It does not prevent [PMIC] or the AMA's competitors from developing comparative or better coding systems and lobbying the federal government and private actors to adopt them. It simply prevents wholesale copying of an existing system."[18]

PMIC apparently did not make the more straightforward argument that the CPT was an unprotectable coding system under section 102(b), which provides: "In no case does copyright protection . . . extend to any idea, procedure, process, system, method of operation, concept, principle or discovery, regardless of the form in which it is . . . embodied in such work."[19] This is curious given that the AMA and the Ninth Circuit repeatedly referred to the CPT as a "system."[20]

Section 102(b) played a more prominent role in a sister case to *PMIC* that arose after Delta Dental published a book containing standard dental procedure nomenclature and associated numbers from the Code on Dental Procedures and Nomenclatures developed by the ADA. ADA sued Delta for copyright infringement and sought an injunction to stop Delta from publishing the ADA's code and money damages for past infringements.

The trial judge ruled against the copyrightability of the ADA Code on Dental Procedures and Nomenclatures,[21] saying it did not qualify for copyright protection because it comprehensively cataloged a field of knowledge, rather than creatively selecting information about it. Although the code's arrangement of data was creative, the arrangement was systematic and highly useful, and hence, unprotectable under section 102(b). The code was, moreover, the collaborative work product of a committee, not an expression of the judgment of an author, and Delta had participated in the drafting of the ADA standard, which further supported its right to reuse the ADA Code on Dental Procedures and Nomenclatures.

Judge Frank Easterbrook, writing for the Seventh Circuit Court of Appeals, disagreed. In his view, ADA's "taxonomy" of dental procedures was creative enough to qualify for copyright protection. "Creativity marks the expression even after the fundamental scheme has been devised."[22] Because there are many different ways to organize types of dental procedures—"by complexity, or by the tools necessary to perform them, . . . or by the anesthesia employed, or in any of a dozen different ways"—the way chosen by ADA was a creative expression not dictated by functional considerations.[23] The usefulness of a taxonomy did not disqualify it from protection, in Easterbrook's view, because only pictorial, sculptural, and graphic works were disqualified from copyright on account of their utility. The trial court's reasoning would imperil copyrights in many other works, such as standards promulgated by the Financial Accounting Standards Board (FASB), the West key numbering system, the uniform system of citation for legal materials, and even computer software.

Easterbrook's opinion went into considerable detail about the perceived creativity of the ADA's numbering system. The ADA assigned five digit numbers to procedures, when it could have made them four or six digits long, and decided the first number should be a zero in order to leave room for future expansion of the code as more procedures were developed or discovered. The second and third numbers represented a particular grouping of procedures, and the remaining two digits identified the specific procedure associated with that grouping. "A catalog that initially assigns 04266, 04267, and 04268 to three procedures will over time depart substantively from one that initially assigns 42660, 42670, and 42680 to the same three procedures."[24] Easterbrook was so taken with the creativity of the ADA code that he opined that the name of each procedure and the number assigned to it were themselves original works of authorship entitled to copyright protection.[25]

To Delta's argument that section 102(b) rendered the ADA's system unprotectable, Easterbrook flippantly responded: "But what could it mean to call the [c]ode a 'system'? This taxonomy does not come with instructions for use, as if the [c]ode were a recipe for a new dish. . . . The [c]ode is a taxonomy, which may be put to many uses. These uses may or may not be or include systems; the code is not."[26]

Easterbrook seemed to think that section 102(b) made unprotectable only those systems presenting a danger of monopolization of a widely used practice such as bookkeeping, as in *Baker v. Selden*. Easterbrook perceived no danger that the ADA would monopolize dental practice. Under section 102(b), dentists were free to use ADA codes in their forms, and even Delta was free "to disseminate forms inviting dentists to use the ADA's code when submitting bills to insurers. But it does not permit Delta to copy the code itself or make and distribute a derivative work based on the code."[27]

Case Law Rejecting Copyright Claims in Numbering Systems
Southco manufactures products such as latches, handles, and rivets. After its competitor Kanebridge reproduced in its catalog product names and numbers from Southco's copyrighted catalog, Southco sued Kanebridge for copyright infringement.[28] Kanebridge's principal defense was that

Southco's numbering system was uncopyrightable under section 102(b). Southco asserted that its names and numbers were original enough to be copyrightable because they were the product of skilled judgment, and since there were many different ways to design numbering systems for such a catalog, there was no "merger" of idea and expression to disqualify the work from copyright.[29]

A retired Southco engineer who designed the Southco numbering system explained the creativity in the numbering system, pointing out that "each particular digit or group of digits signifies a relevant characteristic of the product."[30] The first two digits represented the product type (e.g., 47 = captive screws), while other digits "indicate characteristics such as thread size ("632"), composition of the screw (aluminium), and finish of the knob ("knurled")."[31]

Writing for the Third Circuit Court of Appeals, Judge Samuel Alito (now a justice of the U.S. Supreme Court) held that Southco's numbering system—that is, the pairing of product names with numbers representing the products—was unprotectable under section 102(b).[32] It accepted that Southco "had to identify the relevant characteristics of the products in the class (that is, the characteristics that would interest prospective purchasers); it had to assign one or more digits to express each characteristic; and it had to assign a number or other symbol to represent each of the relevant values of each characteristic."[33] This did require some skill and judgment, but "once these decisions were made, the system was in place, and all of the products in the class could be numbered without the slightest element of creativity."[34] Insofar as any originality could be discerned, it lay in Southco's development of rules for the numbering system, not in the pairing of numbers and products.

In a subsequent case, ATC Distribution, Inc., tried to distinguish its numbering system from Southco's and take cover under *ADA* by characterizing its system as a "taxonomy." As in *Southco*, ATC alleged that its competitor, Whatever It Takes Transmissions & Parts, Inc. (WITTP), was a copyright infringer because it reproduced the taxonomy in the latter's catalog of transmission parts.[35] ATC claimed creativity in

(1) deciding what kind of information to convey in part numbers; (2) predicting future developments in the transmission parts industry and deciding how many slots to leave open in a given subcategory to allow for these developments; (3) deciding whether an apparently novel part that does not obviously fit in any of the existing classifications should be assigned to a new category of its own or placed in an existing category and if the latter, which one; (4) designing the part numbers; and (5) devising the overall taxonomy of part numbers that places the parts into different categories.[36]

The court accepted that "at least some of the decisions made by ATC are arguably 'non-obvious choices' made from 'among more than a few options,'"[37] but nevertheless ruled against the copyrightability of the taxonomy because "the creative aspects of the ATC classification scheme" lay in its ideas.[38] Original ideas, the court held, are not copyrightable under section 102(b). "ATC cannot copyright its predictions of how many types of sealing rings will be developed in the future, its judgment that O-rings and sealing rings should form two separate categories of parts, or its judgment that a new part belongs with the retainers as opposed to the pressure plates."[39]

Nor was the court persuaded that the numbers themselves were original works of authorship entitled to copyright protection. Characterizing *ADA*'s rationale for this holding as "rather opaque,"[40] the Sixth Circuit doubted its soundness. Yet, the court went on to say that even if "some strings of numbers used to designate an item or procedure could be sufficiently creative to merit copyright protection, the part numbers at issue in the case before us do not evidence any such creativity. ATC's allocation of numbers to parts was an essentially random process, serving only to provide a useful shorthand way of referring to each part."[41] The court expressed concern that allowing copyright in part numbers "would provide a way for the creators of otherwise uncopyrightable ideas or works to gain some degree of copyright protection through the back door simply by assigning short numbers or other shorthand phrases to those ideas or works (or their component parts)."[42] The real competition between ATC and WITTP, after all, was in sales of uncopyrightable transmission parts, not in sales of catalogs.

Why Are Systems Uncopyrightable?

The copyright claims previously discussed rested on assertions of creativity in the pairing of particular numbers with discrete phenomena in accordance with rule-based systems for efficiently organizing information for a specific purpose. Three of the four systems were, moreover, promulgated with the intent that they would become industry standards. The Ninth and Seventh Circuits in *PMIC* and *ADA* erred in not seriously analyzing the section 102(b) challenges to these systems. The Third Circuit in *Southco* and the Sixth Circuit in *ATC* correctly recognized that systematic ways of assigning numbers to phenomena are unprotectable by copyright law under section 102(b). Their analyses would have been even stronger had they invoked the long history of copyright cases denying protection to systems and had they discussed policy rationales for excluding systems and their component parts from the scope of copyright protection.

Even before the landmark *Baker v. Selden* decision in which the Supreme Court ruled that bookkeeping systems and their constituent parts (embodied in sample ledger sheets) were unprotectable by copyright law, the Supreme Court ruled that copyright did not protect a symbol system for representing specific types of information on maps of urban areas prepared to assess fire insurance risks.[43] A civil engineer named William Perris, who had mapped certain wards of New York City, sued Hexamer for infringement because the latter used the same symbol system in his comparable map of urban Philadelphia.

The Supreme Court concluded:

The complainants have no more an exclusive right to use the form of the characters they employ to express their ideas upon the face of the map, than they have to use the form of type they select to print the key. Scarcely any map is published on which certain arbitrary signs, explained by a key printed at some convenient place for reference, are not used to designate objects of special interest, such as rivers, railroads, boundaries, cities, towns, &c.; and yet we think it has never been supposed that a simple copyright of the map gave the publisher an exclusive right to the use upon other maps of the particular signs and key which he saw fit to adopt for the purposes of his delineations. That, however, is what the complainants seek to accomplish in this case. The defendant has not copied their maps. All he has done at any time has been to use to some extent their system of arbitrary signs and their key.[44]

The comprehensibility of maps would be impeded if subsequent developers had to use entirely different symbol systems for each map. *Perris v. Hexamer* presents an example of a system held unprotectable by copyright law notwithstanding the fact that its component parts were not "dictated by functional considerations,"[45] as Easterbrook seemed to think was necessary for a system to be ineligible for protection under section 102(b).

In explaining why bookkeeping and other useful systems should not be protected by copyright law, the Supreme Court in *Baker v. Selden* observed that to give the author of a book an exclusive right in a useful art, such as a bookkeeping system, depicted in the book "would be a surprise and a fraud upon the public. That is the province of letters patent, not of copyright."[46] This was relevant in *Baker* because bookkeeper Charles Selden had filed a patent on his bookkeeping system, although no patent had apparently issued. The Court did not want to allow Selden to misuse his copyright by getting patent-like protection for the system through the copyright in his book. Selden could protect his description of the system through copyright, but not the system itself.

Although useful arts can generally "only be represented in concrete forms of wood, metal, stone or some other physical embodiment," the principle that copyright doesn't protect useful systems still applied even when, as with Selden's forms, they are embodied in a book.[47] In *Baker*, the selection and arrangement of headings and columns was deemed too useful to be protected by copyright. Because some systematic organizations of information have been patented,[48] *Baker's* concerns about possible misuses of copyright to obtain patent-like protection may have some significance in information systems cases.

Many cases after *Baker* have applied its system/description distinction. Especially pertinent to the numbering system cases are *Griggs v. Perrin*[49] and *Brief English Systems v. Owen*.[50] In these cases, plaintiffs sued authors of competing books on the shorthand systems each plaintiff had devised. Both systems involved the assignment of particular abbreviations and symbols to represent particular letters, words, phrases, and the like for such purposes as stenographic transcription. The courts ruled against the copyright claims in both cases, citing *Baker*.[51] These cases are notable because in neither case was the particular shorthand system at issue dictated by specific rules or functionality.

When faced with assessing whether a particular information artifact is an uncopyrightable "system," courts should start by recognizing that systems, by their nature, consist of interdependent, interrelated parts that are integrated into a whole scheme. This is true of bookkeeping systems, shorthand systems, burial insurance systems,[52] systems for teaching how to play musical instruments,[53] systems for reorganizing insolvent life insurance companies,[54] systems for issuing bonds to cover replacement of lost securities,[55] systems for consolidating freight tariff information,[56] and systems for teaching problem-solving techniques,[57] among others. Strategies for playing games are another kind of unprotectable system under 102(b).[58] Interestingly, while rules of games structure the players' interactions, outcomes of games are not mechanically deterministic.[59]

Mathematical formulae and the periodic table of chemical elements are other examples of systematic arrangements of information that are unprotectable under section 102(b).[60] Considerable originality may underlie formulae, but mathematical precision and comprehensibility of mathematical ideas are better served by standardizing the language elements of formulae. The periodic table is a useful tool for teaching students about the fields of chemistry and physics precisely because of its standardized representation of atomic phenomena. Gratuitous differences in the fields of mathematics and science would impede effective communication.

Elsewhere I have argued that computer languages, such as the macro command language at issue in *Lotus Development Corporation v. Borland International, Inc.*, are unprotectable systems under copyright law.[61] An earlier lawsuit involving Lotus 1-2-3 recognized that "the exact hierarchy— or structure, sequence and organization—of the menu system is a fundamental part of the functionality of the macros"[62] and that the command hierarchy was an integral part of the Lotus macro command language. Use of exactly the same command terms in exactly the same order and hierarchical structure as in 1-2-3 was necessary for users to be able to reuse macros constructed in the Lotus macros language for commonly executed sequences of functions when using other programs. Users' investments in their macros and their desire to reuse them when using Borland's software was a factor in the First Circuit's ruling that the Lotus command hierarchy was unprotectable under section 102(b).

Thus, it may be relevant that the AMA characterized the purpose of CPT as "to provide a uniform *language* that accurately describes medical, surgical, and diagnostic services, and thereby serves as an effective means for reliable *communication* among physicians, and other healthcare providers, patients, and third parties."[63] Similarly, the ADA had encouraged use of its code by dentists, insurers, and others because "standardization of *language* promotes interchange among professionals."[64] The AMA and the ADA developed uniform standard names and numbers for medical and dental procedures to enable more effective and efficient record keeping and information processing about these procedures. These standards promoted interoperability of data among many professionals who had to exchange information on a daily basis. HCFA mandated use of the CPT to lower its costs for processing Medicare and Medicaid claims, standardize payments to doctors for the same procedures, and avert fraud arising from nonuniform reporting procedures. Facilitating efficient record keeping is among the reasons that copyright law precludes protection of blank forms, and this reinforces the rationale for denying copyright to numbering systems.

Judge Easterbrook may be right that merely calling an intellectual artifact a "system" should not automatically disqualify it from copyright protection.[65] However, if plaintiffs characterize it as a system, as the AMA did in its contract with HCFA and the Ninth Circuit did in *PMIC*, and it fits standard definitions of "system," courts should at least consider whether the artifact is the kind of system that should be ineligible for copyright protection. (Merely calling a numbering system a "taxonomy" shouldn't avert the inquiry. Taxonomies are, by definition, systematic classifications of information that group subcomponents into logical categories based on similarities in clusters of phenomena.[66] The Sixth Circuit in *ATC* recognized the interchangeability of "taxonomy" and "system" in connection with the numbering scheme at issue there.)

Revisiting the claimed creativity in the ADA's "taxonomy" in light of *ATC*, it becomes evident that the creativity of the ADA code also lay in the creation of the system ("the fundamental scheme," as *ADA* calls it[67]). *ADA* says the decision to use five digits instead of four or six was creative. Yet five digits was an obvious choice if dental professionals participating in the code development process thought it likely that new categories of procedures might be developed beyond the four-digit codes already in the ADA Code on Dental Procedures and Nomenclatures. The most reasonable way to accommodate this possibility was to make the first digit a zero. The second and third digits represented a particular category of dental procedures, while the fourth and fifth represented specific procedures within each category.

Restorative procedures, for example, were represented by the number 21. Numbering specific procedures within this category reflected the number of surfaces being restored. 02110, for example, was the number assigned for restorative amalgams for one primary surface, while 02120 was for amalgams for two primary surfaces, and so forth. In general, the ADA code left ten spaces between procedures, presumably because there was some likelihood that in the future new procedures might need to be added in the restoration category or other categories. In some cases, procedures had only one space between them (e.g., 02130 for three-surfaced amalgams, but 02131 for four-surfaced amalgams), but this seems as arbitrary as decisions that ATC made about whether aluminum screws should be numbered 10 or 11. The ADA code, moreover, drew substantially from preexisting codes.

The naming and numbering of dental procedures in ADA's code were also products of an incremental collaborative effort of skilled practitioners in the field that these were (or should be) standard names for dental procedures organized by logical class. Judge Easterbrook may have a point in stating that "blood is shed in the ADA's committees about which [procedure name] is preferable,"[68] but blood is no more a sign of original expression in copyright law than sweat is in the aftermath of *Feist v. Rural Telephone*.[69]

To sum up, industry standard codes promulgated by organizations such as the AMA and the ADA may be unprotectable systems under section

102(b). Such codes or other systematic organizations of information are certainly uncopyrightable if they are dictated by rules or functionality. Yet other factors may be relevant to whether systematic organizations of information are unprotectable under section 102(b): (1) when the system is a useful art and copyright in it would give patent-like protection; (2) when second comers need to use the system to compete or communicate effectively; (3) when systematizing information is necessary to achieve efficiencies; (4) when the system is incidental to uncopyrightable transactions or processes; and (5) when systematizing the information will produce social benefits from uniformity and the social costs of diversity would be high. Standard systems of this sort are born uncopyrightable.

Standards May Be or Become Unprotectable by Copyright under the Scenes a Faire or Merger Doctrines

Alternative theories for deciding that industry standards, such as the AMA and ADA codes, as well as ISO country, language, and currency codes, may be ineligible for copyright protection come from the scenes a faire and merger doctrines and the policies that underlie them. The scenes a faire doctrine, originally developed to recognize that certain plot structures are to be expected from works exploring certain literary or dramatic themes,[70] has been adapted, especially in the software copyright case law, to recognize that expressive choices of subsequent authors may become constrained over time by the emergence of industry standards. The merger doctrine holds that if there is only one or a very small number of ways to express an idea, copyright protection will generally be unavailable to that way or those few ways in order to avoid protecting the idea.[71] While most merger cases involve works that are uncopyrightable when first created, some courts have held that an initially copyrightable work may be disqualified for copyright protection over time, as the Fifth Circuit Court of Appeals did in holding that governmental enactment of a privately drafted model law caused the idea of this law and its expression to merge.[72]

The scenes a faire doctrine struck the concurring Judge Becker in *Southco* as a plausible alternative basis for ruling that Kanebridge's catalog did not infringe Southco's copyright.[73] Southco had "selected characteristics for its system based on customer demand," and once these characteristics were chosen, "values—such as screw thread sizes, screw lengths or ferrule types—were determined by industry standards rather than through any exercise of originality by Southco," and although finishes were specific to Southco, they were "determined by the part identity rather than through some exercise of creative expression."[74] Becker relied on the Tenth Circuit's instructive analysis of scenes a faire in *Mitel, Inc. v. Iqtel, Inc.*[75]

Mitel was in the business of manufacturing call controllers. Long distance carriers buy call controllers to install them on customer premises to "automate that customer's access to the carrier's long distance service."[76] Mitel developed a set of sixty-some four-digit numeric command codes and published them in manuals describing how to program its call controllers with the command codes. Mitel claimed that its copyright in the software and manuals protected the command codes as its creative work product.

Iqtel initially devised its own call controller instruction set, but ultimately concluded that "it could compete with Mitel only if its IQ200+ controller were compatible with Mitel's controller."[77] Iqtel came to realize that "technicians who install call controllers would be unwilling to learn Iqtel's new set of instructions in addition to the Mitel command codes and the technicians' employers would be unwilling to bear the cost of additional training."[78] So Iqtel programmed its controllers to accept the Mitel command codes and translate them into Iqtel codes. Its manual included an appendix that listed and cross-referenced the Iqtel and Mitel command codes. And then it copied Mitel's command codes for all of the call controllers' common functions.

Yet, the Tenth Circuit concluded that Iqtel was not an infringer. In part, this was because the court questioned the originality of the Mitel command codes insofar as the symbols either were arbitrarily assigned to functions or exhibited de minimis creativity. But to the extent the Mitel codes were original, the Tenth Circuit concluded that they were unprotectable under the scenes a faire doctrine. This doctrine "exclude[s] from protection . . . those elements of a work that necessarily result from external factors inherent in the subject matter of the work," such as "hardware standards and mechanical specifications, software standards and compatibility requirements, computer manufacturer design standards, industry programming practices, and practices and demands of the industry being served."[79]

The scenes a faire doctrine "plays a particularly important role [in functional writing cases] in ensuring that copyright rewards and stimulates artistic creativity in a utilitarian work 'in a manner that permits the free use and development of non-protectable ideas and processes' that make the work useful."[80] As applied to the Mitel's command codes, the court concluded that "much of the expression in Mitel's command codes was dictated by the proclivities of technicians and limited by significant hardware, compatibility and industry requirements."[81] The Mitel codes embodied industry standards, and were thus unprotectable by copyright law.

Industry standards serve an important function by allowing those in the industry or field to use the standard for effective communication. The interoperability case law, of which *Mitel* is one instance, recognizes that the design of computer program interfaces may be the product of considerable skill and judgment, and thus might seem to qualify for copyright protection.[82] However, once an interface has been developed, the parameters it establishes for the effective communication of information between one program and another constrain the design choices of subsequent programmers. The interface thus becomes an unprotectable functional design,[83] and the scenes a faire doctrine is often invoked in decisions coming to this conclusion.

Also relevant to determining whether copyright should protect industry standards is the extent of user investments in the standard. In ruling against Lotus's lawsuit against Borland for copying the command hierarchy of 1-2-3, the First Circuit emphasized the significant investments users had made in developing macros with Lotus's macro command language.[84] Although Judge Boudin was not fully persuaded by the majority's 102(b) analysis, he concurred in its holding, observing: "Requests for the protection of computer menus present the concern with fencing off access to the commons in an acute form. A new menu may be a creative work, but over time its importance may come to reside more in the investment that has been made by users in learning the menu and in building their own miniprograms—macros—in reliance upon the menu. Better typewriter keyboard layouts may exist, but the familiar QWERTY keyboard dominates the market because that is what everyone has learned to use."[85]

Professor Paul Goldstein has analogized the copyright case law on industry standards to trademark law's genericide doctrine.[86] Under that doctrine, a once-viable trademark may become unprotectable because widespread public use of the mark as a common name for a product or service causes it to lose its source significance. *Mitel v. Iqtel* and *Lotus v. Borland* demonstrate that industry standards may become unprotectable over time.

Government adoption of a privately drafted standard, such as a model building code, may similarly cause it to become uncopyrightable upon its adoption as law under the merger of idea and expression doctrine, as happened in *Veeck v. Southern Building Code Congress International, Inc.*[87] SBCCI published a standard building code that the towns of Anna and Savoy, Texas, adopted as their laws.[88] Peter Veeck purchased an electronic copy of SBCCI's building code and posted it on his Web site. After receiving a cease and desist letter from SBCCI, Veeck sought a declaratory judgment that SBCCI's code had become uncopyrightable upon its adoption as law. The Fifth Circuit Court of Appeals en banc reversed a grant of summary judgment to SBCCI, holding that "as law, the model codes enter the public domain and are not subject to the copyright holder's exclusive prerogatives."[89]

The Fifth Circuit gave three reasons for its ruling: (1) not protecting enacted codes was consistent with Supreme Court decisions that laws are not subject to copyright protection; (2) upon its adoption as law, the ideas expressed in SBCCI's code had merged with its expression, and the code had, for purposes of copyright law, become a "fact"; and (3) the balance of case law and relevant policies supported its ruling. After enactment, the only way to express the building code laws of Anna and Savoy was with the precise text of SBCCI's code.[90] Hence, the merger doctrine forbade SBCCI to claim copyright in the enacted code. *Veeck* calls into question the Ninth Circuit's ruling in *PMIC* because federal law required use of the AMA's standard, thereby limiting the range of choices of codes that could be used by medical and health professionals.

Thus, industry standards such as the AMA and ADA codes may be unprotectable by copyright law under the scenes a faire or merger doctrines. Considerations that may affect such decisions include (1) whether industry demand or practices effectively constrain expressive choices of subsequent developers; (2) whether reuse of the standard is necessary for effective competition; (3) whether user investments in the standard are substantial enough to give rise to the right to reuse the standard; and (4) whether the government mandates use of the standard or has embodied the standard in its legal code.

Incentives and Competition Policy Concerns about Copyrights in Standards

The principal argument in favor of copyright protection for industry standards is the claim SSOs make that they need copyright incentives to develop standards. The Supreme Court's *Feist v. Rural Telephone* decision, however, informs us that copyright protection is not available to information artifacts just because they are products of industrious efforts and their developers assert the need for copyright incentives. Several considerations reinforce doubts about incentive-based arguments for copyright in standards.

First, SSOs generally have ample incentives to develop standards for use by professionals in their fields.[91] It is simply not credible to claim that organizations like the AMA and ADA would stop developing standard nomenclature without copyright protection. The fields they serve need these standards for effective communication with other health care providers, insurers, and government agencies.

Second, SSOs generally do not actually develop the standards in which they claim copyrights. Rather, they typically rely upon volunteer service by experts in the field to develop standards and require volunteers to assign any copyright interests to the SSOs. The community development of a standard is a reason to treat the standard itself as a shared resource.

Third, SSOs generally use the revenues they derive from selling or licensing the standards to subsidize other activities of their organizations, rather than to recoup investments in the making of the standard. Even without copyright in the standards, SSOs can derive revenues from sales of print materials embodying the standard and value-added products or services.[92]

Fourth, the Internet and World Wide Web now make it very cheap and easy to disseminate standards. Given the rise of volunteer information posting on the Web, there is reason to be confident that users of a successful standard will put the standards online for all to use.

Fifth, once a standard has achieved success through widespread adoption, this very success enables the SSO to charge monopoly rents for use of or access to the code.[93] The availability of copyright protection for standards may give SSOs excess incentives to invest in the creation of standards to get monopoly rents.

Sixth, copyrighting standards may create perverse incentives causing SSOs to invest in persuading governments to mandate use of their standards. *Veeck* illustrates this temptation. Under the deal SBCCI offered, local governments such as Anna and Savoy got royalty-free rights to use the code and one or more copies to make available in a public office. But SBCCI charged anyone else who wanted a copy of the code or access to it a substantial fee, and got referrals from building inspectors and other public officials, making public employees into a kind of free sales force for SBCCI. The perverse incentives problem is of particular concern because of the increasing frequency with which governments are actively encouraging government adoption of privately drafted industry standards.

The long-term credibility of SSOs depends not only on their being able to produce sound standards, but also on producing standards in which the SSOs do not have so strong a financial interest that they succumb to the temptation to abuse the standards process by making a standard into a cash cow that must be purchased by anyone affected by that standard.

Notes

Adapted from Pamela Samuelson, "Questioning Copyrights in Standards," *Boston College Law Review* 48, no. 1 (January 2007): 193–224. I am grateful to Jennifer Lane and Sara Terheggen for research assistance, Robert J. Glushko for guidance, and Boston College Law School Symposium participants for insightful comments and observations.

1. See, e.g., Marcus Maher, "An Analysis of Internet Standardization," *Virginia Journal of Law and Technology*, no. 3 (1998): 5; Geoffrey C. Bowker and Susan Leigh Star, *Sorting Things Out: Classification and Its Consequences* (Cambridge, MA: MIT Press, 2000), 9.

2. Robin Cover, "Standards Organizations Express Concern about Royalty Fees for ISO Codes," cover pages, <http://www.coverpages.org/ni2003-09-20.html>. ISO standard 3166, for example, represents Afghanistan as AF, Albania as AL, Australia as AU, and Austria as AT within this code. ISO standard 639–2 represents the modern German language as deu, modern Greek as gre, Hawaiian as haw, and Italian as ita within this code.

3. Tim Berners-Lee, Dir., W3C, Message to Oliver Smoot, September 18, 2003, <http://lists.w3.org/Archives/Public/www-international/2003JulSep/0213.html>.

4. Kendall Grant Clark, "ISO to Require Royalties?" XML.com, September 24, 2003, <http://www.xml.com/lpt/a/2003/09/24/deviant.html>.

5. Cover, see note 2. The Unicode Technical Committee, the International Committee for Information Technology Standards, and the Internet Architecture Board were among the other objectors.

6. American Medical Association, *Current Procedural Terminology 2004 Standard Edition* (2003) (CPT). The online version of CPT is access controlled.

7. American Medical Association, *CPT Process—How a Code Becomes a Codes* at 1, <http://www.ama-assn.org/ama/pub/category/print/3882.html> (accessed June 2006).

8. Ibid.

9. *Practice Management Information Corp, Inc. v. AMA*, 121 F.3d (9th Cir. 1997) at 517 (hereafter cited as *PMIC*).

10. Ibid. (quoting the contract between the AMA and HCFA).

11. Ibid. at 519.

12. Ibid. The court also perceived PMIC's lawsuit as a vengeful response to the AMA's unwillingness to give it a volume discount. Ibid. at 518.

13. Ibid. at 518.

14. Ibid. The two cases discussed were *CCC Information Services, Inc. v. Maclean Hunter Market Reports, Inc.*, 44 F.3d 61 (2d Cir. 1994), and *Building Officials & Code Admin. v. Code Technology, Inc.*, 628 F.2d 730 (1st Cir. 1980).

15. *PMIC*, 121 F.3d at 520–521.

16. Ibid. at 521.

17. Ibid. at 520, n.8.

18. Ibid. This statement ignores that the very point of developing a standard coding system such as the CPT is to gain the benefits of uniformity.

19. 17 U.S.C. sec. 102(b).

20. *PMIC*, 121 F.3d at 518, 520 n.8. The Ninth Circuit referenced coding systems thirteen times in *PMIC*.

21. *American Dental Association v. Delta Dental Plans Association*, 39 U.S.P.Q.2d (BNA) 1714 (N.D. Ill. 1996), rev. 126 F.3d 977 (7th Cir. 1997) (hereafter cited as *ADA*).

22. *ADA*, 126 F.3d at 979.

23. Ibid.

24. Ibid.

25. "We think that even the short description [i.e., the name of the procedure] and the number are original works of authorship." Ibid. Justin Hughes has criticized *ADA* for treating names of dental procedures and associated numbers as "micro-works" of authorship in contravention of the long-standing copyright policy of not allowing copyright protection for titles, short phrases, and the like. See Justin Hughes, "Size Matters (Or Should) in Copyright Law," *Fordham Law Review* 74 (2005): 575, 595–596.

26. *ADA*, 126 F.3d at 980–981.

27. Ibid. at 981. Professor Justin Hughes has observed that the *ADA* decision "may follow our intuitions on unfair competition and seems to give the ADA an *INS*-like quasi-property right against competitors, but not against individuals. Yet, the distinction makes a hash out of section 106 rights; it would be more sensible to say that an individual's form-filling never produces a work substantially similar to the ADA code as a whole." Hughes, "Size Matters," at 597. Judge Easterbrook, however, considered each number to be an original work of authorship and accompanying text. Under this view, entry of each number in a form, whether by a dentist or by Delta, would arguably be infringement unless saved by fair use. Easterbrook thus makes a hash of sec. 102(b), as well as of sec. 106.

28. *Southco, Inc. v. Kanebridge Corp.*, 390 F.3d 276, 277–279 (3d Cir. 2004) (hereafter cited as *Southco III*).

29. Judge Roth's dissent articulates Southco's arguments. Ibid. at 290–297.

30. *Southco III*, 324 F.3d at 278.

31. Ibid. at 278.

32. Ibid. at 283–285.

33. *Southco III*, 390 F.3d at 282.

34. Ibid.

35. *ATC Distribution, Inc. v. Whatever It Takes Transmissions & Parts, Inc.*, 402 F.3d 700 (6th Cir. 2005) (hereafter cited as *ATC*).

36. Ibid. at 706.

37. Ibid. at 707, quoting from *Matthew Bender & Co. v. West Publishing Co.*, 158 F.3d 674, 682 (2d Cir. 1998).

38. *ATC*, 402 F.3d at 707.

39. Ibid.

40. Ibid. at 708.

41. Ibid. at 709.

42. Ibid. at 709.

43. *Perris v. Hexamer*, 99 U.S. 674 (1878).

44. Ibid. at 676.

45. *ADA*, 126 F.3d at 979.

46. *Baker v. Selden*, 101 U.S. 99, 102 (1880).

47. Ibid. at 105.

48. See, e.g., U.S. Patent No. 6446061 Taxonomy Generation for Document Collections (2002).

49. 49 F. 15 (C.C.N.D.N.Y. 1892) (hereafter cited as *Griggs*).

50. 48 F.2d 555 (2d Cir. 1931), cert. denied, 321 U.S. 785 (1931) (hereafter cited as *Brief English*).

51. *Griggs*, 49 F. at 15 ("complainant has no right to a monopoly of the art of shorthand writing"); *Brief English*, 48 F.2d at 556 ("the plaintiff's shorthand system, as such, is open to use by whoever will take the trouble to learn and use it").

52. *Burk v. Johnson*, 146 F. 209 (8th Cir. 1906); *Burk v. Relief & Burial Association*, 2 Haw. 388 (D. Haw. 1909).

53. *Jackson v. C. G. Conn Ltd.*, 9 U.S.P.Q. (BNA) 225 (W.D. Okla. 1931).

54. *Crume v. Pacific Mutual Life Ins. Co.*, 140 F.3d 182 (7th Cir. 1944), cert. denied, 322 U.S. 755 (1945).

55. *Continental Casualty Co. v. Beardsley*, 253 F.2d 702 (2d Cir. 1958).

56. *Guthrie v. Curlett*, 36 F.2d 694 (2d Cir. 1929).

57. *Kepner-Tregoe, Inc. v. Carabio*, 203 U.S.P.Q. (BNA) 124 (E.D. Mich. 1979).

58. *Landsberg v. Scrabble Crossword Game Players, Inc.*, 736 F.2d 485 (9th Cir. 1984).

59. *Southco III* implies that unprotectable systems are mechanically deterministic, but the game example shows that this is not necessary.

60. The periodic table of elements is in the public domain and is widely available on the Internet. See, e.g., "Public Domain Databases in the Sciences," <http://www.csudh.edu/oliver/pubdomdb.htm>. Hughes agrees that mathematical formulae are uncopyrightable subject matter. Hughes, "Size Matters," at 599.

61. See Pamela Samuelson, "Computer Programs, User Interfaces, and Section 102(b) of the Copyright Act of 1976: A Critique of *Lotus v. Paperback*," *Law and Contemporary Problems* 55 (1992): 311, republished in revised form, *Berkeley Tech. Law Journal* 6 (1992): 209. See also "Brief Amicus Curiae of Copyright Law Professors in *Lotus Development Corp. v. Borland International, Inc.*" (brief to U.S. Supreme Court), *Journal of Intellectual Property Law* 3 (1995): 103; "The Nature of Copyright Analysis for Computer Programs: Copyright Law Professors' Brief Amicus Curiae in *Lotus v. Borland*" (brief to First Circuit Court of Appeals), *Hastings Communications and Entertainment Law Journal* 16 (1994): 657; Pamela Samuelson, "Some New Kinds of Authorship Made Possible by Computers and Some Intellectual Property Questions They Raise," *University of Pittsburgh Law Review* 53 (1992): 685. Languages and their component parts are essential inputs to expression that copyright law ought not to protect.

62. *Lotus Dev. Corp. v. Paperback Software International*, 740 F. Supp. 37, 65 (D. Mass. 1990).

63. American Medical Association, *CPT Process* at 1 (emphasis added).

64. *ADA*, 126 F.3d at 981 (emphasis added). Interchange is, in this context, a synonym for communication. Thus, the ADA's code has essentially the same data interoperability purpose as the AMA's code.

65. Computer programs, for example, may literally be "processes," but they are copyrightable under legislation passed by Congress. See, e.g., *Apple Computer, Inc. v.*

Franklin Computer Corp., 714 F.2d 1240 (1983) (operating system programs held copyrightable).

66. *Webster's Third New International Dictionary* (1993) defines "taxonomy" as "systematic distinguishing, ordering, and naming of type groups within a subject field."

67. *ADA*, 126 F.3d at 979.

68. Ibid. Standards often emerge from tough negotiations. Bowker and Starr, *Sorting Things Out*, 9 (decades of negotiations were required to standardize sizes and capacities of CDs, and the speed, electrical settings, and amplification rules for CD players).

69. *Feist Publications, Inc. v. Rural Tel. Service Co.*, 499 U.S. 340 (1991) (rejecting "sweat of the brow" industrious compilation copyrights).

70. See, e.g., Leslie Kurtz, "Copyright: The Scenes a Faire Doctrine," *Florida Law Review* 41 (1989): 79.

71. See, e.g., Paul Goldstein, *Goldstein on Copyright*, 2nd ed., sec. 2.3.2 (New York: Aspen, 2002), 1.

72. See *Veeck v. Southern Building Code Congress International, Inc.*, 293 F.3d 791 (model building code held unprotectable by copyright law upon its enactment by cities as law) (hereafter cited as *Veeck*); *Building Officials & Code Administration v. Code Technology, Inc.*, 628 F.2d 730 (vacating preliminary injunction because of doubts about the copyrightability of a model code adopted by Massachusetts) (hereafter cited as *BOCA*).

73. *Southco III*, 390 F.3d at 287–289.

74. Ibid. at 288.

75. 124 F.3d 1366 (10th Cir. 1997) (hereafter cited as *Mitel*).

76. Ibid. at 1368.

77. Ibid. at 1373.

78. Ibid.

79. Ibid. at 1375. In support of this conclusion, the court cited *Gates Rubber Co. v. Bando Chemical Industries Ltd.*, 9 F.3d 823, 838 (10th Cir. 1993); *Computer Associates International, Inc. v. Altai, Inc.*, 982 F.3d 693, 709–712 (2d Cir. 1992) (hereafter cited as *Altai*); *Plains Cotton Coop. Association v. Goodpasture Computer Service, Inc.*, 802 F.2d 1256, 1262 (5th Cir. 1987).

80. *Mitel*, 124 F.3d at 1375.

81. Ibid.

82. See, e.g., *Altai*, 982 F.2d at 709–712.

83. See, e.g., Ibid. See also Pamela Samuelson Randall Davis, Mitchell D. Kapor, and J. H. Reichman, "A Manifesto Concerning the Legal Protection of Computer Programs," 94 *Columbia Law Review* 94 (1994): 2308, 2402 (program interfaces are "information equivalents to the gears that allow physical machines to interoperate").

84. *Lotus Development Corp. v. Borland International, Inc.,* 49 F.3d at 818 (hereafter cited as *Lotus v. Borland*).

85. Ibid. at 819–820.

86. Goldstein, *Goldstein on Copyright*, sec. 2.3.2.1. Some courts reject merger defenses if there were more than a few expressive choices when the plaintiff's work was created. However, other courts, notably in the Second Circuit, "appear hospitably inclined to the proposition that merger should be tested at the time the expression was copied rather than at the time it was created."

87. *Veeck*, 293 F.3d 791.

88. Ibid. at 793–794.

89. Ibid. at 793. A Fifth Circuit panel initially ruled to affirm, but upon rehearing, the majority en banc voted to reverse. Ibid. at 793–794. Six judges dissented. See Ibid. at 806–808 (J. Higginbotham, dissenting); Ibid. at 808–815 (J. Weiner, dissenting).

90. Ibid. at 802.

91. See, e.g., Goldstein, *Goldstein on Copyright,* vol. 1, sec. 2.5.2: "It is difficult to imagine an area of creative endeavor in which copyright incentive is needed less. Trade organizations have powerful reasons stemming from industry standardization, quality control, and self-regulation to produce these model codes; it is unlikely that, without copyright, they will cease producing them." Ibid. at 2:51, n.22.

92. *Veeck*, 293 F.3d at 806.

93. See, e.g., "SNOMED Clinical Terms to Be Added to UMLS Metathesaurus," <http://www.nlm.nih.gov/research/umls/Snomed/snomed_announcement.html> (accessed June 2006). The U.S. government paid $32.4 million for a perpetual license to use and allow U.S.-based private organizations to use SNOMED (an acronym of Systematized Nomenclature for Medicine). This license was negotiated to overcome burdensome licensing requirements experienced prior to its adoption. See, e.g., snomed.faq no. 9.

10   Constructing Legitimacy: The W3C's Patent Policy

Andrew L. Russell

You're about to throw away the geek community's respect for the W3C. And we're the people who write software. . . . Don't do this. It's suicidally stupid. We will bypass you. We will surpass you. Will [sic] will make fun of you. And eventually, we will completely ignore you.
—Rob Landley[1]

It is like a finger pointing away to the moon. Don't concentrate on the finger or you will miss all that heavenly glory.
—Bruce Lee[2]

The Web became worldwide because its standards were open. Tim Berners-Lee wrote the first versions of Web browser and server software in the late 1980s and early 1990s. Throughout the 1990s, he took deliberate and repeated steps to ensure that this software remained open and freely available to anyone, no strings attached. In social terms, this strategy made Berners-Lee a champion to open source programmers who shared his commitment to openness; in practical terms it made the Web an accessible and exciting new tool for everybody.

In the autumn of 2001, however, the World Wide Web Consortium (W3C)—the organization Berners-Lee created to preserve the openness and universality of the Web—proposed to turn its back on this open and free character of Web standards. A proposal for a new patent policy, first released on August 16 of that year, recommended that the W3C incorporate patents into Web standards. Chaos ensued. The W3C was besieged by thousands of angry protests from Web programmers, almost universally against patents in W3C standards. Faced with the potentially fatal consequences of a rank-and-file mutiny, the W3C reformed its decision-making process and, by May 2003, reversed course and formally adopted a royalty-free patent policy.

The purpose of this chapter is to examine this flashpoint, and to situate its ultimate result—the W3C's patent policy—within a longer and broader historical context. The quotes in the epigraph set my agenda. The first, from open source programmer Rob Landley, captures the horrified and defiant reaction that the W3C's proposal elicited from the community of Web programmers. The second, from Bruce Lee (no relation to Tim Berners-Lee), underlines my methodological approach: context matters.

We are fortunate to have growing body of quantitative, legal, and pre-scriptive analyses of patents in the standardization process.[3] However, amid the extended academic effort to isolate the precise economic and strategic effects of patent licensing and disclosure, we risk losing sight of how patents and patent policies are linked to fundamental questions of power in a technological society. How is power distributed and exercised? How do governing institutions demonstrate their legitimacy? Who decides? In short, what rules are necessary to exercise democratic control over technology?

These are difficult questions, even for expert agencies such as the Federal Communications Commission or Environmental Protection Agency whose rules are backed by the force of law.[4] However, the voluntary character of Web and Internet standards creates an additional dimension of complexity. By definition, voluntary consensus standards bodies lack any inherent authority to enforce the use of their standards. Instead, authority is con-ferred through legitimacy, which arises through a social process constructed over time, in the face of competing jurisdictional efforts.[5]

This social construction of authority and legitimacy has two interrelated dimensions, one cultural, one economic. Due to his position as the Web's inventor and champion, Berners-Lee's status was what one observer in 1998 called "a moral authority that is the closest thing the Internet has to law."[6] When he created the W3C in 1994, Berners-Lee accepted that he would be presiding over a social experiment, one that would attempt to institutionalize his moral authority and place the founding values of the Web in the care of the broader community of Web developers. During the patent policy dispute in 2001, the charged rhetoric of the open source community suggested that this social experiment was placing the open and free Web—as well as the legitimacy of the W3C—in great peril.

Landley's threat to "bypass, surpass, and ignore" the W3C reminds us of the economic issues that coexist with the cultural. The ultimate success or failure of a voluntary consensus standard is determined by market demand and acceptance. Within the market for standards, any participant in the process can choose from three options: loyalty, voice, or exit.[7]

Viewed from this perspective, the W3C's patent policy marked a strategic turning point where the group could either maintain or squander its leading position in the market for Web standards.

When faced with an open source revolt over its proposed policy to incorporate patents into its standards, the W3C reformed its rule-making process to be more open—although, as we will see, it stopped short of embracing absolute transparency. For scholars and practitioners alike, this episode is significant because it advanced a sharp critique of closed and proprietary standards, and demonstrated the practical and ideological merits of open standards and an open process. As such, it reinforces a major theme developed in this volume—that standardization is simultaneously technological, economic, cultural, and political. This combination of contexts is history unfolding.

A Brief History of Open Web Standards

Berners-Lee invented the Web when he worked as a software engineer at CERN, a European physics research laboratory located in Geneva. Berners-Lee, having observed how scientists communicated and shared ideas in a nonhierarchical, networked fashion, decided that CERN needed a system for cataloging information that could mimic these physical interactions. He first developed a proposal for a hypertext-based system that he called the "WorldWideWeb" in 1989, and by the end of 1990 he had set up the first Web server and created a program for browsing and editing hypertext pages. The technical foundations of his Web server and browser software included a language for rendering hypertext pages—the HyperText Markup Language, or HTML—and a protocol for sending hypertext documents over a network—the HyperText Transfer Protocol, or HTTP.[8]

The Web's initial growth was a direct consequence of Berners-Lee's open source strategy, which was in turn guided by a mix of ideological and practical concerns. Berners-Lee's ideal for a collaborative approach to Web development was shaped by his background in science (he earned a physics undergraduate degree from Oxford in 1976) as well as Richard Stallman's crusade for free software. In a note circulated in a CERN computing newsletter, Berners-Lee wrote, "A source of much debate over recent years has been whether to write software in-house or buy it from commercial suppliers." He continued, "Now, a third alternative is becoming significant in what some see as a revolution in software supply. Richard Stallman's almost religious campaign for usable free software led to the creation of the Free Software Foundation and GNU General Public License." In addition to the idealism contained in Stallman's "third alternative," Berners-Lee was drawn to the scientific and academic characteristics of this approach. "Just as we publish our physics for free," he wrote, "should we not in certain cases 'publish' our software?"[9]

The academic ideal for open Web standards also suited a bureaucratic imperative: it bypassed the costly and time-consuming licensing process. Convinced by the ideals and effectiveness of the free software approach, Berners-Lee posted a description of his browser and server software—as well as a link to their source code—on several mailing lists and online discussion groups in August 1991.

Over the next two years, Berners-Lee's decision to release the browser's source code and ask others to collaborate and experiment with it—to "harness the geeks," as one account put it—sparked a tremendous amount of interest in the Web. The number of Web servers and browsers grew by leaps and bounds. Berners-Lee later attributed this explosive growth to "a grassroots syndrome. . . . A very significant factor was that the software was all (what we now call) open source. It spread fast and could be improved fast—and it could be installed within government and large industry without having to go through a procurement process."[10]

This reference to the "procurement process" again reminds us of the bureaucratic choices that shaped the Web's early development as an open information platform. In addition to the intellectual merits of allowing free access to the Web's source code, there were also significant practical benefits to this approach. In early 1993, the fate of another online information system—the gopher system developed at the University of Minnesota—further confirmed Berners-Lee's skepticism of proprietary strategies for developing software. Gopher enjoyed a growing user base in the early 1990s. However, in February 1993, Minnesota announced a plan to charge users (apart from nonprofit and academic users) an annual fee to use gopher. The plan backfired. According to Berners-Lee, "This was an act of treason in the academic community and the Internet community. Even if the university never charged anyone a dime, the fact that the school had announced it was reserving the right to charge people for the use of the gopher protocols meant it had crossed the line. To use the technology was too risky. Industry dropped gopher like a hot potato."[11]

Berners-Lee immediately was pressed by members of the Internet community who wondered if CERN would follow in Minnesota's footsteps and require a license to use the Web. Berners-Lee was convinced that any licensing requirements would suffocate the Web—gopher provided the proof—and renewed his effort to have CERN place the Web technology in the public domain, with no strings attached. In April 1993, CERN administrators agreed to a public domain release that Berners-Lee and his collaborators and managers at CERN celebrated as a key moment that ensured the continued growth of the Web.[12]

During this same period in the early 1990s, several Web browsers—alterations of Berners-Lee's original design—were under development, including Midas, Erwise, Viola, and NCSA Mosaic. Berners-Lee recognized that, absent some sort of institutional effort to coordinate these divergent projects, the Web might balkanize into a variety of incompatible standards. As the Web's inventor, he was in a unique position to lead such an institutional initiative. However, since CERN administrators clearly were not interested in providing the resources to support the growth of the Web, Berners-Lee began to contemplate entrepreneurial options outside CERN. One traditional option in such situations is to create a private company that can internalize transaction costs and provide greater managerial coordination.[13] Berners-Lee and his collaborator Robert Cailliau briefly contemplated this option, but quickly rejected it as too much of a financial risk and unlikely to prevent the balkanization of Web protocols.

Instead, Berners-Lee decided that an alternative institutional form—some sort of standardization body—would provide the best means for promoting the universality of the Web. One obvious venue was the Internet Engineering Task Force (IETF), a large and respected body that had developed the core Internet protocols. However, Berners-Lee was discouraged by his initial efforts (in 1992 and 1993) to set standards through the IETF process because it forced him to compromise important aspects of his vision for the Web. Moreover, although he was anxious to move quickly, progress in the IETF was slow, due in part to "endless philosophical rat holes down which technical conversations would disappear."[14]

In early 1994, a meeting with Michael Dertouzos, the director of MIT's Laboratory for Computer Science, convinced Berners-Lee that he should start his own standards consortium. Dertouzos based his suggestion on a prior success: he had overseen the creation of the X-Consortium to coordinate the development of X-Windows that, like the Web, was an academic project that grew and attracted interest from a broad and diverse community. After meeting with Dertouzos in February 1994, Berners-Lee agreed to move to MIT to be the director of the World Wide Web Consortium (W3C).

For Berners-Lee, the W3C was the best option in his menu of institutional choices. Such a consortium would allow him to focus on the Web's proliferation from a "neutral viewpoint," as opposed to the competitive life of corporate employment. Instead, the strength of the group would come from Berners-Lee's ability to convince corporate developers of Web technologies to apply for Membership in the W3C—at the cost of $50,000 per year. As the director of this massively collaborative effort, Berners-Lee could keep a close eye on the Web's development, but not be forced into becoming a centralized point of authority or control. Indeed, he thought that the Web should be "out of control." As he summarized in 1999, "Starting a consortium, therefore, represented the best way for me to see the full span of the Web community as it spread into more and more areas. My decision not to turn the Web into my own commercial venture was not any great act of altruism or disdain for money, of which I would later be accused."[15] Indeed, the W3C provided a way for Berners-Lee to leverage his status as the Web's inventor and stay at the heart of the action—hardly an altruistic or selfless gesture.

Berners-Lee envisioned that the W3C itself would be a social experiment. He borrowed heavily from the IETF's structure and process as he designed his own consortium. The Internet's success as an information platform was due to the fact that its standards were open and freely available for anyone to implement or improve. In 1992, Dave Clark (another computer scientist at MIT), famously summarized the Internet's philosophy of standardization: "We reject: kings, presidents and voting. We believe in: rough consensus and running code." This model of open participation, with its rapid and informal specification process, appealed to Berners-Lee. He did not, however, share the IETF's wholesale rejection of "kings"; he simply thought that kings should preside over a technological style of parliamentary democracy. As he remarked in 1998, "A lot of people, including me, believe in the 'no kings' maxim at heart. . . . The wise king creates a parliament and civil service as soon as he can, and gets out of the loop."[16] He did, however, agree with the IETF tradition of using informal labels to refer to the products of consensus: "We wrestled over terms—whether the consortium should actually set a 'standard' or stop just short of that by issuing a formal 'recommendation.' We chose the latter to indicate that getting 'rough consensus and running code'—the Internet maxim for agreeing on a workable program and getting it out there to be tried—was the level at which we would work."[17]

Once the W3C was established and its initial structure and process was in place, the major problems for Berners-Lee's vision came from the explosion of commercial interest in the Web—manifest most visibly in the "browser wars" between Netscape Navigator and Microsoft Internet Explorer. In 1999, Dertouzos wrote that Berners-Lee's "consistent aim was to ensure that the Web would move forward, flourish, and remain whole, despite the yanks and pulls of all the companies that seemed bent on controlling it."[18] Beyond the browser wars, a new threat to the unified development of the Web—patents—began to worry Berners-Lee and his collaborators. "Software patents are new," Berners-Lee lamented in 1999. "The Internet ethos in the seventies and eighties was one of sharing for the common good, and it would have been unthinkable for a player to ask for fees just for implementing a standard protocol such as HTTP. Now things are changing."[19]

Berners-Lee understood that open standards—that is, standards that could be designed through a quasi-public collaborative process and implemented free of patent restrictions—fueled the growth of the Web. He had always been willing to experiment with the design process in the W3C, but he was consistent in his opposition to fees and patents in standard protocols. He saw no reason to alter these founding values of the Web, and warned that he would continue to advocate keeping the Web open to the widest possible group of users: "If someone tries to monopolize the Web— by, for example, pushing a proprietary variation of network protocols— they're in for a fight."[20]

Patent Policy Working Group: October 1999–May 2003

Corporate IT strategists should think very carefully about committing to the use of features which will bind them into the control of any one company. The [W]eb has exploded because it is open. It has developed so rapidly because the creative forces of thousands of companies are building on the same platform. Binding oneself to one company means one is limiting one's future to the innovations that one company can provide.

—Tim Berners-Lee, 1996[21]

For the first ten years of the Web's existence, tradition and Berners-Lee's personal feelings had prevented the use of proprietary specifications in Web standards. By 1999, however, the pressures of the dot-com economy— most visible in the heavily corporate membership of the W3C as well as patent holders outside the W3C membership—challenged this tradition.[22] Beginning in 1999, the W3C's technical work had experienced delays due to patent claims over aspects of W3C "Recommendations." These claims included allegations from a W3C member company, Intermind, that aspects of the W3C's Platform for Privacy Preferences (P3P) infringed an Intermind patent. Additionally, W3C Members Microsoft and Sun

Microsystems held patents on technologies that were to be included in other W3C Recommendations. These practical concerns—which threatened to derail and delay the W3C's work—pushed the W3C to look more closely at its patent policy and, ultimately, articulate new rules for the use of patents in W3C Recommendations.[23]

In August 1999, the W3C chartered the Patent Policy Working Group (PPWG) to study the role of patents and create a clear policy to govern the use of patents in W3C Recommendations. Berners-Lee chose Daniel Weitzner, the leader of the W3C's Technology and Society Domain, to chair the PPWG. Weitzner brought to the W3C his experience in working at the intersection of public and corporate interests: before joining the W3C in September 1998, he had worked as a policy analyst at the Electronic Frontier Foundation and was a cofounder and deputy director of the Center for Democracy and Technology. In an interview published soon after he joined the W3C, Weitzner noted that the "W3C has done a progressively better job of engaging outside constituencies and experts," but added that there was still more work to be done. At the W3C, he emphasized, he would embrace the opportunity to "do everything I possibly can to engage people who are interested in these technology-and-society issues."[24]

Although Weitzner had hoped to devote his time to helping the W3C develop ways to ensure greater online privacy, the patent claims surrounding the W3C's P3P recommendation meant that the W3C's patent policy—with its significant implications for technology and society—became one of his primary tasks. At first, the W3C appointed only six people to the PPWG: Weitzner (the chair), representatives from W3C member companies Microsoft, Hewlett-Packard, Philips, and Apple, and a patent attorney retained by the W3C who worked on the P3P patent dispute. The group took a long time—almost two years—before publishing a "Working Draft" on August 16, 2001, that proposed a new W3C patent policy.[25]

The Working Draft, edited by Weitzner, proposed three specific changes to W3C patent policy. The first change would establish clear ground rules by requiring W3C Working Groups to articulate in their charters whether the W3C Recommendation would be licensed under reasonable and non-discriminatory (RAND) or royalty-free (RF) terms. The second change sought to flush out potential "submarine" patents by requiring all W3C Members to disclose relevant patent claims within their contributions to the W3C's work. The third change attempted to guard against patent extortion by requiring all W3C Members to commit to RAND licensing terms. By this point, the W3C and its Members simply could not afford to leave these issues undefined: any policy would be better than no policy. However, by endorsing royalty-generating patents in W3C Recommendations, the W3C proposed a stunning departure from the Web's tradition and Berners-Lee's founding ideals.[26]

Perhaps in anticipation of the resistance to come, the Working Draft also acknowledged that the patent policy was "of significant interest to the community-at-large," and thus requested members of the community to direct their comments to www-patentpolicy-comment, a public mailing list maintained by the W3C. In keeping with a recent change to the W3C's procedural rules, the PPWG pledged to compile a list of public comments at the end of the Last Call period on September 30, 2001, and respond to all substantive issues. The W3C's commitment to responding to substantive objections stemmed from a change in the W3C process in February 2001. Before the change, no formal mechanism existed for a nonmember minority or dissenting party to plead his or her case. Previously, reporting and archiving of minority views was entirely at the discretion of the Working Group chair—not exactly a model of a democratic or radically open governance process.[27]

Despite these careful preparations to accommodate public comments, the "public" seemed to have been mostly unaware of the issue and the forum until late September. The list archives record only one comment in the two weeks following the August 16 draft. However, on September 29 and 30—the final days before the end of the Last Call period—747 more comments were submitted.[28]

A vast majority of the comments displayed emotions ranging from measured displeasure to outright disgust. Many feared that the W3C's decision to open its standards to patents was a sign that it had lost touch with the open source development community, or, even worse, surrendered its founding traditions of free and open code to a future controlled by corporate capital. Microsoft—a company that had allegedly vowed to "embrace, extend, and extinguish" open standards—was a chief target of criticism. Microsoft and IBM employees posted notes to www-patentpolicy-comment that supported patents in general and the RAND policy in particular, which only added fuel to the fire.[29] However, representatives from other W3C member companies, such as Sun Microsystems, came out in support of a royalty-free policy. For these companies, the economic case for a royalty-free policy was more convincing than any anti-patent ideology. Indeed, Sun and other W3C Members held extensive patent portfolios; they simply argued that a royalty-free Web would provide a platform for better growth and revenue opportunities down the road and at the edges of the Web.

Many comments also projected a bitter defiance toward the W3C. For example, one person declared: "Basing your standards on patented methods will fragment the web and destroy your organization. If you succeed in forcing such debased standards on the web, your corporate masters will no longer need you. If you fail, you will be irrelevant. Either way W3C loses."[30]

With the seemingly imminent demise of the W3C as the steward of open Web standards, several open source programmers welcomed the challenge of creating open source alternatives. The ongoing success of open source projects such as the Apache server software and Linux operating system had given the open source community confidence in its technical and organizational capabilities. Apache's dominant position in the market for Web server software—over 60 percent market share, almost three times more than Microsoft's competing product—further emboldened the community, and provided compelling evidence that its radically decentralized and modular style of open source development was economically and technologically viable.[31]

Other critics, writing to www-patentpolicy-comment and in the trade press, charged that the W3C tried to sneak its RAND proposal past an unsuspecting public. Although the W3C had established a mailing list along with its August 16 announcement, none of the leading industry news Web sites—such as Slashdot, LinuxToday, The Register, or CNet—had covered or reacted to the announcement. The fact that so many comments were submitted in the final days of September—within hours of the Last Call deadline—added an additional sense of drama, urgency, and even conspiracy to their collective alarmist tone.[32]

In response to these concerns about the transparency and integrity of the W3C's public outreach, the PPWG extended the comment period through October 11. In the meantime, Weitzner sounded concerned. In an interview published on October 2, he echoed a prominent objection from the posts to www-patentpolicy-comment: a RAND policy in the W3C would push the open source community to abandon the W3C and create its own open source alternatives to the patent-encumbered W3C Recommendations. The consequences of such an organizational split would spell the end of Berners-Lee's mission, developed over the past decade, to avoid the balkanization of Web standards by presiding over an authoritative consortium.[33]

In an attempt to avoid this disastrous split, Weitzner introduced greater transparency in the PPWG's deliberative process—including major changes aimed at winning back the trust of the open source community and maintaining the W3C's legitimacy. At the end of the extended Last Call on

October 12, Weitzner invited Eben Moglen and Bruce Perens, two prominent open source advocates who had publicly bashed the W3C for its
RAND proposal, to join the closed internal deliberations of the PPWG. The
PPWG also created a public homepage to make policy documents—such
as summaries of working group meetings—widely accessible. For his part,
Weitzner agreed to participate in online and face-to-face public forums,
and restated the PPWG's commitment to responding to the substantive
issues raised from the more than two thousand emails sent to
www-patentpolicy-comment.[34]

Throughout all the commotion, Berners-Lee had been conspicuously
quiet. He broke his silence on October 24, with a post to www-patentpolicy-comment titled "Why I have not spoken personally about the patent
policy issue." His main point was to endorse the consensus-building
process. He noted that his views on patents in general were well known,
and even provided a link to an excerpt from his autobiography where he
referred to patents as a "great stumbling block for Web development." He
also addressed critics who hoped he would take a decisive stand on patents
by explaining that his "silence arises from the fact that I value the consensus-building process at W3C. I am not (contrary to what some of the
pundits might suggest! ;-) a dictator by role or nature and so prefer to wait
and let the community resolve an issue."[35]

Given the evolving nature of Berners-Lee's role as "facilitator" (not
"dictator"), it is difficult to know how much influence he exerted in the
subsequent internal W3C discussions: although the mailing list for comments on the W3C patent policy is open to the public, internal W3C
deliberations are not. What we do know is that, after three days of meetings from October 15 to October 17, the PPWG announced that its members
could not reach a unanimous decision. They decided to seek guidance from
the W3C Advisory Committee—a group that theoretically consists of a
representative from each of the W3C's Members (at this time it had over
three hundred Members) and meets twice a year. No public records exist
from the Advisory Committee meeting in mid-November, but one can
imagine that the patent policy debate dominated the meeting.

After the meeting concluded, Weitzner posted an "action item" sent by
the Advisory Committee to the PPWG that introduced a new direction for
the debate. The Advisory Committee, after acknowledging the broad con-
tinuum of views on the respective merits of RAND and royalty-free licenses,
instructed the PPWG to "develop as a first priority . . . an RF patent policy."
Although Weitzner's note emphasized "this does NOT mean that the W3C
has made a final decision in favor of a RF-only policy," the reality of the

situation was that the Advisory Committee shifted the terms of debate from RAND-friendly to RF-friendly ground.[36]

After several more teleconferences and meetings, the PPWG issued a revised proposal on February 26, 2002, outlining a royalty-free patent policy. Weitzner summarized this policy as a legally binding commitment for anyone participating in W3C Recommendations to make any relevant patents available on a royalty-free basis. The new policy was a remarkable change: in less than six months, the W3C had assessed consensus—among its staff, Members, and the interested public—and reversed course. The consensus of the community, as judged within the closed deliberations of the W3C, determined that a royalty-free process would best facilitate widespread development of Web applications, and simultaneously would minimize the significant transaction costs associated with licensing negotiations and intellectual property lawyers. Although practical concerns were paramount for W3C staff, defenders of the ideals of open source claimed victory and concluded that the W3C had averted building "a tollbooth on the Internet."[37]

The final version of the W3C patent policy, released on May 20, 2003, assured that "Recommendations produced under this policy can be implemented on a Royalty-Free (RF) basis." The W3C stopped short of an exclusive RF policy by including an exception clause that would allow for patented technologies to be included in Recommendations if no royalty-free alternative existed. Berners-Lee, in his commentary that endorsed the W3C patent policy, was careful to point out that royalty-encumbered technologies could still, in theory, be included in W3C Recommendations. However, this would occur only in exceptional circumstances, after "considerable deliberation" with the "substantial consensus of both those participating in developing the technology and the W3C Membership." Hardly a victory for RAND advocates, Berners-Lee noted that the "exception process is only designed to be used in the rarest cases," and should be seen as a tool for the W3C to maintain flexibility in its technical solutions if a lack of royalty-free solutions would halt the development of W3C technologies.[38]

The revised policy was touted as a success for both constituencies of the W3C: where the open source community could claim victory over corporate control, the member companies of the W3C took comfort that the new patent policy rendered the W3C and its Members less vulnerable to costly litigation and submarine patents. Any policy was better than no policy, but the best policy was one that maintained the loyalties of the various constituencies in the W3C. Yet one has to pause at the irony of this episode of reform: the decision to keep the W3C's standards open was made behind closed doors.

Given the W3C's dramatic and very public about-face, one can only wonder how much Berners-Lee influenced the Advisory Committee's deliberations, despite his stated preference to let the community resolve the issue. Weitzner dutifully rejected this notion: "If Tim [Berners-Lee] were going to impose his own view as the policy, he would have done that two and a half years ago and saved us all the trouble." Weitzner—who, we should recall, was handpicked by Berners-Lee to lead the PPWG—continued, "He's watched this group work, looked at our product, and I think he'll respect the process we're going through."[39] In the end, the W3C patent policy decision turned out to be consistent with its founder's idealistic views of patents and software. It surely was no accident that Berners-Lee's personal views aligned with the convictions of the open source Web developing community: after all, Berners-Lee was the original open source Web developer.

Conclusion: Meritocracy, Democracy, and the Market

It is, of course, too soon to evaluate the long-term significance of the W3C's royalty-free patent policy. In the meantime, anecdotal evidence from the short and medium term suggests that the W3C has thrived in some ways but fallen short of its goals in others. To its credit, the W3C anticipated the growing appetite for royalty-free licenses in Web standards, and has maintained its leadership in this arena.[40] It has also demonstrated the importance of a vigilant stance on issues that could disrupt its authority as an institution, and has slowly and incompletely opened some of its decision-making processes. However, the market for standards continues to be a crowded and contested organizational field. Patent holders continue to litigate aggressively, and companies such as IBM, Apple, and Microsoft, despite some goodwill gestures, continue to seek alternative venues—competitors to the W3C such as OASIS—that will give them greater control over the terms and pace of standardization.[41]

How can we ensure that this competitive global market for standards can reflect, embody, or even advance fundamental human values such as democracy and equality? This question begs the more basic questions I posed at the outset: How is power distributed and exercised? What steps are necessary to exercise democratic control over technology?

The W3C's experience provides some grounds for generalization, and possibly for pointing a way forward. The legitimacy problem, that is, the tension between meritocracy and democracy, is exacerbated by the decentralized structure and competitive nature of markets for information and communication technology (ICT) standards.

Meritocracy—which, in this context, we might define roughly as leadership by trusted technical elites—can work well, but only within small projects that "fly under the radar" (such as the Internet in the 1970s or the Web in the early 1990s) or in projects with relatively homogenous social norms (such as the Linux kernel). Democracy, on the other hand, helps to ensure that rules for an expanding and diverse constituency are created with the consent of the governed. However, centuries of political history show us that the practice of democratic reform can be fraught with difficulties. Some of the toughest questions come when measures to democratize and enhance participation grow from informal ad hoc solutions—as with the inclusion of open source advocates into the PPWG in October 2001—into more formal and bureaucratized measures. One does not have to be a devotee of Joseph Schumpeter to recognize that bloated and bureaucratic institutions often stifle innovation. Inertia and momentum can render an organization vulnerable to the gales of creative destruction; newer, nimbler, and more flexible organizations usually emerge after the storm and begin to take control over innovation and, eventually, standardization.

We should not be surprised, then, if an institution such as the W3C resists openness and transparency in order to preserve its ability to change course quickly. We may hear enthusiasts celebrate the open and democratizing characteristics of the Web, but beneath this rhetoric lies a more complex reality of the opaque and undemocratic control overseen by Sir Berners-Lee and his civil servants in the W3C.

Notes

Earlier versions of this chapter were presented at the Telecommunications Policy Research Conference in 2003 in Arlington, Virginia, and at the Business History Conference in 2007 in Cleveland, Ohio. I acknowledge gratefully the comments and suggestions provided by Hyungsub Choi, Michael Aaron Dennis, Shane Greenstein, Thomas Haigh, Deborah Hurley, Brian Kahin, Eric Nystrom, Joseph M. Reagle, and Philip J. Weiser. Remaining errors are of course my responsibility alone.

1. Rob Landley, "Proprietary Standards" (September 30, 2001), <http://lists.w3.org/Archives/Public/www-patentpolicy-comment/2001Sep/0305>.

2. *Enter the Dragon* feature film (1974).

3. See for example Benjamin Chiao, Josh Lerner, and Jean Tirole, "The Rules of Standard Setting Organizations: An Empirical Analysis," *CEPR Discussion Papers* 6141 (February 2007); Mark A. Lemley, "Intellectual Property Rights and Standard-Setting Organizations," *California Law Review* 90 (2002): 1889–1980; Timothy S. Simcoe, "Open Standards and Intellectual Property Rights," in *Open Innovation: Researching a New Paradigm*, ed. Henry Chesbrough, Wim Vanhaverbeke, and Joel West, 161–183 (New York: Oxford University Press, 2006), and Andrew S. Updegrove, "The Essential Guide to Standard Setting Organizations and Standards," <http://www .consortiuminfo.org/essentialguide> (accessed February 28, 2011).

4. See for example Sheila Jasanoff, "Science, Politics, and the Renegotiation of Expertise at EPA," *Osiris*, 2nd series, vol. 7, Science after '40 (1992): 194–217; Jody Freeman and Laura I. Langbein, "Regulatory Negotiation and the Legitimacy Benefit," *NYU Environmental Law Journal* 9 (2000): 60–138; and the papers at "Reforming the FCC," a conference hosted by Silicon Flatirons, Public Knowledge, and the Information Technology & Innovation Foundation, <http://fcc-reform.org>.

5. See for example Raymund Werle and Eric J. Iversen, "Promoting Legitimacy in Technical Standardization," *Science, Technology & Innovation Studies* 2 (2006): 19–39; A. Michael Froomkin, "Habermas@Discourse.Net: Toward a Critical Theory of Cyber- space," *Harvard Law Review* 116 (2003): 751–873; Craig Murphy and JoAnne Yates, *The International Organization for Standardization (ISO): Global Governance through Voluntary Consensus* (New York: Routledge, 2009); and Andrew L. Russell, "'Industrial Legislatures': Consensus Standardization in the Second and Third Industrial Revolu- tions" (PhD diss., The Johns Hopkins University, 2007).

6. Simson L. Garfinkel, "The Web's Unelected Government," *Technology Review* 101 (November/December 1998): 42.

7. Albert O. Hirschman, *Exit, Voice, and Loyalty: Responses to Decline in Firms, Orga- nizations, and States* (Cambridge, MA: Harvard University Press, 1970).

8. This section draws primarily on three accounts: Tim Berners-Lee, *Weaving the Web: The Original Design and Ultimate Destiny of the World Wide Web by its Inventor* (San Francisco: HarperSanFrancisco, 1999); James Gillies and Robert Cailliau, *How the Web Was Born* (New York: Oxford University Press, 2000); and Dan Connolly, "A Little History of the World Wide Web," <http://www.w3.org/History .html>.

9. Berners-Lee, quoted in Gillies and Cailliau, *How the Web Was Born*, 209.

10. Gillies and Cailliau, *How the Web Was Born*, 215; Berners-Lee, quoted in Paul Festa, "Charting the Web's Next Transformation," *CNet News.com* (December 12, 2001), <http://news.com.com/2102-1082-276939.html>.

11. Berners-Lee, *Weaving the Web*, 73. See also Philip K. Frana, "Before the Web There Was Gopher," *IEEE Annals of the History of Computing* 26 (2004): 20–41.

12. The CERN declaration may be seen at <http://tenyears-www.web.cern.ch/tenyears-www/Welcome.html>.

13. Ronald H. Coase, "The Nature of the Firm," *Economica*, New Series 4 (1937): 386–405; Alfred D. Chandler Jr., *The Visible Hand: The Managerial Revolution in American Business* (Cambridge, MA: Belknap Press, 1977).

14. Berners-Lee, *Weaving the Web*, 61–63; Tim Berners-Lee, "Universal Resource Identifiers in WWW," RFC 1630 (June 1994), <http://www.ietf.org/rfc/rfc1630.txt>; Roy Rada, "Consensus Versus Speed," *Communications of the ACM* 38 (October 1995): 21–23.

15. Berners-Lee, *Weaving the Web*, 85, 89, 99.

16. Berners-Lee, quoted in Garfinkel, "The Web's Unelected Government," 47. See also Andrew L. Russell, "'Rough Consensus and Running Code' and the Internet-OSI Standards War," *IEEE Annals of the History of Computing* 28 (July–September 2006): 48–61.

17. Berners-Lee, *Weaving the Web*, 98. See also Charles Vincent and Jean Camp, "Looking to the Internet for Models of Governance," *Ethics and Information Technology* 6 (September 2004): 161–173.

18. Michael Dertouzos, foreword to Berners-Lee, *Weaving the Web*, x. See also Thomas Haigh, "Protocols for Profit: Web and Email Technologies as Product and Infrastructure," in *The Internet and American* Business, ed. William Aspray and Paul E. Ceruzzi, 105–158 (Cambridge, MA: MIT Press, 2008).

19. Berners-Lee, *Weaving the Web*, 197.

20. Ibid., 108.

21. Tim Berners-Lee, "W3C and Standards, 1996," <http://www.w3.org/People/Berners-Lee/FAQ.html#standards>.

22. Anne Eisenberg, "What's Next: Legal Squabbles in Path of Internet," *The New York Times* (December 9, 1999), p. G14.

23. Daniel J. Weitzner, Testimony before the United States Department of Justice and United States Federal Trade Commission Joint Hearings on Competition and Intellectual Property Law and Policy in the Knowledge-Based Economy, April 18, 2002, <http://www.ftc.gov/opp/intellect/020418weitzner.shtm> (accessed February 28, 2011). Joseph M. Reagle and Daniel J. Weitzner, eds., "Analysis of P3P and US Patent 5,862,325" (October 27, 1999), <http://www.w3.org/TR/P3P-analysis>. See also Patrick Feng, "Designing a 'Global' Privacy Standard: Politics and Expertise in Technical Standards-Setting" (PhD diss., Rensselaer Polytechnic Institute, December 2002).

24. Weitzner, quoted in Garfinkel, "The Web's Unelected Government," 43.

25. The Working Draft listed as authors the PPWG members listed here, as well as members from IBM, Reuters, Sun Microsystems, The Open Group, two additional Microsoft representatives, two representatives from Nortel Networks, and three additional members of the W3C staff.

26. Daniel J. Weitzner, ed., "W3C Patent Policy Framework: W3C Working Draft 16 August 2001," <http://www.w3.org/TR/2001/WD-patent-policy-20010816>.

27. Weitzner, "W3C Patent Policy Framework." See also "4.1.2 Group Consensus and Votes," <http://www.w3.org/Consortium/Process-20010208/groups.html# WGVotes>.

28. See <http://lists.w3.org/Archives/Public/www-patentpolicy-comment/>.

29. See the W3C's extensive analysis of the comments, "Public Issues for Patent Policy Framework of 20010816," <http://www.w3.org/2001/11/PPF-Public-Issues .html>.

30. William Hill, "Patents in Your Standards" (September 30, 2001), <http://lists .w3.org/Archives/Public/www-patentpolicy-comment/2001Sep/0457>.

31. See for example Russ Mitchell, "Open War," *Wired* 9 (October 2001): 135–139.

32. Karsten M. Self, "Re: Janet Daley's Comments to LinuxToday" (September 30, 2001), <http://lists.w3.org/Archives/Public/www-patentpolicy-comment/ 2001Oct/0025>; Margaret Kane and Mike Ricciuti, "W3C Patent Plan Draws Protests," *CNet News.com* (October 1, 2001), <http://news.com.com/2102-1023- 273752.html>.

33. Andrew Orlowski, "Web Standards Schism 'Terrible'—W3C Patent Policy Boss," *The Register* (October 2, 2001), <http://www.theregister.co.uk/2001/10/02web _standards_schism_terrible_w3c>.

34. Daniel J. Weitzner, "Next Steps in W3C Patent Policy Process" (October 12, 2001), <http://lists.w3.org/Archives/Public/www-patentpolicy-comment/2001Oct/ 1559.html>.

35. Tim Berners-Lee, "Why I have not spoken personally about the patent policy issue" (October 24, 2001), <http://lists.w3.org/Archives/Public/www-patentpolicy- comment/2001Oct/1642.html>.

36. Daniel J. Weitzner, "FW: Action Item from Advisory Committee Discussion on Patent Policy" (November 21, 2001), <http://lists.w3.org/Archives/Public/ www-patentpolicy-comment/2001Nov/0147>.

37. Daniel J. Weitzner, ed., "Patent Policy Working Group: Royalty-Free Patent Policy" (February 26, 2002), <http://www.w3.org/TR/2002/WD-patent-pol- icy-20020226/>; Bruce Perens, "Perspective: The Patent Threat to the Web," *CNet News.com* (October 7, 2002), <http://news.com.com/2010-1071-961018.html>.

38. Daniel J. Weitzner, ed., "W3C Patent Policy" (May 20, 2003), <http://www. w3.org/Consortium/Patent-Policy-20030520.html>; Tim Berners-Lee, "Director's Decision, W3C Patent Policy" (May 20, 2003), <http://www.w3.org/2003/05/12-director-patent-decision-public.html>.

39. Paul Festa, "At the Center of the Patent Storm," *CNet News.com* (September 24, 2002), <http://news.com.com/2102-1082-959180.html>.

40. Paul Festa, "Patent Holders on the Ropes," *CNet News.com* (December 2, 2002), <http://news.com.com/2100-1023-975587.html>; and Michael Calore, "Big Guns Jump on Open-Source Bandwagon for New Web Apps," *Wired* (May 11, 2007), <http://www.wired.com/software/webservices/news/2007/05/open_source>.

41. D. Linda Garcia, "Standards for Standard Setting: Contesting the Organizational Field," in *The Standards Edge: Dynamic* Tension, ed. Sherrie Bolin, 15–30 (Ann Arbor, MI: Sheridan Press, 2004); Steve Lohr, "Setback for Microsoft Ripples through the World Wide Web," *The New York Times* (September 17, 2003); Neal Levitt, "Are Web Services Finally Ready to Deliver?" *IEEE Computer* 37 (November 2004): 14–18.

11 Common and Uncommon Knowledge: Reducing Conflict between Standards and Patents

Brian Kahin

Standards have become critical for advancing technology and new markets in the information and communication technology (ICT) sector. At the same time, patents have become easier to obtain, more potent, and readily available for software and business methods. The low thresholds and opacity of the patent system have made inadvertent infringement commonplace, dramatically increasing opportunities for "patent trolls" to threaten ICT standards. Because these standards have much the same investment rationale as intellectual property, standards that meet minimum requirements of openness should be accorded protection from patent predators. Patent holders should assert their rights promptly—or waive the opportunity to sue those who merely practice the standard.

In March of 2007, Alcatel-Lucent won a record $1.52 billion patent infringement judgment against Microsoft. The award pertained not to proprietary technology but to MP3, a universal audio encoding standard developed in the early 1990s. In 1994, Microsoft licensed a patent underlying the MP3 standard for $16 million from the Fraunhofer Institute,[1] only to discover thirteen years later that it owed another patent holder, Lucent, nearly one hundred times as much for another MP3-related patent. The verdict has become a poster child for more disciplined calculation of damages awarded in litigation, a controversial issue in patent reform. Although the verdict was later set aside, it demonstrates how vulnerable companies, indeed entire sectors, are to attacks from patent holders who do not participate in developing or setting the standard.

It is remarkable how little policy-level attention is accorded standards given their strategic importance to the IT sector—and given the importance of IT to innovation, economic growth, and national competitiveness. IT standards do not merely serve traditional goals such as improving safety, reducing consumer confusion, or promoting compatibility. They also are platforms for advancing technology and creating markets—

well-known, well-defined tides that lift many boats. They are essential architectural elements for complex information systems and infrastructure. Standards assure buyers that they are investing in technology that works with and adds value to other investments, value that will not disappear at the whim of a particular vendor.

The time-critical, market-making nature of IT standards has led to a variety of alliances and consortia, rather than formal standards development organizations, for developing many of the most important IT standards. These entities do not seek accreditation and validation from the American National Standards Institute (ANSI), although they may ultimately choose to submit a standard to an ANSI committee. Open to international participation, they look to the global IT marketplace, which does not fit with the nationally based framework for de jure standards. They often forego formalities in favor of speed and flexibility.

While other countries participate in the International Organization for Standardization (ISO) through national agencies, the U.S. participates through the private organization ANSI. Members of ANSI include government agencies such as the National Institute for Standards and Technology (NIST), as well as private companies and associations. The U.S. government's involvement in standards policy is therefore less direct, less consistent, and more laissez-faire and reactive than other national governments. IT standards setting is further insulated from U.S. policy making by virtue of its strong market orientation and global scope. Although many IT standards are developed or ultimately validated through formal channels, IT standards development as a whole, vast as it is, is fragmented, context dependent, and lacks significant political presence.

Even within firms, standards activities are often widely dispersed among operating divisions. Despite rising awareness of the strategic importance of leadership in setting standards, there is seldom a natural locus for addressing standards as a matter of corporate strategy or policy—in marked contrast to patents. Standards suffer from a history and reputation as common denominators in a world where market presence and competitive strength have historically been defined by differentiation and control.

Yet in IT, standards are essential to technological and economic progress. Innovations are cumulative, building on each other and on the shared systems and ecologies in which they participate. In a world where lock-in and stranded investments are the stuff of legend, customers demand assurance that they can connect and use components from a wide choice of contractors and vendors.

The Paradigm of Complementarity

The Internet's spectacular success attests to the value of open standards as platforms for innovation. Anyone has been free to build on openly available nonproprietary protocols with no permission required. This openness has spurred innovation in products and services on a vast, unprecedented scale. No single company had the resources, ingenuity, and entrepreneurship to create the Internet explosion on its own. The Internet succeeded because standardized protocols and interfaces allowed hundreds of thousands of firms and individuals to invest and innovate simultaneously. Just as a common language makes possible the richness of literature, a common technological platform makes possible a wealth of proprietary implementations. If the platform is to be recognized as open rather than controlled by particular private interests, defining the platform is necessarily a collective process. Participants must be concerned about how the standard will evolve in the future, given that IT standards often continue to evolve as surrounding technologies change. If patented technology is included, implementers may owe royalties to competitors, tilting the market for products and perhaps discouraging competition. Even if implicated patents are licensed royalty-free, the patent holder may confine the license to the practicing of the standard as written, in effect limiting free implementations and further evolution of the standard.

If a standard is relatively simple and abstract, as may be the case for an interface specification, it may be free of patents. A complex compression program containing many functional elements is likely to include many patented processes. The dynamics are then quite different. As a practical matter, a patent pool may be needed to assemble a marketable package so that implementers do not have to face patent holders one by one. The MPEG-2 pool, for example, includes 102 U.S. patents plus hundreds of similar patents issued in other countries.

The Relationship between Patents and Standards

A good standard should be largely invisible. It can be taken for granted. Its value stems from commonality and ubiquity—*not* exclusivity or scarcity as in the case of conventional goods. Companies rely on standards as much as they rely on their wholly owned property. Yet despite their role in generating future revenue, standards cannot be treated as assets because they cannot be controlled or traded.

By contrast, patents have gained much attention as intangible assets that can be controlled, traded, licensed, securitized, and collateralized. Yet a patent is only a right to exclude, *not* a right to exploit. The ability to exploit the patented technology may depend on an underlying patent that belongs to someone else and may or may not be available for license. In the United States, patented technology cannot even be tested or experimented with without the patent holder's permission. Yet the patent itself can be invalidated at any time by prior art that the patent holder is not aware of.

Twenty years ago, simple specifications rarely involved patented technology. Since then, the patent-specialized Court of Appeals for the Federal Circuit in the United States has abolished limitations on patentable subject matter and lowered standards of patentability. While standards have assumed unprecedented importance, patents have become easier to acquire, more versatile, and more powerful. In fact, the growth of standards-dependent investments has encouraged patent applicants to use creative tactics to track and capture emerging standards.

These changes enable "patent trolls" (best defined by a business model of "being infringed"[2]) to extract large settlements from companies with products on the market. The possibility of an injunction means that producers risk having to shut down an entire product line if a single patented function (among the tens of thousands of functions a complex information technology product performs) is found to infringe. Although this risk is presently lower than before the U.S. Supreme Court struck down the Federal Circuit's automatic injunction rule, the threat of injunction enables the patent holder to seek a settlement far beyond the original value of the patented technology.

For patented technology embedded in standards, the economic risk is far worse. Not only is the standard likely to be deeply embedded and impractical to excise, it will be implemented widely, perhaps by every firm in the global market. Since all implementations, including downstream uses, are potential targets, the incentives to ambush are high. A patent infringed by an adopted standard becomes far more valuable in time than it would have been had the standards developers known about it when they had the ability to work around it.

Could the standards developers have searched for the patent, found it, and designed around it in the first place? Possibly, but the cost would have been enormous and risks would have remained. Panelists in the 2002 Federal Trade Commission (FTC) hearings on patents and innovation indicated that even large companies had abandoned product clearances because they were not cost-effective. Relevant patents must first be identified, no small task in an IT product that may contain tens of thousands of possibly patentable functions and components. In 2005, validity opinions cost an average of $13,000. An opinion on whether a particular component or process infringes a particular patent costs another $13,000.[3] Even if all issued patents and published patent applications that might affect the product could be identified, unpublished applications will be missed. On the other hand, many IT patents are ultimately invalid because there is prior art out there somewhere, even though it may be difficult to find. Knowing this, it does not make much sense to expend vast resources to clear every function and component.

Participants in standards-setting efforts are commonly asked to disclose patents that might be relevant to the standard under discussion. However, many companies are reluctant to commit to full disclosure. As Frederick J. Telecky of Texas Instruments (TI) explained: "TI has something like 8,000 patents in the United States that are active patents, and for us to know what's in that portfolio, we think, is just a mind-boggling, budget-busting exercise to try to figure that out with any degree of accuracy at all."[4]

By the same token, however, it is unreasonable to expect an uncapitalized standards effort to figure out the potential effect of thousands of patents that may be held by companies inside or outside the process— especially when it is impossible to identify unpublished or yet-to-be-filed applications. The low standards of inventiveness combined with the richness of the technology means that there are far too many questionable patents out there, and the special penalties for willful infringement discourage looking.

In addition to having made patents more potent, more plentiful, and difficult to defeat, the Federal Circuit has favored patent holders against standards development efforts. It has held that a duty of good faith cannot be implied and that disclosure obligations should be narrowly construed.[5] Astoundingly, the Federal Circuit has even endorsed amending patent applications to deliberately capture the work of others: "[T]here is nothing improper, illegal or inequitable in filing a patent application for the purpose of obtaining a right to exclude a known competitor's product from the market; nor is it in any manner improper to amend or insert claims intended to cover a competitor's product the applicant's attorney has learned about during the prosecution of a patent application."[6]

Standards organizations try to mitigate potential problems by asking all participants to agree to license any of their patents that may be needed to practice the standard on a reasonable and nondiscriminatory (RAND) basis.

However, standards organizations are technically oriented; they lack the will and capacity to oversee or enforce this requirement. The patent holder is free to negotiate licensing terms privately, licensee by licensee, according to its own definition of "reasonable and nondiscriminatory" terms while precluding public disclosure of the terms. This may not be a problem for companies that hold large patent portfolios and are already mutually cross-licensed. But small companies, including startups, have little bargaining power and may be forced to relinquish exclusivity for the few patents they hold. They will most certainly not be inclined to take the dominant patent holder to court to contest the meaning of "reasonable and nondiscriminatory" in their particular cases.

Potential users of standards quite reasonably want to know the cost differential between competing approaches, along with any differences in licensing terms and conditions. Markets for standards should be robust and transparent—no less than other markets. In "ex ante licensing" all factors—technology, price, license terms—should be on the table in a timely manner, just as they are in other business decisions. Ex ante licensing helps participants reach decisions that make business sense and avoid the uncertainties and abuses of RAND licensing. A recent report by the FTC and the Department of Justice argues that ex ante licensing can be pro-competitive and should not be considered a per se antitrust violation.[7]

However, neither a RAND commitment nor ex ante licensing is effective against patent holders outside the standards-setting process, since they are not bound by any disclosure or licensing commitments. Once the standard is chosen and many firms have embedded it in products that have been designed, manufactured, and widely distributed, the "highest and best use" of the inadvertently infringed patent will be to extract, or "extort," as much as possible of the sunk investments based on the standard.

Opportunities for conflict and ambush have increased, as both standards and patents have expanded in scope and significance. But while standards are disciplined by the market, patents have proliferated by legislative, judicial, and administrative fiat. The 1952 Patent Act framed patents as an entitlement that had to be allowed unless the examiner could show that the subject matter was obvious to a person having ordinary skill in the art. This threshold was further lowered by the Court of Appeals for the Federal Circuit by making it difficult to show obviousness in combinations,[8] exalting secondary factors that favored nonobviousness, and by enhancing the presumption of validity, making it hard to show obviousness in court.

In addition to creating legal stumbling blocks for other innovators, low-quality patents dilute the value of patents for conveying knowledge. Patent documents may be available for free on the Internet, but large numbers of low-quality patents raise more questions than they answer. Unlike spam, patents cannot be ignored or deleted.

In contrast to the murky patent landscape, standards development demands highly focused and explicit communication and generation of specific knowledge that is easy to understand and implement. The need for certainty and economy cautions against duplicative, potentially incompatible standards-setting efforts. The standards process must produce, validate, and publicize useful information. Its value is affirmed when multiple firms adopt and implement the standard successfully.

Standards as an Asset

The invisibility of economic value in today's economy is not unique to standards. It is partly expressed by the "intangibles" problem as measured in the growing discrepancy between a firm's stock market valuation and the much lower value of the asset base on the corporate books. Intangible assets include intellectual property, R&D, human capital, organizational capital, and customer capital. The very limited ability of the firm to trade, control, exploit, or monetize these assets makes it difficult to assign them a dollar value. In many cases, the economic value is speculative or contingent. Or it may be derived from sources, relationships, and emerging opportunities outside the firm.

Standards are shared intangible assets for a market segment, an entire industry, or even multiple industries. A standard may promise a large future market for new technology, products, and services, but it depends on who is pushing the standard, complementary advances, and competition from other standards and technologies. Standards are essential but beyond the control of individual users. Now consider the value of the standard from the point of view of the owner of a patent that has been inadvertently embedded in a complex technology. Holding up deep-pocketed companies like Microsoft is, in real estate parlance, "the highest and best use" of the patent. The private value that can be realized from the patent is roughly equal to the staggering costs that can be imposed on the rest of the world.

The patent holder can realize this opportunity by avoiding full disclosure within the standards process, but that is risky as the FTC made clear in the Dell case.[9] Nonparticipants have no obligation to disclose patents and, indeed, no obligation to license at all, under RAND terms or otherwise. By surreptitiously tracking deliberations of a standards process, perhaps through an ally inside the process, a nonparticipant can shape a patent application to capture the standard.

Sadly, the more open the process, the more information will spread to nonparticipants and the more vulnerable the standard will be. The value of a standard is in its ubiquity, but that is also a measure of its vulnerability. Hidden patents can undermine the rational business expectations of millions of integrators, packagers, resellers, service producers, and users—including users of complementary products and services and all the way down the value chain. Although patents are touted as an incentive to investment, they can also undermine legitimate market-oriented investments by encouraging investment in arbitrage and extortion. The result is a systemic bias against open collaborative innovation and in favor of bad faith behavior and legal maneuvering. All the more remarkably, this is happening in a sector in which the value of individual patents is diluted by numbers and less important other means of securing returns from innovation.

Reforms to mitigate the threat of extortion in the IT sector have been opposed by industries (especially biotechnology and pharmaceuticals) in which individual patents are extremely important—and by the patent bar, which is economically interested in keeping patents as powerful and plentiful as possible.

Yet just as patents are uniquely important to the pharmaceutical industry, standards are uniquely important to the IT sector. IT standards are so critical, so time sensitive, so market oriented and strategic that they do not fit well within the international standards system. And because so many IT standards are developed outside the system, the IT sector is politically underrepresented within the system. No organization represents the business and policy interests of the many IT standards entities not accredited by ANSI. With little coordination among standards organizations, there has been no collective response to the problem of participants who act in bad faith or to the problem of ambush by nonparticipants. Despite the strategic importance of standards in information technology, standards setting remains largely a function of an engineering community with an underappreciated relationship to business strategy and public policy.

The fragmentation and institutional weakness of the IT standards enterprise is especially striking in the face of a deeply and broadly institutionalized patent system. IT standards are increasingly hostage to a one-size-fits-all patent system that defies empirical observation and inevitably leads to discriminatory results. Furthermore, the cottage industry in ambush and extortion preys not only on IT but also on the benefits that IT brings to every sector in the economy. If the IT sector wants reform, it must seek reform of the entire patent system—against the wishes of deeply invested and motivated interests that believe that any diminishment of patent power and scope, tactical, strategic, political, or otherwise, will have a direct impact on their bottom line. In effect, a monolithic system cross-subsidizes industries where patents work well at the expense of those where patents work poorly.

The limited monopoly of patents is intended to promote public disclosure of new knowledge. Patent information should be instant, clear, and significant. In reality, it is delayed, opaque, of indeterminate value, costly to evaluate, and a source of liability for willful infringement. Patents are negotiated privately between the applicant's patent attorney and a government employee, and the applicant is entitled to patent unless the examiner can show otherwise. There is no requirement for a working model or other evidence that the technology performs as claimed. Even with publication after eighteen months, there is virtually no third-party input into the examination process.

By contrast, the development of open standards occurs only if there is a shared, focused conviction that a standard is worth investigating, negotiating, and implementing. The inputs and outcomes in IT standards are subject to constant scrutiny and testing through expert deliberation, reference models, conformance testing, competing implementations, and commercial use. The knowledge instilled in standards is documented by and for those who will use this information for its intended purpose, unmediated by lawyers.

Encouraging and protecting investment form the principal rationale of intellectual property and IT standards. Standards-driven investments are all the greater because they are multiplied across companies; they extend down value chains and across networks of complements. Open standards processes further ensure the quality and accessibility of the knowledge behind the standard. Open licensing ensures the broadest and deepest use and reliance on the standard, and therefore the greatest possible investment. Yet the more open the process and the more open the licensing, the more vulnerable the standard is to free riding by patent trolls, who, if they are lucky, are able to exploit immense investment made by others in reliance on the standard.

Patents and standards both create investment-backed expectations that merit recognition as intellectual property. The final report of the National Innovation Initiative observes: "From an intellectual property perspective, open and proprietary IP models should not be seen as mutually exclusive; rather the IP framework must enable both approaches."[10] The burdens of disclosing and learning about potential conflicts should be managed so that standards and patents work productively together rather than as two disconnected systems, one run by engineers and the other by lawyers.

Aligning Patents and Open Standards

Today, we have a system in which patent holders hold all the cards, while those invested in standards face unknown and practically unforeseeable patent land mines. Yet standards, too, deserve protection by virtue of the great investment that is needed to make IT products, systems, and infrastructure work as users expect.

One approach to the problem would be to raise the threshold of "nonobviousness" beyond the statutory standard, which is tied to the "person having ordinary skill in the art." While the U.S. Supreme Court recently interpreted this standard more stringently,[11] it needs to be raised further to a proper expert standard. Only then will IT patents be good enough and few enough so that engineers will read and respect them. In addition, penalties for "willful infringement" should be limited so that engineers are not discouraged from reading patents. If patents embodied advances sufficient to be recognized by other innovators, there would be little risk of inadvertent infringement. This approach would solve much more than the problem of standards ambush, but by the same token, it would be difficult to achieve. Patents are rationalized by scale of investment, rather than genuine invention, and patent departments and firms are addicted to a volume-driven patent system. Any attempt to substantially reduce the volume of IT patents would meet with great resistance.[12]

A more tailored approach would give standards some measured relief from the patent holder's ability to extract damages and enjoin unwitting infringers. Patents hold unique leverage against standards, and if patent holders wish to threaten investments on industry standards, they should at least be obliged to make their rights known in a timely manner. If not, they should lose the ability to sue those who do no more than practice an open standard. It is far more efficient to put patentees, who presumably know the field in which they are patenting, on notice of a relatively small

number of open standards than to put multitudes of standards implementers and users on notice of multitudes of patents.

Like ex ante licensing and patent disclosure by participants, clearing
standards against ambush would add to the transparency and efficiency of
the market. It would encourage participation in standards development
processes by patent applicants and holders who might otherwise prefer to
stay back and monitor the process, while avoiding any commitments that
would limit their ability to hold standards-based products and services
hostage.

Of course, a clearing mechanism would apply only to standards that
meet threshold criteria of openness and broad participation, so that patent
holders could reasonably be charged with notice. The more open the
process, the more vulnerable the standard will be to unscrupulous patent
applicants who monitor the process and adapt their patent application to
capture the standard. Clearly, standards developed by the Internet Engineering Task Force (IETF) or the World Wide Web Consortium (W3C) are
public and open enough to qualify as protected standards.

This is nothing more than specific application of the venerable doctrine
of "laches." The laches doctrine limits enforceability based on the principle
that people should not sit on their rights, whether idly or cunningly, while
others make huge investments on top of them.

The danger of individual patents holding standards hostage is a growing
concern shared by businesses and consumers. IBM circulated a "safe
harbor" proposal explaining the incentives for the patent holder to refrain
from acting until standards are deeply embedded and widely adopted—and
suggesting an adaptation of laches as a partial solution.[13] The Consumer
Project on Technology's "Proposed WIPO Protocol for the Development of
Open Standards" has proposed a similar procedure for protecting standards
from ambush.[14]

Conclusion

Standards and patents are complements in the unfolding digital architecture. One unifies, the other differentiates. Although each is driven by its
own logic and culture, they need to work together in an efficient and
transparent manner. Each in principle encourages innovation, but each
suffers from distinctive pathologies that can discourage innovation. In
particular, standards that are too ambitious, too embedded, or even too
adaptable can preempt new ways of doing things. Patents by definition

block others from following particular paths, and broad or abstract patents can preempt many technological paths.

But today the problem is that in the case of digital technology, the patent system went on a binge. Judges of the new Court of Appeals believed they had a charter to revitalize the patent system and made decisions that expanded its scope and scale. The extraordinarily rich functionality of IT opened up immense prospects for patenting, with little to distinguish what was obvious or what was not. IT companies aggressively pursued large portfolios, not only for defensive purposes, but also in the hope that licensing would prove lucrative and rewarding. The U.S. Patent and Trademark Office was for a long time happy to accommodate, proclaiming that its mission was "to help customers get patents." The patent bar and innumerable consultants touted patents as the currency of the knowledge economy.

Those who created the technology and wrote code coped by ignoring patents. As patent scholar Mark Lemley observes: "Both researchers and companies in component industries simply ignore patents. Virtually everyone does it. They do it at all stages of endeavor. From the perspective of an outsider to the patent system, this is a remarkable fact. And yet it may be what prevents the patent system from crushing innovation in component industries like IT."[15] But standards cannot be ignored. They are the common knowledge that producers and users depend on.

Notes

Revised January 2010; an earlier version of this chapter appeared in Sherrie Bolin, ed., *The Standards Edge: Golden Mean* (Ann Arbor: Sheridan Books, 2007), pp. 85–92.

1. Douglas Heingartner, "Patent Fights Are a Legacy of MP3's Tangled Origins," *New York Times* (March 5, 2007), <http://www.nytimes.com/2007/03/05/technology/05music.html?ei=5090&en=72ad80392c70cd63&ex=1330750800&partner=rssuserl and&emc=rss&pagewanted=print>.

2. Markus G. Reitzig et al., "On Sharks, Trolls, and Other Patent Animals—'Being Infringed' as a Normatively Induced Innovation Exploitation Strategy," working paper (February 2006), <http://ssrn.com/abstract=885914>.

3. American Intellectual Property Law Association (AIPLA), "Report of the Economy Survey" (2005).

4. Frederick J. Telecky, "Statement at FTC/DOJ Hearings on Competition and Intellectual Property Law and Policy in the Knowledge-Based Economy," Federal Trade

Commission/Department of Justice hearings (February 28, 2002), <http://www.ftc
.gov/opp/intellect/020228telecky.pdf>.

5. *Rambus v. Infineon*, 318 F.3d 1081 (Fed. Cir. 2003).

6. *Kingsdown Medical Consultants v. Hollister*, 863 F.2d 867, 874 (Fed. Cir. 1988).

7. U.S. Department of Justice and Federal Trade Commission, "Antitrust Enforcement and Intellectual Property Rights: Promoting Innovation and Competition"
(2007), pp. 49–56, <http://ftc.gov/reports/innovation/P040101PromotingInnovation
andCompetitionrpt0704.pdf>.

8. The so-called teaching-suggestion-motivation test was recently overruled by the
Supreme Court in *KSR v. Teleflex*, 550 U.S. 398 (2007).

9. *Dell Computer Corp.*, 121 F.T.C. 616 (1996).

10. Council on Competitiveness, "Innovate America, Thriving in a World of Challenge and Change," National Innovation Initiative Summit and Report (December
2004), p. 44.

11. *KSR International v. Teleflex*, 550 U.S. 398 (2007).

12. The organized patent bar has consistently argued for a lower threshold of nonobviousness. See amicus briefs in the seminal cases of *Graham v. John Deere*, 383 U.S.
1 (1966), and *KSR International v. Teleflex* (see note 8).

13. IBM Issue Paper, "Toward an Open Standards Based Innovation Economy,"
(unpublished, 2005). On file with the author.

14. Consumer Project on Technology, "Proposed WIPO Protocol for the Development of Open Standards (PDOS) Version 1.0" (2005), <http://www.cptech.org/a2k/
pdos.doc>.

15. Mark Lemley, "Ignoring Patents," *Michigan State Law Review* 2008, no. 19
(2008); quotation from abstract at <http://papers.ssrn.com/sol3/papers.cfm?abstract
_id=999961>.

IV Interoperability and Openness

12   ICT Standards Setting Today: A System under Stress

Andrew Updegrove

The modern standards development infrastructure is largely the product of the industrial age and evolved to address the needs of such an economy. The requirements of a world that is increasingly based upon information and communications technology (ICT), however, are far different, and include demands for faster standards development, more vulnerability to uncooperative owners of necessary patent claims, and a greater need for universal, global adoption of core enabling standards. These needs have been partially addressed through several organic developments, such as the proliferation of consortia, the evolution of more detailed intellectual property rights policies, and the passage of the World Trade Organization's Technical Barriers to Trade Act. But the advent of the Internet and the Web, and the continuing introduction of new ICT-based products and services in ever shorter and more frequent product cycles, are exposing the fact that a system that retains strong roots in the nineteenth century is ill suited to meet the demands of the twenty-first. In this chapter, I survey some of the areas of inadequacy inherent in the current system, the ways in which society is being impacted by new standards-dependent technologies, and the situations in which governments may feel called upon to intervene.

Introduction

For most of the first hundred years of the modern era of standards setting, standards developers focused their attention on the attributes of tangible objects. The standards they developed specified dimensions, materials, and other physical attributes, and to the extent that they addressed intangibles, those elements were result oriented, such as targeting performance and safety. Similarly, interoperability standards were physical standards, intended to ensure that part A would fit with part B.

These standards were created by domain experts and by interested parties within the market niches that produced the products involved. Usually, problems requiring standards solutions could be addressed within a single standards-setting organization (SSO).

In a world of physical objects, standards development could conveniently lag behind product development. Only after screws, steam power, and electric lights had proven to be popular did a demand develop for standards to establish common thread gauges, boiler safety guidelines, and light socket dimensions. Even in the case of networks, the same held true, as railroads, power companies, and telephone services were all launched as local enterprises, using available proprietary implementations. Not until these discrete networks were joined did the need for national and global interoperability standards arise.

Such after-the-fact nonurgent standards setting could, and sometimes did, have advantages. For example, products that were inherently well designed and successful were more likely to become the models for de facto or de jure standards. Similarly, when cycles of innovation are widely spaced and their results long lasting (Edison's light bulbs, in comparison to yesterday's floppy disks, remain in use today), taking time to achieve the best standards result represents a wise investment due to the length of time that the market will be "locked in" by the decisions made.

Because of communication, travel, and trade constraints, most of the SSOs that were founded to meet evolving standards needs were national in scope (with notable exceptions, such as the International Telecommunication Union, or ITU). But after the Second World War, the internationalization of standards increased under the auspices of several global standards bodies that were formed in addition to the ITU, most notably the International Organization for Standardization (ISO) and International Electrotechnical Commission (IEC). But domestic standards can be used to protect domestic manufacturers from the competition presented by foreign goods, and at times this provided a disincentive to locally implement useful standards, even after a global authority had adopted them.

In a world of primarily performance, material, and physical interoperability standards, patent infringement was rarely an issue for most SSOs. Instead, when intellectual property rights (IPR) were mentioned, if they were mentioned at all, it was copyrights that were usually under discussion, since most SSOs funded their efforts in whole or in part through the sale of paper versions of their work product. When IPR policies were eventually created and adopted, they were high-level statements of principles, and lacked implementational details. Moreover, for many standards there was no proprietary advantage to be gained by any stakeholder as a result of a given standard coming out in one way rather than another.

In short, the initial standards-setting infrastructure that evolved to serve the needs of the maturing industrial age was adequate, but also limited, to the specific demands that were placed upon it by the commerce of the day.

With the advent of the computer age, the need arose for new types of consensus-based specifications that have as much in common with non-technical standards as with the historical work products of SSOs (computer languages being an example). As technological innovation increased in many disciplines, the need for new standards implemented in software, silicon, wireless broadcasts, fiber optics, and hardware emerged to serve the needs of (in particular) the ICT industries, and that need soon expanded dramatically. With the explosive success of the Internet, the utility and value of globally accessible, networked products, services, and content have today become enormous.

Our new, networked world holds unprecedented opportunities for individuals who have hitherto been denied access to modern education, information, and opportunities. It also offers a platform that both public as well as private entities are enthusiastically embracing, resulting in a world where ICT access is becoming a prerequisite to enjoying the full rights and opportunities of society, democracy, and the economy. That access is only feasible, however, if standards exist to address local character sets, languages, and physical disabilities. Concerns such as these are far different from those encountered in developing standards for networking, and most existing ICT SSOs are neither interested in nor even highly aware of such needs.

At the same time, single standards can no longer solve many of the problems that new ICT opportunities are presenting nor can suites of standards created by a single SSO. Instead, increasingly complex collections of standards created by many SSOs, often with very different rules regulating IPR, must be cobbled together in order to do what needs to be done.

Who, then, should—and who is competent—to develop the standards required to feed the needs of this brave new ICT-enabled world? Is the traditional standards-setting infrastructure adequate to the task, either technically or democratically? And to the extent that it is not, how, and by whom, and to what results will its shortcomings be addressed?

In this chapter I will review some of the principal ways in which the traditional standards-setting infrastructure is inadequate to the task of supplying the ICT standards of the future. I will also describe some of the organic solutions that have already been developed by industry participants, and provide thoughts on how those issues that remain unresolved might be productively addressed.

Standards Challenges

When one examines the ICT standards needs of the future, it becomes immediately apparent that almost none of the dynamics that led to the evolution of the traditional standards-setting infrastructure remain unchanged today. Consider, for example, the following factors.

Interoperability Demands

Unlike physical products, the fruits of ICT technologies require a large number of interoperability standards in order to function and flourish. This offers vendors the choice of trying to dominate a market, through the creation of a de facto standard (e.g., the VHS video format, and reaping large royalty rewards), or of collaborating with other vendors to develop a consensus-based standard that may more quickly and certainly create a new market that is shared by all. When vendors choose to roll the dice on the former approach, damaging standards wars can result.

Innovation Cycles

As noted, technology generations in many areas are becoming shorter with each cycle. This results in pressure to create and deploy standards more quickly. Otherwise, they may be useless by the time that they are released. As a result, it is less feasible for standards creation to follow product introduction, because the useful life of the standard is short. The only way to dramatically reduce time to market with a standard is to develop both the standard as well as the products that will comply with it on a concurrent basis.

All will be well if those that are interested in a new product space decide to collaborate on a single standard. But if there are competing technologies, then each may wish—or indeed have no choice, if the technologies are fundamentally different—to create its own standard(s) as a precondition to testing its products in the marketplace. The result can be either a healthy standards "competition" that enables multiple technologies to test themselves in the marketplace, with each finding its respective niche (as has occurred with the Wi-Fi and Bluetooth standards, each of which was initially in competition with the other, but has now settled into the respective uses for which it is best suited) or a standards war between standards that may have little useful differentiation in consumers' eyes (as is currently the case with the Blu-Ray and HD-DVD next-generation video standards).

Network Prevalence

More and more ICT technologies must be used in connection with networks, but nonproprietary networks cannot form until the standards that enable them are created. It is axiomatic that the larger a network becomes, the more value can be derived by those who are connected. This drives up the value of the network as well as the products and services that can be linked to, or provided through, the network, and which therefore become more attractive to potential purchasers. To the extent that one standard's solution favors one vendor more than another, an incentive is therefore created to influence the outcome. In the case of the increasing number of patent "trolls" that develop or purchase IPR solely for the purpose of reaping licensing revenues, placing a patent claim in the way of the implementation of such a standard has the potential to reap huge rewards.

Freedom from Lock-in

End users have become more conscious of the fact that requiring the implementation of "open standards" in the ICT products they purchase can lead to wider choices, cheaper prices (through competition), and real protection from vendor lock-in. Such standards create opportunities for new entrants into product and service areas, but also threaten incumbents that may currently control those niches. As a result, some industry participants will have more to gain by blocking and delaying standards efforts than by promoting and supporting them.

IPR Infringement

ICT standards are unusually susceptible to infringing the patents of SSO members, and of greater concern, nonmembers. Increasingly, standards must address areas of intense patent activity, often referred to as "patent thickets." Because owners of patents infringed by a standard can charge royalties or impose specific license terms on implementers of that standard, they may try and cause such infringement to occur during the development process. But if SSO IPR policies are tightened to lessen this possibility by requiring all such patents to be disclosed before a standard is adopted, participants with large patent portfolios become concerned that they may be required to undertake burdensome patent searches in order to avoid their IPR becoming subject to obligatory licensing requirements.

Convergence

Historically, standards were created and used by the same vendors, allowing those vendors to evolve whatever rules and licensing practices they wished within a single SSO and industry niche. But in ICT, dozens of capabilities and hundreds of standards can be utilized in a single device (e.g., a state-of-the-art cell phone may have 3G telephone, video, Web browsing, wireless, PDA, and other capabilities; may utilize any of a number of operating systems; and can host multiple programs and services). Some of these standards are based upon patent pools, while others may have been developed by SSOs with strict royalty-free policies. If even a small fraction of these standards bear royalties, the cost of such a device could become prohibitive. If too many IPR owners require unique licenses, the burden of obtaining and negotiating necessary rights can become excessively burdensome.

Globalization

Trade, travel, production, and utilization are increasingly becoming global. In ICT in particular, the concept of a national standard has become archaic. As a result, there are great needs as well as great incentives to achieve global consensus on the types of uniform standards that can permit products to be sold and used anywhere. At the same time, the specific standards that are adopted can favor some participants more than others, and therefore some nations and regions (such as the EU) have incorporated standards into their global trade strategies. Those governments therefore dedicate resources and government attention toward standards strategies as well, and interweave these considerations into other international policy decisions.

Other forces can complicate globalization. Some standards bear significant royalty loads, which can empower some parts of the world (e.g., the West) with significant trade advantages, because their vendors can sell high-margin, branded products, while nations in other regions (e.g., emerging countries) are relegated to the status of low-cost, low-margin job shops that can supply finished goods to the owners of the patents that underlie controlling standards, but cannot sell similar goods, at high margins, directly to end users. Such advantages can tempt those with large markets and production capabilities (e.g., China) to create their own domestic standards in order to level the economic playing field, notwithstanding the constraints on such behavior contained in the Technical Barriers to Trade Act among World Trade Organization member nations.

More Complex Standards Problems

The problems that require standards solutions today are increasingly large and complex, even when the business case being addressed may appear deceptively simple. Wirelessly printing a picture from a cell phone camera, for example, requires the use and coordination of a variety of standards, each of which was created by a different SSO with different considerations in mind. As a result, printer, camera, mobile device, and other vendors must all decide which set of standards could perform the desired task, and then each agree to implement that subset of the resulting standards "profile" that relates to their particular products, before their customers can enjoy the type of simple features that will enrich their product experience—while also enriching the vendors that wish to sell more printer paper, ink, and camera-enabled cell phones.

Standards Tools

Unfortunately, the infrastructural tools available to deal with these challenges are in many respects inadequate. The ICT standards infrastructure today comprises the following principal parts, with the limitations identified.

Accredited Standards Development Organizations (SDOs)

Nations throughout the world have variously complex systems of domestic SDOs. In some cases, they are "top down" governmental, or quasi-governmental bodies (as in Germany and China), while others are "bottom up" organizations (as in the United States) formed primarily by private industry and other stakeholders, and accredited by a national body (in the United States, that body for most purposes is the American National Standards Institute, or ANSI). But while some SDOs, such as ASTM International (originally known as the American Society for Testing and Material) are becoming global in scope, others remain national. As a result, they are to an extent in competition with the SDOs of other countries either to create and promote domestic standards, or to promote their standards for adoption (in preference to those of other countries) on a global basis. In addition, since global adoption is necessarily a two-step process, the time between chartering an SDO working group and final global adoption (often following some period of market implementation) can be protracted.

While independent in governance, budget, and activities, SDOs have multiple points of contact, both domestically as well as internationally. In the United States, for example, ANSI runs multiple forums, panels, and programs in which both SDO members (corporate, government, university, etc.) as well as SDO management members participate. Internationally, IEC, ISO, and ITU have regular plenary and other meetings, and multiple committees and other working groups are active on standards activities, all of which are peopled by member representatives from around the globe.

Consortia

Among all SDOs, only a small number are prominent in the ICT sector. Nonaccredited SSOs ("consortia"), however, have proliferated wildly in the information technology, and to a lesser extent, the communication technology sectors since the late 1980s. Today, there are more than five hundred such organizations in operation, ranging from small, closed vendor clubs that operate on an invitation-only basis, to very large, institutionalized, global, open membership organizations. Some (such as the Object Management Group [OMG], World Wide Web Consortium [W3C] and the Organization for the Advancement of Structured Information Systems [OASIS]) have broad and coordinated programs that can enable the accomplishment of comprehensive technical goals. But many others have been formed to develop and maintain a single standard. The largest consortia have dozens of staff, but the vast majority operate on a very limited budget, and have only one or a few full-time employees, if they have any human resources at all beyond their members' own staff.

Unlike SDOs, which have various points of formal contact, there is no umbrella organization of any type for consortia, or other formal means by which they meet en masse to address matters of common interest.

The "Big Is"

The three best-known global standards bodies—the ITU, IEC, and ISO—play a variable role in ICT standards setting, with more communications than IT standards arising in SDOs for eventual international adoption. Far more IT standards are created today in consortia than in SDOs, and only a small percentage of their standards are introduced to the accredited system, despite the creation of avenues such as the Publicly Available Standard (PAS) process for that purpose. When consortium-developed standards are offered for formal adoption, they are usually submitted to a subcommittee of IEC/ISO Joint Technical Committee 1 (JTC 1), which was originally formed to consider (and still processes) SDO-originated IT standards.

Because most consortia both court and admit members globally, and due to the fact that consortia are commonly founded by transnational companies in the first instance, they are often able to achieve wide international adoption of their standards without seeking the imprimatur of the global accredited standards infrastructure at all. Increasingly, however, consortium members are urging these SSOs to qualify as PAS submitters so that particular standards that are of significant interest to particular customer groups (such as European governments) that favor, or require, ISO/IEC standardized products, can achieve that status.

Liaison Relationships

These many SDOs and consortia are interlinked by a loose network of one-on-one liaison relationships, each typically formalized by a brief, high-level "Memorandum of Understanding," if they are formalized at all. While these relationships can be adequate for maintaining communication and, to a degree, avoiding needless duplication of activities, they are rarely multiparty, and therefore not typically capable of delivering comprehensive solutions to complex problems (such as the camera/printer example noted earlier). Moreover, maintaining such relationships well is time consuming and resource intensive, and a typical ICT SSO may maintain twenty to forty such relationships. An SSO with a large full-time staff can task a full-time employee with managing and maintaining such relationships, but a typical consortium is too lightly resourced to afford dedicating a staff person to such a purpose. As a result, liaison relationships are frequently served by member volunteers, with a greater risk that any given relationship may languish, and that overall cohesiveness will suffer.

Participation

While both SDOs as well as most consortia espouse many of the same open standards principles, some of those principles are honored to a greater or lesser extent in word rather than in the breach. In the case of SDOs, which are by definition committed to the participation of all those affecting, and affected by, standards ("stakeholders"), the greatest challenge can be attracting all stakeholders into participation. After all, creating technical standards is not likely to be of great appeal to the average consumer, nor to consumer advocates or to government personnel with more immediate concerns. Only a few consortia (such as the W3C) include societal concerns and broad noncommercial participation in their charters at all. In the case of standards that have only societally neutral elements to be specified, this limited participation is not problematic. But in those areas where the interests of all those affected are not congruent, the absence of a watchdog for the unrepresented can be of concern.

In summary, the modern ICT standards infrastructure is a lightweight, highly distributed, and only loosely connected system. As such, it is democratic, reasonably responsive, and economically efficient. But it is also ill suited to address complex problems, and democratic only for those that find it sufficiently in their self-interest to participate. Moreover, some SSOs are vulnerable to manipulation by the individual companies, and groups of companies, that are willing to dedicate the time and resources needed to support their operations.

Societal Challenges

At the same time that challenges are increasing for the ICT standards, infrastructure, society, commerce, and governments are rushing pell-mell toward greater and greater dependence on ICT in general, and on the Internet and the Web in particular. With astonishing speed, vital services and facilities, such as international banking, communications, travel, utilities, and, indeed, just about everything else of significance in the modern world, have either been redeployed across the Internet, or have become dependent upon the uninterrupted availability of the Internet for their own viability.

That viability is in the first instance enabled by the protocols and standards that together support the Internet and the Web. These specifications function as the synapses through which information flows in what has come to be described as the "cyberinfrastructure."

But is the infrastructure that creates and maintains these standards—as well as the many others that enable the services, software, and devices that run on top of the Internet and the Web—the right infrastructure to robustly, democratically, and securely support the cyberinfrastructure on which we are increasingly dependent? There are multiple reasons to believe that it is not, of which the following are examples:

• Years after the disastrous events of 9/11 exposed the inadequacy of first-responder communications, wireless equipment is still incapable of permitting fire, emergency, and police responders to reliably and seamlessly communicate.

• China is developing multiple standards for domestic use in areas such as 3G telephone, wireless communication, and video compression due to perceived inequities in the costs of implementing patent-encumbered global standards, arguably in violation of its obligations under the Technical Barriers to Trade Act. If this practice becomes more common in China, 1.3 billion of the world's inhabitants will be utilizing different standards than the rest of humanity.

• Governments are becoming aware that their wholesale conversion to electronic document production and archiving is leaving them vulnerable to proprietary lock-in, as well as future inability to access documents. OpenDocument Format (ODF), an OASIS-developed standard, has been adopted as an ISO/IEC standard to meet that concern, and it has been implemented in multiple proprietary and open source products.

• The legislatures of U.S. states have considered bills that would mandate the use by government of office software based on "open document formats." Similar efforts have occurred in several nations.

• SSOs have not been successful in adopting IPR policies that are sufficiently stringent to provide real protection against the emergence of "submarine patents," at least without the need for implementers to engage in hugely expensive defensive litigation against the owners of those patents. (Submarine patents are patent claims that are not revealed and asserted by their owners against the implementers of a standard until it has already become widely adopted and difficult—or impossible—to change.)

• There is no consensus on the definition of "open standards" at a sufficiently useful level of granularity. New challenges, such as the increasing popularity of open source software, are widening the gap.

• There is a similar lack of uniformity regarding the terms of IPR policies among SSOs. To the good, a one-size-fits-all approach would be unnecessarily restrictive, but to the bad there are needless inconsistencies among policies that are each attempting to say the same thing. This increases complexity in converging technologies.

• There are an increasing number of commercial disputes over whether a patent owner that has made a commitment to license that IPR on reasonable and nondiscriminatory (RAND) terms is violating that pledge.

• The IPR policies of most consortia that develop software are inadequate to ensure the implementation of such standards in open source software.

• There is no mechanism for consumers or other stakeholders to participate, or to make their concerns known, in most ICT SSOs, despite the increasing impact that ICT standards have on their welfare.

• In some countries such as the United States, government remains both disengaged from as well as largely unaware of the increasing importance of ICT standards outside of traditional telecommunications boundaries.

• The importance of the Internet and the Web has been recognized by the United Nations, which chartered the World Summit on the Information Society (WSIS). However, that multiyear process became mired in a dispute over the continuing right of the U.S. government, via the Department of Commerce, to oversee the Internet Corporation on Assigned Numbers and Names (ICANN).

• While the benefits of the Internet are being made available to more people around the world, little progress has been made thus far in implementing accessibility standards (even by governments), to ensure that those with disabilities will be able to enjoy those benefits wherever they may live.

• Standards continue to be created in "silos" by vendors, while end users increasingly need solutions to larger problems that can only be solved by a more holistic approach.

What Is to Be Done

To be sure, the standards world has responded in a few instances both organically as well as deliberately. The following are examples.

IPR Policy Convergence
There are multiple efforts ongoing, and even accomplished, to achieve greater uniformity and coherence among IPR policies. Fairly recently, the ITU, IEC, and ISO announced a unified IPR policy. In the case of open document formats, the ODF Alliance, an organization formed to promote governments' open document format uptake, has created a model statute as a starting point for governments considering enacting legislation to encourage or require the usage of open document formats. Finally, a subcommittee of the American Bar Association Science and Technology Section has recently completed a multiyear project directed at creating an extensively annotated IPR policy, in part to assist SSOs in creating IPR policies with more uniform terminology.

Metastandard Consortia
A few consortia have been formed to assemble suites of standards capable of solving complex problems. The camera/printer business case described earlier is a real-world example, and has been addressed by the Mobile Imaging and Printing Consortium (MIPC), a client of

the author's. Another client, the Network Centric Operations Industry Consortium (NCOIC) is undertaking a far more complex challenge: assembling the standards needed to enable members of the U.S. armed forces and those of U.S. allies to identify themselves to a single network and gain instantaneous access to information that becomes known to that network.

Simultaneous Innovation and Standardization

The commercial rewards anticipated from new technologies have been sufficiently attractive to provide the incentive for industry to invest in standards setting simultaneous with innovation, even where it is far from certain that the resulting standard and products will be successful. Perhaps the best example of this practice can be found in the case of wireless technologies, where a first wave of innovation gave rise to several contenders to dominate the home network space. One entrant, called HomeRF, failed, despite being supported by a consortium effort. Another, Wi-Fi, developed by IEEE and SDO, succeeded in taking the original prize, while the third, Bluetooth, originally developed by Ericsson Mobile Phones and then supported by the Bluetooth Special Interest Group, failed to establish itself in that space, but has become dominant in mobile and certain other devices. Now a second wave of standards is reaching the market, targeted at other discrete uses, such as Nearfield Communications, a very short-range standard being used in (for example) contactless payment cards. Meanwhile, competing standards will allow home entertainment and computer peripheral equipment to shed their connecting cables, WiMAX will provide intermediate range wireless networks, RFID tags and readers are reaching the supply chain, and mesh network standards are being developed to allow the digital home to become a more sophisticated reality.

The development of such standards "swarms" allows the marketplace to simultaneously innovate, productize, and standardize, and at the same time for competing technologies to vie for supremacy in the marketplace. Absent such behavior, new technology-based products and services would reach the marketplace far more slowly, and a less robust and rich range of choices would be available.

The Future

Useful though these developments may be, they are evolutionary rather than revolutionary. They do not fundamentally challenge or reorder any existing power relationships among standards stakeholders or bring any new stakeholders into the process. Nor do they significantly identify or serve to address societal interests that are impacted by ICT progress and at risk as the importance of cyberinfrastructure grows.

This dilemma gives rise to many questions: Is revolutionary change needed, or will the infrastructure of the past in fact be sufficient to address the cyberinfrastructural demands of the future? And if such change is required, how will it manifest itself? Will government expand its actions beyond its traditional health- and safety-related regulatory function? If so, will it limit its actions to simply leading by example, as it appears to be doing in the case of open document formats? Or will it in fact expand its regulatory function as well? Following the completion of the initial phase of the WSIS process, the United Nations retreated, rather than advanced, commissioning the Working Group on Internet Governance (WGIG) more as a discussion group than a new body with a remit to act. Will that group become more substantive, or will it simply debate?

The answers to questions such as these may have much to do with public perceptions of the challenges that will need to be addressed, and the importance that is placed upon those challenges. Considering how these challenges should be viewed and addressed gives rise to further questions:

• Will Internet access achieve the legal status of a public utility? Should it?
• Will governments extend accessibility laws to the Web? If so, will governments defer to SSOs to create not only the standards by which accessibility can be achieved, but also the definition of when it has?
• Will eminent domain laws be extended to cover IPR, if that IPR is asserted to block or unduly tax the usage of essential, standards-based ICT services?
• Should the development of some ICT standards, such as those that relate to voting, privacy, and medical and financial records, be subject to greater public participation, and if so, how can that participation be achieved?
• Will the Technical Barriers to Trade Act and the WTO complaint resolution process adequately address standards-based trade disputes?
• Will the United States voluntarily surrender its remaining control over ICANN?
• Will ISO/IEC and their national bodies make their processes more transparent, given that they are exercising a quasi-governmental function (e.g., by making all contradictions, responses, and minutes public)? Should

consortia and SDOs be required to do the same for certain types of standards?

• Will courts and regulators take a more active interest in standards-related activities (e.g., by imposing stricter duties of good faith and right conduct on standards participants, and permitting stricter penalties when those duties are violated)?

• Will governments make it safer to participate in standards setting (e.g., in the United States, by expanding the benefits of the National Cooperative Research and Production Act to participants in standards development, instead of just to SSOs themselves)?

• Should government provide greater support for standards setting in the public interest (e.g., by offering tax incentives to participate in SSOs that maintain open processes and provide public participation, or perhaps by subsidizing the operations of such SSOs, where the public interest has been identified as being of importance)?

• Will industry create new ways to address convergence, so that a more cohesive, efficient process of standards setting results?

Given the current status of the standards-setting infrastructure, it is difficult to imagine that the concerns underlying many of these questions will be addressed by industry voluntarily. It is equally difficult to imagine that many of the governmental actions postulated here would occur in the United States, with its laissez-faire, bottom up approach to standards setting. But it is quite conceivable that such actions could happen elsewhere, perhaps most obviously in Europe.

Conclusion

Governments have already begun to venture into the realm of ICT standards in new ways, most notably as regards open document formats and privacy, and as they relate to open source software. Whether this is the beginning of an ongoing and extending period of engagement by government in cyberinfrastructure-related matters remains to be seen, but there are logical reasons to assume that it is.

How extensive such a movement will be will have much to do with how responsibly and effectively the private sector acts on its own. Given the history of standards setting to date and the fact that ICT standardization occurs primarily in consortia today, it would appear that at minimum the leading consortia that are influential in creating cyberinfrastructure would be well advised to consider adopting a greater sensitivity to social concerns, if they wish to retain their independence of action when they create standards in that domain.

Note

This chapter is updated from the April 2007 issue of the *Consortium Standards Bulletin* (now called *Standards Today*) at <http://www.consortiuminfo.org/bulletins/apr07 .php#feature> (accessed January 5, 2011).

13   Software Standards, Openness, and Interoperability

Robert S. Sutor

Global debates about open standards for document formats dominated the information technology (IT) world in the opening decade of the twenty-first century. Unfortunately, there remains basic confusion between what a standard does and what the rules are when one implements it. In certain open standards debates, I've been told secondhand that some people were even informed that "if you implement that standard, then all your software has to be given away for free." This, of course, was wrong and confused, if it wasn't, in fact, outright FUD (creation of Fear, Uncertainty, and Doubt).

To clarify this, let's talk about what a standard is, what an *open* standard is, and how this relates to interoperability. We'll see how more confusion has been introduced into discussions around this last topic.

A *standard* is like a blueprint. It provides guidance to someone when he or she actually builds something. Standards are not limited to software, but are an important part of computer hardware, telecommunications, health care, automobiles, aerospace, and many areas of manufacturing.

One of the reasons an architect produces a blueprint is so that a builder, an engineer, or an inspector can look at it and say, "If you build according to this plan, it will be safe and the house won't fall down." In the same way, some standards are for safety, especially where they involve electrical or electronic components.

A standard is more than just a blueprint, though, because it has to be something with which a lot of people agree. Something that may not have this sort of "blessing," or common agreement, is usually called a *specification*. By abuse of language, we will sometimes call a standard a specification. Put another way, all standards are specifications, but not all specifications are standards.

Standards are also employed when we have to ensure that things made by different people will either work together or work in the same way. I live in the United States, and when I go to the store and buy a telephone,

I know that the telephone wire will plug into the jack in my wall. I don't need different jacks for phones made by different vendors. The design of the telephone jack and the plug are not control points for any phone vendor. I make my choice based on the features of the phone, the color, the price, whether it is wireless or not, and so on.

There are standards that describe the "blueprints" for the plugs and jacks, but the standards themselves are not the actual plugs or jacks. We separate the ideas of "a standard which may be implemented" and "something that is an implementation of a standard."

To bring this back to a software example, the OpenDocument Format (ODF) is a standard, a blueprint, created by a technical committee of independent global experts at the Organization for the Advancement of Structured Information Standards (OASIS) consortium. It is not software, but rather a description of how you should write out the information in word processing documents, spreadsheets, and presentations should you ever need to put them on disk or, say, attach them to emails. The same description also tells you that if someone gives you a document, spreadsheet, or a presentation and tells you it is in ODF (perhaps via the file extension), then your software applications know what to expect when they read the file.

Because it is a standard, the information can be used by anyone who builds software that complies with the standard. No one vendor can arbitrarily change it, and that provides a lot of security for people who save their documents in ODF.

Another important standard is HTML (Hypertext Markup Language), the rules by which you format pages for the World Wide Web. Although there were vendor differences in HTML in the mid-1990s, most people no longer think that it is reasonable to allow vendors to break interoperability by implementing too little of the standard or doing their own special things. We don't need different browsers to view Web pages from different people, though some browsers like Firefox and Opera are known to adhere to the Web standards, essentially the blueprints for the Web, better than other browsers. To extend my earlier analogy, we know that a Web page ("the plug") will fit into the browser ("the jack") and then I can see and interact with the page ("I can talk on the phone").

Just as we said in the 1990s that no vendor should have a control point by having its own flavor of HTML, in the twenty-first century we say the same thing about document formats. In fact, since word processors have been with us a lot longer than the Web, it's surprising that standards weren't created, if not demanded, there earlier.

So, to summarize, a standard is a blueprint or a set of plans that can be implemented. Where do standards come from?

A *de facto standard* is a specification that became popular because everyone just happened to use it, possibly because it was implemented in a product that had significant market acceptance. The details of this specification may or may not be available publicly without some sort of special legal arrangement.

The basic problem with a de facto standard is that it is controlled by a single vendor that can—and often does—change it whenever the vendor decides to do so. This frequently happens when a product goes from one major version to another. At that point, everyone else who is trying to interoperate with the information created in that vendor's product must scramble to make their own software work again. This is easier, of course, if they can actually see the new specification and there are no impediments, legal or otherwise, to implementing it. The owning vendor gets a time-to-market advantage, possibly increasing its market share, again.

Traditionally, it was not in the interest of the owner of a de facto standard to make the details too widely available because they didn't want to make it easier for anyone else to move into their market space. They would say, "Why would I voluntarily let other people build products compatible with my data? They might steal away my customers!" To turn this around, it is not in the best interests of customers to be locked into de facto standards controlled by a single vendor. The customer might say, "I may have used your software, but it is my information, and I very much want and demand the freedom to use any application I want to process my information." De facto standards decrease customer empowerment and choice, though they linger on.

The second kind of standard I'll mention is something I'll call a *community standard*. As you might guess, this is something created and maintained by more than one person or company. The members of the community may work for companies or governments, or belong to organizations, or may be experts who are otherwise unaffiliated. The standards creation process involves negotiation, compromises, and agreement based on what is best for the community and the potential users.

It is a classic fallacy to think that this necessarily creates a "lowest common denominator" or unsatisfactory compromise. Smart people can make good decisions together, even if they don't all work for the same company. Conversely, people who all work for the same company don't necessarily always make smart decisions. They might, for example, produce de facto standards that have security vulnerabilities and are difficult to use with common software tools.

Community standards usually get blessed, as I termed it earlier, by being created or submitted to a Standards Development Organization, or SDO. While it does happen that people may get together and write a standard from scratch in an SDO, it is very likely that one or more parties will bring drafts to the table as a starting point. It is usually expected that the developing standard will change over time as more minds are directed at the problem that the standard is expected to help solve.

A standard may go through multiple versions: it is not uncommon for the first version to take one to two years, and then to take about the same amount of time for each of the next one or two iterations. At some point the standard will stabilize and either become fairly universally used or else become eclipsed by an alternative way of tackling the same general problem. For example, the new Web services standards are starting to be used for distributed computing, replacing older standards as Service Oriented Architecture becomes more broadly deployed.

I want to return to this "community" idea for a moment. If you bring something to an SDO, you take a risk that others may change the specification, perhaps in ways that interfere with your product plans. One word: tough. Working within a community does not mean walking in and saying, "I'm the king (or queen) and you can't change anything unless I say it is okay." Under no circumstances should a vendor be able to dictate to a reputable standards organization that the developing specification remain 100 percent compatible with that vendor's products.

The value of creating a standard in a community is that products from different sources can work together to build solutions that solve real customer problems. If you can't compete by creating superior, higher performing, more scalable and more secure products and perhaps the services to give the customers what they need, then I would suggest you have problems beyond not controlling the creation of a standard.

What you are basically saying is "I can't win on a level playing field." Your customers might be interested in hearing that. Some SDOs are de jure organizations: they have particular credentials in national or international settings. Some governments have laws that make it very difficult to use standards that do not come from de jure organizations. ANSI, ITU, and ISO are examples of de jure organizations while groups like the World Wide Web Consortium (W3C), OASIS, and the Object Management Group (OMG) are usually just referred to as consortia.

Sometimes a standard produced by a consortium will be submitted and blessed by a de jure organization to make it more palatable for government procurements. Of course, de jure organizations, like all standards groups, must be very careful what they bless because they have reputations for quality and relevance that they hope to maintain. The OpenDocument Format is an international standard as well as an OASIS standard, namely ISO/IEC 26300:2006.

You may have heard of an "open standard." What does this mean? I think we need to consider five aspects of standards and ask some important questions about each of them:

1. How is that standard created?
2. How is it maintained after Version 1.0?
3. What is the cost of getting a copy of the standard?
4. Are there restrictions on how I can implement the standard?
5. Can I use just a part of the standard or extend it and still claim compliance?

In answering these, we need to think in terms of transparency, community, democracy, costs, freedoms and permissions, and restrictions:

• The more transparent the standards process is, the more open the standard is.
• The more the community can be involved and then actually is involved, the more open the standard is.
• The more democratic the standards process is, where the community can make significant changes even before Version 1.0, the more open the standard is.
• The lower the standards-related cost to software developers who want to use the standard, the more open it is.
• The lower the standards-related cost to the eventual consumer of software that happens to use the standard, the more open it is.
• The more generous the standard's licensing is in the freedoms and permissions it provides, the more open the standard is.
• The more onerous the standard's licensing is in the restrictions it imposes, the less open the standard is.

From these and perhaps other criteria, we should be able to come up with some sort of "Standards Openness Index." In the meanwhile, use them when deciding for yourself how open a particular standard is. I don't think openness is a binary situation: there is a range from being completely closed to being completely open. "Open" has become a standard marketing term, so make sure you ask good questions of those who are trying to convince you that they are as open or more open than the other guy.

Now let's look at interoperability. In mathematics the phrase "by abuse of terminology" is sometimes used in advanced books and lectures. There is no dishonesty intended, it's just a simple way of saying, "I'm omitting some of the details and it's not quite exactly what I mean, but close enough for us to talk about." Since we are discussing mathematics, you can always follow up with a more complete treatment where everything is proved before you agree to the conclusion. That is, no one is getting fooled.

In the same way, some words such as "normal" are used in many different areas of mathematical study. At first it seems almost random, but the more you learn about the subjects, the more you realize that you're really talking about the same things, just through a different lens, if you will.

Alas, if this were only true in IT. There, we should be saying "the terminology is being abused" when appropriate, but rarely do. Similarly, what is "normal" to a market leader might not be at all normal to everyone else. Luckily, things are starting to change, particularly as communities rise up and start fighting for proper behavior and description.

In the opening decade of the century, we saw this around the word "open." It no longer became appropriate for a single vendor to declare something open because (1) the vendor created it, and (2) the vendor will call it anything it wants. This might have been accepted behavior before, but it is not now, nor will it be in the future.

I think the word "interoperability" is now being similarly abused. When a single vendor or software provider makes it easier to connect primarily to his or her software, this is more properly called *intraoperability*. In the intraoperability situation, one product is somehow central and dominant, either by market share, attitude, or acquiescence. The connectivity is supported by protocols and data formats that favor the central software, and the provider often prescribes those. The goal is to suck all-important data and processing into the central software ecosystem, and it is in this sense that we use the prefix "intra."

So when the software provider comes out and says "we just created a consortium to provide interoperability with our products," he or she is really saying "we want you to help us keep our product at the center of the world, and help us increase sales." Nice deal if you can get it. And a deal it is, when we are talking business and financial arrangements. The protocols and formats somehow always work best with the central software and aren't really conducive for others to use when the central software is not being accessed.

You may need special licensing to use the protocols or formats, and the central vendor may even try to standardize the specifications with weird rules stating that you can't break compatibility with their products. The licensing might even prevent the use of the formats, protocols, or even a user interface by competitors or creators of open source software. It may be in the immediate economic interest of the other players to participate, but they do so with the tacit agreement that they are agreeing to play in an asymmetric environment where the primary advantages go to the one in the center.

In this real interoperability situation, we use truly open standards that do not favor any one software provider. They allow two pieces of software to work together as they do any two others. Certainly one of the providers might have a superior market position, but it is not given or maintained by the asymmetrical intraoperable situation.

Software succeeds because the application or service is faster, more reliable, more secure, and more scalable, has a better user interface, or, more generally, provides a better quality of service. It does not succeed because a provider abuses the word "interoperability" and convinces others that they play on a field that is level.

Interoperability driven by open standards increases competition, provides more choice of applications to customers, and drives down prices. Customers can interchange, or substitute, one piece of software from one provider for another. The central provider in the middle of an interoperability situation hates this true, open interoperability. Customers love it.

The next time you hear about interoperability, ask yourself if this isn't really intraoperability. If so, further ask yourself if this is best for you or best for that provider in the middle. It doesn't have to be that way. We need to force software providers to stop abusing terminology.

To be clear, I'm talking about software interoperability. Technically, that boils down to the formats used to exchange information, the protocols by which the formatted information is exchanged, and the application programming interfaces (APIs) that software implements to allow the interchange to concretely take place. Collectively I'll call these "interchange formats and methods."

Interoperability is the ability for two different and independent software applications to exchange information without loss of data, semantics, or metadata. To approximate this in plain English, this means that I'm going to give you some information, I'm going to share what I know about the inner relationships within that information, and I'm also going to tell you everything I might happen to know about where the information came from, and how and when it was massaged and by whom.

The words "fidelity" and "faithfulness" are often used when discussing interoperability. These synonyms both mean the exchange of information without loss or extraneous additions. Just as I can compose two sentences that mean exactly the same thing, there are multiple ways of formatting information so that fidelity can be maintained when sharing it. However, when a single collection of interchange formats and methods can be developed and maintained by a broad community of independent users, interoperability becomes much easier.

For interoperability to work, I need everything necessary in order to understand and fully implement the processing of the information. Therefore if you give me information and include something coming from somewhere else, then I must have full access to everything I need to handle that other data. This has implications about the openness and freedom from intellectual property (IP) legal entanglements of all interchange formats and methods involved.

Here are ten ways in which you can tell whether you will be able to get more or less interoperability among software applications:

1. You will have more interoperability when all interchange formats and methods are fully developed as and described by community-driven open standards, including formats and methods included by reference.

2. You will have less interoperability when the interchange formats and methods are incompletely or ambiguously specified.

3. You will have more interoperability when the interchange formats and methods are factored into smaller pieces that can be independently processed yet composed to add greater functionality.

4. You will have less interoperability when there is likely to be one and only one implementation that can fully and completely implement the interchange formats and methods, either by virtue of complexity, large size of the specifications or required implementation, or lack of availability of necessary intellectual property.

5. You will have more interoperability when common features needed in multiple places are extracted and reused when necessary.

6. You will have less interoperability when the interchange formats and methods are redundant and use unnecessarily different representations for the same type of data in different places.

7. You will have more interoperability when the interchange formats and methods do not reflect historical processing errors in one particular software application.

8. You will have less interoperability when the interchange formats and methods tie the implementations in any way to one particular platform, such as an operating system.

9. You will have more interoperability when the interchange formats and methods aggressively make use of other preexisting open interchange formats and methods wherever possible rather than using any duplicatively developed in a proprietary way.

10. You will have less interoperability when the open standards process is abused to promote interchange formats and methods that only serve to perpetuate a single software provider's market share and network effects.

Open standards are insurance policies for customers, including governments. They guarantee that the information created today will be accessible and processible in the future. They avoid private deals with and promises from vendors. They force vendors and other software providers to compete. This creates better products at lower prices. Open standards help avoid single-supplier situations and all the problems they have historically created.

If a vendor tells you that there might be better ways of achieving software interoperability than open standards, ask to take a look at his or her calendar. Make sure they know they are living in the twenty-first century, not the twentieth. Open standards ensure that information will live on for centuries to come.

14   Open Standards: Definition and Policy

Ken Krechmer

Technical standards represent a powerful way for society to influence the use of technology. In the past decade, the need for technology to be responsive to the changing needs of society has emerged. Technical standards that are more responsive to the changing needs of society are called "open standards." But what does open standards mean? Multiple sources of implementations? No intellectual property costs? Standardized in a recognized standardization committee? The standard is the same worldwide? Backward compatibility is maintained? The standard is supported as long as users desire? Open standards mean different things to different people.

Understanding what an open standard is depends on the vantage point of the viewer and the type of technology being standardized. Public standardization organizations, private standardization organizations, different legal communities, economists, software developers, original equipment manufacturers, end users, and different governments have quite different views of open standards and how to achieve them. This chapter explores these viewpoints.

A "technical standard" is defined as a codified (an independent model or written representation) and quantified (measurable) rule, imposed by an authority, committee, or market (Hayek 1973). Using this definition, this chapter describes the requirements that bear on the openness of a standard and proposes changes for the policies and procedures of different organizations associated with both standardization and intellectual property rights (IPR) associated with standards. As these changes occur, standards will become more open. But openness is a direction, not a destination. As will become clear, there are few standards that are completely open.

Developing the Requirements for Open Standards

Different groups focus on specific indications of openness of a standard and the related standardization process. Table 14.1 lists the different groups that may have an interest in a standard and what indications are most associated with openness within each group. This is the first step toward developing the requirements of open standards.

It should be clear that the seventeen indications of open standards listed in table 14.1 are reasonable and desirable in the view of each identified

Table 14.1
Indications of open interface standards by interest group

	Interest group	Indications of open standards
1.	Standards-setting organization	A fair standardization process including:
1.1		Open meeting
1.2		Consensus
1.3		Due process
1.4		Changes only by consensus
1.5		Available and identified conformance procedures
2.	Commercial implementers	Supports fair competition:
2.1		Standard does not favor a competitor
2.2		Private functions are allowed
2.3		Does not make obsolete prior implementations
2.4		Standard applies to all markets
2.5		Acceptable standards documentation costs
3.	End user of implementation	Supports implementation user's desires for:
3.1		Multiple procurement sources
3.2		Standards maintained over the implementation service life
3.3		Standard maintains compatibility with earlier versions
4.	Economists	Enhances communications, commerce, or trade.
4.1		Increases trade
4.2		Reduces asymmetric transactions
5.	Legal profession	Intellectual property rights are not forced or prevented by the standard:
5.1		Controlled intellectual property is possible
5.2		Private features are allowed

interest group. While the viewpoints of governments are certainly important, these viewpoints are not addressed because they are amalgamations
of the viewpoints of the interests identified earlier. The relative importance
of each indication of open standards changes depending upon which interest group is asked. Table 14.2 resolves the seventeen indications into ten
requirements by removing the overlapping indications.

To test the reasonableness of these ten requirements, table 14.3 relates
the ten requirements to three interest groups: creators, implementers, and
users, and compares their requirements with requirements proposed by
the European Union (EU) body for Interoperable Delivery of European
eGovernment Services to public Administrations, Businesses and Citizens
(IDABC). The IDABC listing of requirements is taken from an International
Data Corporation (IDC) technology assessment report, *The Road to Open
Documentation Standards* (October 2006).

The IDABC requirements do not address one world requirements for
the same standard for the same function worldwide, as this is a contentious
issue impacting even the sovereignty of nations that could be required
to support international standards over national ones. The other three
requirements not identified by IDABC—for open interfaces, open
access, and ongoing support—are emerging requirements for open
standards.

How many of these indications of an open standard in table 14.3 are
necessary for a standard to be considered open? Some say standards are
open when they do not include controlled intellectual property (e.g.,
World Wide Web Consortium, or W3C). Of course, this may be unfair to
those who have worked to create useful intellectual property. Some say
standards are open when they are standardized in a recognized standardization committee (e.g., formal standardization organizations such as the
International Organization for Standardization (ISO). However, it is now
recognized that the difference between formal standardization organizations and consortia is often slight (Egyedi 2003). The IDABC notes that
interoperability is a very important objective, yet does not address the
requirement of open interfaces to achieve interoperability. It appears there
is considerable confusion about what an open standard is, as well as how
to achieve it.

Open standards are not an idle desire. The search for open standards
indicates people's need to influence standards that affect them. The pace
of technology appears very fast to people not involved with the standardization processes because they do not recognize how standardization paces
the introduction of technology. Reviewing the history of standards shows

Table 14.2
Condensing the 17 indications into 10 requirements

17 indications of open standards	Open meeting	Consensus	Due process	One world	Open IPR	Open change	Open documents	Open interface	Open access	Ongoing support
									10 requirements of open standards	
1.1	x									
1.2		x								
1.3			x							
1.4						x				
1.5									x	
2.1					x					
2.2					x					
2.3								x		
2.4				x						
2.5							x			
3.1	Each requirement increases the likelihood of multiple procurement sources									
3.2										x
3.3								x		
4.1				x						
4.2				x						
5.1					x					
5.2					x					

Table 14.3
Comparing different views of open standards

	Rights/area of interest	Creator	Implementer	User	IDABC
1	Open meeting	x			x
2	Consensus	x			x
3	Due process	x			x
4	Open IPR	x	x	x	x
5	One world	x	x	x	
6	Open change	x	x	x	x
7	Open documents		x	x	x
8	Open interface		x	x	
9	Open access		x	x	
10	Ongoing support			x	

how standards pace technology and can maintain a balance between public and private value.

The Successions of Standards

Over the course of history, different standards have supported each wave of civilization (e.g., agrarian, industrial, information). The range of standards required to support a new wave of civilization and the associated technologies is termed a succession of standards (Krechmer and Baskin 2006). Each succession of standards utilizes different means to balance public and private interests. Successive standards necessary to support the industrial age are those that define the similarity of objects or processes; these are similarity standards. During the industrial revolution, the importance of creating public similarity standards was understood (Industrial Standardization 1929, 11). The use of patents emerged during the same period as a means to offer value to the entrepreneur. Similarity standards created in standardization organizations that supported consensus and due process, and when coupled with patents, offered a successful balance of the public and private interests.

In the information age, the standards necessary to define interfaces have emerged as the compatibility standards succession. A fair balance of public and private interests has yet to be achieved here. Compatibility standards began with the development of private interfaces. Such private interfaces were controlled by patents or proprietary information. Patents on interfaces have a winner-take-all effect, assuring a very large private gain to the innovator who controls a high-volume interface. Many have recognized the need for open standards for high-volume interfaces. But creating open standards for such interfaces is more difficult than creating open similarity standards.

The open creation, open implementation, and open use of compatibility standards are necessary to create pubic interfaces. To achieve this, a change in approach and policy about interface standards is needed. Different patent examination procedures (e.g., higher requirements for claims bearing on interfaces), different patent policies (e.g., no patents on adaptability mechanisms, shorter patent periods for claims on algorithms), different standardization organization procedures (e.g., only allow intellectual property rights on interface options, evaluate costs of IPR versus performance gain), and adaptability mechanisms are approaches to better balance the public value of an open standard with the private gain possible on necessary interfaces defined by compatibility standards.

A better balance of public and private interests on compatibility standards also requires recognition that similarity and compatibility standards have very different impacts on society. Organizations that deal with both successions of standards need to have different approaches and policies to address similarity and compatibility standards. Compatibility standards define interfaces. Communications interfaces created in standardization committees are mutual agreements, not inventions; therefore the intellectual property claims on the implementations of compatibility standards that define interfaces should be minimized.

In the post-information age a new succession of standards has emerged. When interfaces are computer controlled, they can adapt to different requirements. The standards that define how to identify, negotiate, and select among different interface requirements are termed adaptability standards. Developing and using adaptability standards offer new means to achieve a successful balance of public and private interests for compatibility standards.

Where algorithms controlled by IPR are desired to optimize the performance of such interfaces, such algorithms could be optional, thereby making the interface more open. Adaptability mechanisms allow the selection of such options. Standardization organizations should only standardize controlled interfaces where it is clear that the public good—increased performance of the interface using controlled technology—is greater than the private gain desired by the owners of the controlled technology. The market is the best means to determine if a controlled (via IPR) performance enhancement of an interface provides sufficient value given its cost. Market determination, a basic means to support open interfaces, can only function if the controlled technology is optional in any interface standard.

Ten Requirements of Open Standards

The ten requirements developed in tables 14.2 and 14.3 are fundamental to the broadest concept of open standards. Placing each requirement in context helps explain the requirements and identify where different policies and procedures to support each requirement are needed. The requirements follow, beginning with:

1. Openness—all stake holders may participate in the standardization process.
2. Consensus—all interests are discussed and agreement found, no domination.
3. Due process—balloting and an appeals process may be used to find resolution.

These first three requirements of open standards are related to the standardization process. In the early twentieth century, these requirements emerged to prevent exploitation of the standardization process by dominant organizations or factions. This was very important during the period when there was a single dominant railroad, car company, telephone company, and so on, in each major country of the world. As trade and travel have expanded, the market dominance of such companies has declined, helped in part by active antitrust concerns. The participants of standardization meetings are also more aware of these issues now and more able to counter attempts by one faction to dominate a standardization process.

4. One world—same standard for the same function, worldwide.

These first four requirements of open standards are at the heart of the World Trade Organization (WTO) Agreement on Technical Barriers to Trade, Code of Good Practice (<http://www.wto.org/english/tratop_e/tbt_e/tbtagr_e.htm#Annex%203>). The fourth requirement, the same standard for the same function worldwide, is an important requirement to prevent technical barriers to trade (TBT). Yet, many interface standardization committees create standards for a specific geographic area (e.g., ATIS [USA], ETSI [Europe], TTC [Japan]). The creation of compatibility standards by country or region does not make common worldwide communications easier. One way to address this dichotomy of national and regional

standardization organizations and the need for communications worldwide is to utilize adaptability standards to negotiate among multimode
devices supporting multiple national or regional compatibility standards.

Common worldwide adaptability standards need to be developed in
international standardization organizations and should be required wherever two or more compatibility standards compete to define the same
interface. This should be a new WTO requirement under the TBT requirements. Such a requirement would allow national standards, such as China
and the United States desire, yet support the negotiations necessary to
identify a common communications interface.

5. Open IPR—low or no charge for IPR necessary to implement the basic
standard. IPR is allowed for options and proprietary extensions.

The existing procedures for addressing IPR issues in standardization organizations were created to deal with IPR relating to similarity standards;
they do not work well for IPR relating to compatibility or adaptability
standards. The IPR relating to similarity standards and the IPR relating to
compatibility standards have very different economic impacts. The existing reasonable and nondiscriminatory (RAND) rules of standardization
organizations for IPR are appropriate for IPR on similarity standards yet
are often ineffectual for IPR relating to compatibility standards. IPR issues
have not yet been identified for adaptability standards.

As an example, a cell phone implementer invents and patents a new
battery that provides more use per charge. The IPR relates to the chemistry
of each battery. If the new battery performance were standardized (as
minimum usage time per charge), the standard would be termed a similarity standard. If another inventor created a different battery chemistry that
provided as much usage per charge, that battery would meet the requirements of the standard also. Finally, each user can decide if the additional
cost for longer battery life is warranted by the value it offers. Properly
written similarity standards offer both the implementer and user flexibility
in their choice of new technology.

The case with compatibility standards that define interfaces is quite
different. If the cell phone implementer holds IPR on the compatibility
standard that defines the air interface of the cell phone system, all who
wish to use that cell phone system *must* pay for that IPR without any decision on their part about the value of that IPR to them. Using patents to
control compatibility is effectively an expansion in the applicability of the
patent system and impacts the rights of others. This unplanned expansion
of the patent system must be recognized and addressed.

Computer-based standardized interfaces should include an adaptability mechanism whenever multimode operation is desired. When IPR included in an interface standard is optional, the implementers of the equipment on each side of the interface standard (e.g., cell phone and cellular base station) will have to choose if an option is worth including in their implementations. This gives the implementers a practical negotiating position. Conversely, if a controlled option significantly improves the system's performance, any implementers that did not choose to include that option in their implementations would run the risk of not being competitive with implementers that did include the option. In this manner a market-based negotiation is supported by requiring that IPR in compatibility standards be optional.

Far too often each participant in the standardization process accepts others' IPR into a new interface standard if their IPR is also accepted into the standard. This serves to ensure that the key participants in the interface standardization process gain a part of the royalties that may accrue. While this allows consensus to be achieved, it is not fair to those who have not participated in the standardization process. It is also unfair to users who will ultimately bear the cost of the IPR, often without any input in determining if the IPR included in a standard is desirable to them. It is the high-tech equivalent of taxation without representation.

National courts, governments, and many international organizations do not appear to be fully aware of the impact of an interface standardization process. The conversion of public telephone utility companies (PT&Ts) to private companies offers one example. When PT&Ts have submitted controlled technology to standardization committees for inclusion in an interface standard, it has usually been with the assumption (sometimes stated) that no royalties would be charged because they were a public utility. Where patented technology of the PT&T is already included in public compatibility standards, the future value of that patented technology is assured. When a PT&T patent portfolio is transferred to a private company, the private company receives a windfall (increased private gain from the future patent royalties). In effect, it is a transfer of value previously in the public domain to private enterprise. In 1996, a significant portion of the AT&T Bell Labs patent portfolio was transferred to its private successor, Lucent. After this transfer, Lucent began charging for patents that had previously not been enforced (Lucent 1997). The open use of AT&T's patents included in existing public compatibility standards was an issue that should have been considered in the transfer of these patent rights from AT&T, formally a public utility, to Lucent, a private company.

When multiple companies in an industry gather together to support a specific technology to be standardized, this can be an indication of market dynamics working or it can be an indication of a collusion that prevents other useful technologies from being considered. Where there is controlled IPR and active cross-licensing, standardization of the controlled technology may become a means to prevent others (without a cross-license) from competing. The current government policies do not minimize such practices.

Many of these problems can be minimized by a policy change in the standardization organizations. All controlled IPR should be optional in compatibility standards (see requirement no. 8, open interfaces, to follow), and prevented in adaptability standards. When controlled IPR emerges after the standard is issued, the standard should be changed to make such IPR optional. When compatibility standards can be automatically upgraded over the Internet, making such changes in the standard after it is issued is practical.

6. Open documents—all may access and use committee documents, drafts, and completed standards for their intended purpose.

Committee documents, completed standards, and software documentation should be readily available. This requirement allows any interested party to see any documents that relate to an open standard. In practice, the openness of a standardization meeting is closely related to the availability of the documents from the meeting. All technical documentation falls into two classes: work-in-progress documents (e.g., individual technical proposals, meeting reports) and completed documents (e.g., standards, test procedures). Different interest groups need access to these different classes of documents. Standards implementers and software developers need access to work-in-progress documents—to understand specific technical decisions—as well as access to completed standards. Implementation testers (including users and their surrogates) also need access to completed documents.

The Internet Engineering Task Force (IETF) has pioneered new standards development and distribution procedures based on the Internet. Such procedures have made the IETF perhaps the most transparent standardization organization. Using the Internet, the IETF makes available on the Web both its standards (termed RFCs) and the drafts of such standards at no charge. Using the facilities of the Internet, IETF committee discussion and individual technical proposals related to the development of standards can be monitored by anyone and responses offered. This transparent development of IETF standards has been successful enough that many other standardization organizations are now doing something similar.

Ultimately, as technology use expands, everyone has an interest in technology and the technical documents that describe it. Using the Internet, access to documents and discussion may be opened to all. In this way, informed choices may be made about being involved in a specific committee or project, and potential new participants could evaluate their desires to participate. Open documents deserves to be a requirement for any standardization organization that wishes to be considered open.

7. Open change—all changes are proposed and agreed in the standardization organization.

To maintain openness, all changes to existing standards need to be presented and agreed in a standardization organization supporting the previous six requirements of open standards identified earlier. Controlling changes is a powerful tool to control interfaces when system updates are distributed over the Internet and stored in computer memory. Even with the most liberal of IPR policies, Microsoft would still be able to control its Windows Application Programming Interfaces (APIs) by distributing updates (changes) to users that update both sides of each API at the same time. Competing vendors' products on one side of the same API, without a similar distribution *at the same time*, would be rendered incompatible by such a Microsoft online update. Users recognize the potential of Microsoft updates to cause incompatibilities in non-Microsoft software systems and often avoid using non-Microsoft software in Microsoft environments.

The only way that interfaces can remain open is when all changes are presented, evaluated, and approved with a common distribution plan in a standardization committee that supports the first six requirements already identified. Considering how computers are connected over the Internet, identifying and requiring mutually agreed changes are vital to the concept of open standards. This is not widely understood.

The original U.S. judicial order to break up the Microsoft PC-OS and application software monopoly did not address this key issue (Krechmer and Baskin 2000). On March 24, 2004, the European Commission (EC) announced its decision to require Microsoft to provide its browser (Explorer) independently of the Windows operating system and make the related Windows APIs available to others (European Union 2004). This decision also did not address the necessity for mutually agreed change. "On 10 November 2005, following input from the European Commission's technical advisers (OTR) and an extensive market test, the Commission issued a

Decision pursuant to Article 24(1) of Regulation 1/2003 ('the Article 24(1) Decision'). This decision concluded that Microsoft was not complying with its obligation pursuant to the Decision to (i) supply complete and accurate interoperability information and (ii) make that information available on reasonable terms" (European Union 2006). Unfortunately this decision also does not address the need for mutually agreed changes to maintain "accurate interoperability information." It appears that neither the U.S. judiciary nor the EC OTR understands that a computer-controlled interface cannot be mandated to be an open standard. For such a standard to be open, it must be created and maintained in an open standardization process.

8. Open interfaces—support migration (backward compatibility) and allow proprietary advantage, but standardized interfaces are not hidden or controlled.

The user's economic interests are best served when manufacturers or service providers compete. Without competition a seller becomes dominant and the user's interests, economic and otherwise, are often not addressed. Standards represent a means to help balance the buyers' and sellers' interests, but when everything about a transaction is standardized there is no longer any product competition, only price competition. While price competition is desirable, the manufacturer or service provider also needs to have the possibility of feature competition to motivate innovation. In similarity standards, a balance can be achieved by standardizing some aspects of a product or service but allowing others to be proprietary. For example, a brick's size may be standardized, but color, texture, or strength can be proprietary features. Compatibility (interface) standards also require a balance to offer the greatest value to society. Unfortunately, many people think that all interfaces of a specific type must be the same to ensure compatibility. This is not correct. Interfaces can be made adaptable to support proprietary advantage (private gain) as well as compatible operation (public good).

Interfaces that are not hidden or controlled and support migration can also support proprietary advantage. Such interfaces, which exhibit both proprietary and public advantages, are an emerging approach to interface standards used between programmable systems. Programmable systems with changeable memory make possible multimode interfaces that can be changed to support backward and forward compatibility as well as compatibility to other modes of operation. The idea that open interfaces should embody both public and private advantage is relatively new. But interest is increasing due to the considerable success of open interfaces in facsimile

(T.30), telephone modems (V.8 and V.32 auto baud procedures), and Digital Subscriber Line (DSL) transceivers (G.994.1 handshaking).

One way of achieving open interfaces is to implement a newer technique called an *etiquette* (Krechmer 2000). Etiquettes provide

• connectivity, negotiating between two or more devices in different spatial locations to determine compatible protocols;
• a means to allow both proprietary and public enhancements to the interface that do not impact backward or forward compatibility;
• adaptability, so that one communications system can become compatible with a different communications system (e.g., by uploading the needed software); and
• easier system troubleshooting by identifying specific incompatibilities.

As long as the etiquette itself is common between the equipment at both ends, it is possible to receive the code identifying each protocol supported by the equipment at a remote site. Checking this code against a database of such codes on the Web or in a manual, the user can automatically or manually select compatible operation or determine what change is necessary in their system or the remote system to enable compatibility.

One of the earliest etiquettes is ITU Recommendation T.30, which is used in all Group 3 facsimile machines. Part of its function includes mechanisms to interoperate with previous Group 2 facsimile machines while allowing new features (public as well as proprietary) to be added to the system without the possibility of losing backward compatibility. Another etiquette is the ITU standard V.8, which is used to select among the V.34 and higher modem modulations. More recently ITU G.994.1 provides a similar function in DSL equipment.

As an example of the usefulness of open interfaces, consider Microsoft APIs. Assume that an open standard based upon a Microsoft Windows API is created. Then any vendor could create an operating system (OS) to work with Microsoft's applications or create applications to work with Microsoft's OS that utilize that API. If any vendor (including Microsoft) identified a new function such as a music delivery service or IPTV that was not supported across the basic API, that vendor could then offer the new function, as an identified proprietary feature across the API, to users who have purchased that vendor's OS and appropriate applications, while not impacting compatibility for those who have not. Since an open interface supports proprietary extensions, each vendor controls the way the new function is accessed across the API, but does not change the basic compatibility of the API. In this manner any implementer—including Microsoft—is able to maintain control and add value, based on the desirability of the new functions they offer.

An open interface offers a means to address recent political concerns:

• The French government's concern that only Apple iPods can download music from Apple iTunes Web sites.
• The Chinese government's push for their own communications technology in Chinese communications systems (Qu and Polley 2005).
• The European Union and previous U.S. antitrust actions over Microsoft's proprietary software interfaces (Krechmer and Baskin 2000).

In each of these cases, Open Interfaces that support adaptable operation could resolve the political concerns without any direct government involvement in standardization. David (1987) notes that government action mandating a specific standard tends to produce poor results.

9. Open access—objective conformance mechanisms for implementation testing and user evaluation.

Implementation assessment covers all possible parameters that may need to be identified as conforming for accurate, safe, and/or proper use. Such parameters could include physical access (e.g., access by people with disabilities), safety (e.g., CE or UL mark, the European and U.S. indications that equipment is designed safely), and correct weights and measures (e.g., certification of scales and gasoline pumps) as well as interface compatibility indicated by noting a term that indicates the type of interface (e.g., V.92, WiFi, Bluetooth, GSM). Implementation assessment may be as simple as identifying a known brand or it may require specific testing by implementers, regulators, users or their testing agencies. Conformance may be displayed by a known and controlled identification mark (e.g., UL, CE) or just a specification calling out existing standards.

For products that conform to similarity standards, a simple mark of conformity is often sufficient. In the European Union (EU), the CE marking is the manufacturer's indication that the product meets the essential (mostly safety) requirements of all relevant EU Directives. This specific marking indicating compliance reduces the user's safety concerns. For products that have standardized interfaces, such as communications equipment or communications software, an interoperability event may be needed (often termed a plug-fest) to test whether different implementations interoperate.

The complexity of multilayer communications products makes compatibility more difficult to achieve, let alone identify. Such more complex compatibility standards would benefit greatly from adaptability mechanisms (as discussed under requirement no. 8, open interfaces). These adaptability mechanisms could help achieve the highest level of compatibility. The same mechanisms could identify incompatibility in a manner that would allow upgrades (automatic or manual) to achieve compatibility. Adaptability standards require new levels of testing to verify their long-term ability to maintain backward compatibility. While all other implementations are tested to verify conformance to a standard, implementations of adaptability standards also need to be tested to verify that they ignore what they do not recognize, that is, any extensions to the standard that occur in the future. This level of testing is rarely being done currently; it represents a new criterion for conformance testing for organizations concerned with the conformance of implementations supporting adaptability standards. This brings us to the tenth and final requirement.

10. Ongoing support—standards are supported until user interest ceases.

Users desire that their products, services, and related software be supported until their interest in them ceases, rather than when implementer interest declines. Ongoing support of hardware, software, and services, and their associated standards, is of specific interest to end users as it may increase the life of their capital investment in equipment or software. The support of an existing standard, which directly impacts any products that utilize the standard, consists of five distinct phases (see table 14.4).

It is difficult to interest users in the first phase of standards development (Naemura 1995). Even the second phase, fixes, may be of more interest to the creators and implementers than the users. The next three phases,

Table 14.4
Standards life cycle

Phase	Activity	Description	Major interest group
1.	Create standard	The major task of SSOs	creators
2.	Fixes (changes)	Rectify problems identified in initial implementations	implementers
3.	Maintenance (changes)	Add new features and keep the standard up to date with related standards work	users
4.	Availability (no changes)	Continue to publish, without continuing maintenance	users
5.	Rescission	Removal of the published standard from distribution	users

however, are where users have an interest in maintaining their investment. Currently few standardization organizations actively address maintaining their standards based on user desires. Greater user involvement in the ongoing support of standards would be practical by taking advantage of the Internet to notify users of potential changes in specific standards. Increasing the users' involvement with the maintenance phases of the standardization process may also represent new economic opportunities for standardization organizations. For example, users could, for a small fee, register on the Internet their interest in a standard or group of standards; then whenever a new support phase of those standards was being considered, the users would be notified and could raise any concerns. Much like any concerns raised in the standardization process, the users concerns could be addressed as part of considering the support phase change. Over time such treatment might also increase the users' preference for standards from the standardization committees that offer such policies.

The ITU-T Telecommunications Standardization Bureau Director's Ad Hoc IPR Group report, released in May 2005, includes "on-going support—maintained and supported over a long period of time" as one element of its open standards definition (International Telecommunication Union 2005). Recognition that ongoing support is a part of open standards is increasing.

Policy and Procedure Recommendations

As society becomes more technologically based, standards and standardization become more important. Standardization and intellectual property processes are always evolving and because of this flexibility the standardization systems have worked well. To create and maintain standards that move toward the ten requirements of Open Standards requires further evolution of the policies and procedures of standardization organizations, organizations that address antitrust or anticompetition issues, national patent offices, the World Intellectual Property Organization (WIPO), and the World Trade Organization (WTO).

Essential changes that standardization organizations need to make in their policies and procedures are as follows:

• Identify open changes as a requirement for compatibility standards for microprocessor-controlled interfaces accessible over the Internet.
• Each standardization organization should maintain and publish a listing of how they address each of the ten open standards requirements.

• Only allow IPR as an option in compatibility standards. When such IPR emerges after standardization, change such controlled requirements to options where practical.
• Standardization of adaptability standards to be addressed only in international standardization organizations.
• Offer users the means to participate in the maintenance of standards.

Recommended changes to WTO policies:

• Define as barriers to trade the lack of open change procedures and open interfaces of microprocessor-based compatibility standards.

Recommended changes to EC competition and antitrust policy:

• When interfaces are required to support competition, empower a standardization organization to create and maintain them.

Recommended changes to WIPO policies:

• WIPO should help evaluate IPR claims on international interface standards and make recommendations on when controlled technology should be optional in interface standards.

Recommended changes to individual countries' patent policies:

• Require greater demonstration of uniqueness for patent claims that control interfaces.
• Impose shorter term on patent claims that may control interfaces (e.g., algorithms).

The wide applicability of the policy and procedure changes suggested here indicates the importance of gaining greater understanding of how standardization impacts modern high-technology societies. Perhaps the most important change of all would be to teach the requirements for open standards in appropriate engineering, business, law, political science, and economics courses.

Note

This chapter addresses the policy implications of open standards more than my previous papers on the subject, but the ten requirements of open standards was developed previously, most recently in "Open Systems in Digital Convergence," a chapter in *Strategies and Policies in Digital Convergence*, ed. Sagin Park (Hershey, PA: Idea Group Reference, 2007). In turn that chapter is an expansion of an earlier *Journal of IT Standards and Standardization Research* paper (Krechmer 2006). The latter paper is a significant revision of one published in the *Proceedings of the 38th Annual*

Hawaii International Conference on System Sciences (HICSS), January 2005. In turn, the HICSS paper is a major expansion of Krechmer 1998.

References

David, P. A. 1987. Some New Standards for the Economics of Standardization in the Information Age. In *Economic Policy and Technology Performance*, ed. P. Dasgupta and P. Stoneman, 206–239. Cambridge, UK: Cambridge University Press.

Egyedi, T. M. 2003. Consortium Problem Redefined: Negotiating "Democracy" in the Actor Network on Standardization. *International Journal of IT Standards and Standardization Research* 1 (2) (July–December): 22–38.

European Union. 2004. EU Commission Concludes Microsoft Investigation, Imposes Conduct Remedies and a Fine (March 24, 2004), 45/04. Delegation of the European Commission to the United States. <http://www.eurunion.org/news/press/2004/20040045.htm>.

European Union. 2006. The European Commission's Microsoft Case. <http://ec.europa.eu/comm/competition/antitrust/cases/microsoft/index.html>.

Hayek, F. A. 1973. Cosmos and Taxis. *Law, Legislation and Liberty*, vol. 1: *Rules and Order*. London: Routledge & Kegan Paul Ltd.

Industrial Standardization. 1929. New York: National Industrial Conference Board, Inc.

International Telecommunication Union (ITU), TSB Director's Ad Hoc IPR Group. 2005. Definition of "Open Standards." <http://www.itu.int/ITU-T/othergroups/ipr-adhoc/openstandards.html>.

Klein, Arthur H. 1974. *The World of Measurements*. New York: Simon and Schuster.

Krechmer, K. 1998. The Principles of Open Standards. *Standards Engineering* 50 (6) (November/December): 1–6.

Krechmer, K. 2000. The Fundamental Nature of Standards: Technical Perspective. *IEEE Communications Magazine* 38 (6) (June): 70.

Krechmer, K. 2006. Open Standards Requirements. *International Journal of IT Standards and Standardization Research* 4 (1) (January–June): 43–61.

Krechmer, K., and E. Baskin. 2000. The Microsoft Anti-Trust Litigation: The Case for Standards. *Society for Engineering Standards*. <http://www.ses-standards.org/display-common.cfm?an=1&subarticlenbr=56>.

Krechmer, K., and E. Baskin. 2006. The Entrepreneur and Standards. In *International Standardization as a Strategic Tool: Commended Papers from the IEC Centenary Challenge 2006*, 143–154. Geneva, Switzerland: International Electrotechnical Commission.

Lucent. 1997. Lucent Technologies Announces Plans to License Intellectual Property for High-speed Modem Technology. <http://www.alcatel-lucent.com/wps/portal/ !ut/p/kcxml/04_Sj9SPykssy0xPLMnMz0vM0Y_QjzKLd4y3cAsFSYGZzgH6kShiBvGO CJEgfW99X4_83FT9AP2C3NCIckdHRQB02b-I/delta/base64xml/L3dJdyEvd0ZNQUF zQUMvNElVRS82X0FfQkdS?LMSG_CABINET=Docs_and_Resource_Ctr&LMSG _CONTENT_FILE=News_Releases_LU_1997/LU_News_Article_006356&lu_lang _code=en_WW>.

Naemura, K. 1995. User Involvement in the Life Cycles of Information Technology and Telecommunications Standards. In *Standards, Innovation and Competitiveness*, ed. R. Hawkins, R. Mansell, and J. Skea, 206–239. Hants, England: Edward Elgar Publishing Limited.

Qu, P., and C. Polley. 2005. The New Standard-Bearer. *IEEE Spectrum, NA* 42 (12) (December): 49–52.

Contributors

Stacy Baird   Stacy Baird is a technology, intellectual property, and public policy advisor living in Hong Kong and Hollywood. Baird recently concluded concurrent appointments as a visiting fellow, Faculty of Law, The University of Hong Kong, and visiting scholar, University of Southern California School of Letters, Arts and Sciences. He has served as senior policy advisor to U.S. Senator Maria Cantwell, member of the Senate Commerce Committee. Baird served as technology and intellectual property counsel to the senator when she was a member of the Senate Judiciary Committee. He worked on landmark legislation including the U.S. Patriot Act, the Homeland Security Act, 2002 immigration and border security reform, the Intelligence Reform and Terrorism Prevention Act, and Cantwell's legislation to assist victims of identity theft. Previously, Baird was Brookings Legislative Fellow to U.S. Representative Howard Berman, ranking Democrat on the Courts and Intellectual Property Subcommittee of the House Judiciary Committee. He advised Berman on the Internet and intellectual property issues arising with the advent of Napster. He was responsible for Berman's 1999 patent reform bill to address Internet "business-method" and biotech patents, and was a principal negotiator on the Electronic Signatures in Global and National Commerce Act (E-SIGN Act).

Laura DeNardis   Laura DeNardis, Internet governance scholar and author, is an associate professor in the School of Communication at American University. DeNardis is the author of *Protocol Politics: The Globalization of Internet Governance* (MIT Press, 2009), *Information Technology in Theory* (2007, with Pelin Aksoy), and numerous publications. She is an affiliated fellow of the Yale Information Society Project and served as its executive director from 2008 to 2011. She received a PhD in science and technology studies from Virginia Tech, a master of engineering degree from Cornell

University, and a bachelor of arts degree in engineering science from Dartmouth College.

D. Linda Garcia   Linda Garcia is the former director of the Communication, Culture and Technology Program at Georgetown University, and a current member of the faculty. Prior to assuming the directorship of the 150-plus student graduate program in 1996, she was project director and senior associate at the U.S. Congress Office of Technology Assessment. There, she directed studies on electronic commerce, intellectual property rights, national and international telecommunications policy, standards development, and telecommunications and economic development. In 1997, Garcia received her doctorate from the program in social science informatics at the University of Amsterdam. She received her master's in international affairs from Columbia's School of International Affairs in 1965, and was ABD in the Department of Political Science. In 1963, she received her bachelor's degree from Syracuse University where she majored in international affairs.

Rishab Ghosh   Born in New Delhi, Rishab Ghosh is head of the Collaborative Creativity Group at the Maastricht Economic Research Institute on Innovation and Technology (MERIT) at the University of Maastricht and United Nations University, the Netherlands. He is cofounder and vice president for research at Topsy Labs, Inc., a San Francisco startup. He moved to the Netherlands in 2000, where he researched innovation, technology, and open collaborative production, in particular Free/Libre/Open Source Software (FLOSS) through a series of global research projects. He studied the use of open source software and ICT in Asia, Africa, America, and Europe. His research is funded by the European Union and the U.S. National Science Foundation. He is a founding editor of *First Monday*, the peer-reviewed journal of the Internet, and in 2005, he published *CODE: Collaborative Ownership and the Digital Economy* with the MIT Press. In January 2007, the European Commission published a major study led by him on the impact of open source on the economy, competitiveness, and innovation. Since 2005 he has been on the board of the Open Source Initiative.

Brian Kahin   Brian Kahin is senior fellow at the Computer & Communications Industry Association in Washington, DC, where his work focuses on patent policy, standards, open source, and innovation policy. He is also adjunct professor at the University of Michigan School of Information and a research fellow at the Mossaver-Rahmani Center for Business and Government at the Harvard Kemedy School. Kahin's writing addresses public policy and the political economy of knowledge, innovation, information technology, and intellectual property. Reflecting his own background in academia, industry, and government, he stresses the importance of policy debate and analysis that reflect diverse perspectives, the need for informed, empirically grounded, multidisciplinary policy development, and the need for academic research that is accessible and useful to the national and international policy community. He has edited ten books, including *Standards Policy for Information Infrastructure* with Janet Abbate (MIT Press, 1995) and, most recently, *Advancing Knowledge and the Knowledge Economy* with Dominique Foray (MIT Press, 2006). Kahin was previously general counsel for Interactive Multimedia Association, founding director of the Information Infrastructure Project at Harvard's John F. Kennedy School of Government (1989–1997), and senior policy analyst in the White House Office of Science and Technology Policy from 1997 to 2000. He is a graduate of Harvard College and Harvard Law School.

Brenden Kuerbis   Brenden Kuerbis is pursuing a doctorate in information science and technology at Syracuse University's School of Information Studies. He is currently a researcher and operations director for the Internet Governance Project. He is also a member of the Noncommercial Users Constituency at ICANN, serving as its North America region Executive Committee member. As part of his research, Kuerbis actively follows and analyzes work occurring in global forums such as ICANN, Regional Internet Registries, IETF, ITU-T, and the Internet Governance Forum, as well as domestic venues like NTIA and the U.S. Congress. His dissertation research focuses on the security of critical Internet resources, specifically the development and deployment of Internet standards to secure the DNS and routing system (i.e., DNSSEC, RPKI). He is employing the theoretical tools of institutional analysis and standardization, as well as historical and social network analysis methods. Other projects he has worked on include the governance of global identity systems (e.g., service provider identity [SPID]), and conducting social network analysis of transnational policy advocates involved in the area of Internet governance. His work has been presented at TPRC, ICA, and ITS, and appeared in *Telecommunications Policy, The Information Society*, the *International Journal of Communication*, Circle ID, and on IGP Blog.

Ken Krechmer   Ken Krechmer (krechmer@csrstds.com) is a lecturer at the University of Colorado in Boulder. He taught a three-credit unit course on the theory of standards. He was program chair of the Standards and Innovation in Information Technology (SIIT) conference in 2001 (Boulder, CO), 2003 (Delft, Netherlands), and 2007 (Calgary, Canada), and co-program chair of SIIT 2009 (Tokyo, Japan). In 2006 he received a joint second prize in the IEC Centenary Challenge paper competition. In 1995 and 2000 he won first prize at the World Standards Day paper competition. From 1990 to 2002 he was the founding technical editor of *Communications Standards Review*, a technical journal reporting on standards work in progress in the Telecommunications Industry Association (TIA), the ITU, and the European Telecommunications Standards Institute (ETSI). He has also been secretary of TIA TR-29 (facsimile standards) from 1990 to 1995 and a U.S. delegate to ITU-T Study Group 8 (fax), 14 (previous modem standards), 15 (xDSL), and 16 (modem, video, conferencing) meetings. He consulted on standardization strategies from 1980 to 2000 for clients including France Telecom, British Telecom, NEC, Dialogic, Intel, Ascend Communications, and Pacific Telesis. He is a senior member of the IEEE and a member of the Society of Engineering Standards.

John B. Morris Jr. John B. Morris Jr. is general counsel at the Center for Democracy & Technology (CDT), and is the director of its Internet Standards, Technology and Policy Project. Prior to joining CDT in 2001, Morris was a partner in the law firm of Jenner & Block. At both CDT and Jenner, he has litigated groundbreaking cases in Internet and First Amendment law. He was a lead counsel in the successful 1996–1997 challenge to the Communications Decency Act, in which the Supreme Court extended to speech on the Internet the highest level of constitutional protection. Since 2001, Morris has been actively involved in the intersection of public policy and technical standards, working in both the Internet Engineering Task Force and the World Wide Web Consortium. He is a coauthor of IETF RFCs 3693, 3694, 4745, and 5606. Morris received his BA magna cum laude with distinction from Yale University and his JD from Yale Law School, where he was the managing editor of the *Yale Law Journal*. Prior to becoming a lawyer, he had significant experience in the computer industry.

Milton Mueller Milton Mueller is a professor at Syracuse University's School of Information Studies and professor at Delft University of Technology, the Netherlands. He is the author of *Networks and States: The Global Politics of Internet Governance* (MIT Press, 2010), *Ruling the Root: Internet Governance and the Taming of Cyberspace* (MIT Press, 2002), and other books. Mueller teaches and does research on the political economy of communication and information. He uses the theoretical tools of property rights analysis, institutional economics, and both historical and quantitative social science methods. He has a long-standing interest in the history of communication technologies and global governance institutions. His research has been cited and utilized by policy makers in the United States, Europe, Hong Kong, and New Zealand. He is on the international editorial boards of the journals *Telecommunications Policy*, *The Information Society*, and *Info: The Journal of Policy, Regulation and Strategy for Telecommunication, Information and Media*. Mueller received the PhD from the University of Pennsylvania in 1989.

Andrew Rens   Andrew Rens thinks and writes about the interaction of law, knowledge, and innovation, and blogs his thoughts at <www.aliquidnovi .org>. Currently based in Cape Town, Rens works as legal consultant and conducts research through Intellectual Property Law Research at the University of Cape Town; he is teaching a master's course in telecommunications law at the University of Cape Town Law School. He has worked in academia, private practice, and the nonprofit sector. He was the founding legal lead of Creative Commons South Africa, a cofounder and former director of The African Commons Project, a charter member and director of Freedom to Innovate South Africa, a fellow at the Stanford Center for Internet and Society, and a research associate at the LINK Center at the School of Public and Development Management, University of the Witwatersrand, Johannesburg. Rens qualified as an attorney in South Africa, and was awarded a master of laws from the Law School at the University of the Witwatersrand where he subsequently taught master's courses in intellectual property, telecommunications, broadcasting, space and satellite, and media and information technology law, before spending several years in San Francisco. Rens recently completed a three-year fellowship as the Intellectual Property Fellow at the Shuttleworth Foundation.

Andrew L. Russell   Andrew L. Russell is an assistant professor in history in the College of Arts & Letters at Stevens Institute of Technology in Hoboken, New Jersey, where he teaches American history, the history of science and technology, and social aspects of information and communication technologies. He is a graduate of Vassar College (BA in history, 1996), the University of Colorado at Boulder (MA in history, 2003), and the Johns Hopkins University (PhD in history of science and technology, 2007), and worked in the Harvard Information Infrastructure Project in Harvard University's Kennedy School of Government from 1997 to 1999. His research and writing have been supported by the Interdisciplinary Telecommunications Program at the University of Colorado, the Charles Babbage Institute at the University of Minnesota, the IEEE History Center, and the John Hope Franklin Humanities Institute at Duke University. He has published articles and book chapters on standardization in the Bell System, the American system of voluntary standards, the Internet-OSI standards war, and digital cellular networks in the United States and Europe. His current project is a book manuscript, "An Open World: History and Ideology of Network Standards," that explores the changing rhetoric, rules, and practices of standardization that have sustained American information networks.

Pamela Samuelson   Pamela Samuelson is the Richard M. Sherman Distinguished Professor of Law and Professor of Information Management at the University of California, Berkeley, and director of the Berkeley Center for Law and Technology. Samuelson is recognized as a pioneer in digital copyright law, intellectual property, cyberlaw, and information policy. She serves on the board of directors of the Electronic Frontier Foundation (since 2000) and on advisory boards for the Electronic Privacy Information Center, Public Knowledge, and the Berkeley Center for New Media. She is a fellow of the Association for Computing Machinery (ACM), a contributing editor of *Communications of the ACM*, a past fellow of the John D. and Catherine T. MacArthur Foundation, an honorary professor of the University of Amsterdam, and received the Woman of Vision Award for Social Impact in 2005 from the Anita Borg Institute. Samuelson holds a JD from Yale Law School.

Robert S. Sutor   Robert S. Sutor is the vice president of open source and Linux for the IBM Corporation. In this role he has the responsibility for driving the IBM strategy, sales enablement, and technical presales for software running on Linux and other open source environments. He works with customers, partners, government leaders, analysts, and the press to understand the value of adopting business-critical open source and Linux. He is also responsible for driving and executing the cross-company business and policy strategy for open standards as they relate to software, hardware, services, vertical industries, and emerging markets. A twenty-seven-year veteran of IBM, Sutor worked for fifteen years in IBM Research, specializing in symbolic mathematical computation and Internet publishing. He coauthored the books *Axiom: The Scientific Computation System* (1992) and *The LaTeX Web Companion* (1999). Sutor was a coauthor of the W3C Recommendation "Mathematical Markup Language (MathML)" as well as the W3C Recommendation "Document Object Model Level 1." In 1999 Sutor moved to the IBM Software Group and focused on jump-starting industry use of XML. This led to positions on the board of directors of the OASIS standards group and vice chairmanship of the ebXML effort, a joint OASIS/United Nations endeavor. Sutor then led IBM's industry standards and Web services strategy efforts. He is a widely read blogger and a frequent speaker around the world on open source, Linux, open standards, virtual worlds, and cloud computing. He is frequently cited in the press; was featured in interviews in the *Harvard Business Review*, *CNET*, *eWeek*, and *InfoWorld*; and was quoted in the *Wall Street Journal* and the *Economist*. In 2006 Sutor was named as one of *Computer Business Review*'s "Open Source VIPs." He has an undergraduate degree from Harvard College and a PhD from Princeton University, both in mathematics.

Nicos L. Tsilas Nicos Tsilas is senior attorney at Microsoft. He is also a guest lecturer at the University of Washington School of Law in Seattle where he teaches IP licensing, interop, and standards in the software industry. A graduate of Georgetown University Law Center, he has a bachelor of engineering in electrical engineering and a master of science in engineering management from Stevens Institute of Technology. His publications include "Enabling Open Innovation and Interoperability: Recommendations for Policy-Makers" (United Nations University), "The Perils of Imposing Compulsory IP Licensing to Achieve Interoperability" (The Metropolitan Corporate Counsel), and "Towards Greater Clarity and Consistency in Patent Disclosure in a Post-Rambus World" (*Harvard Journal of Law and Technology*). Prior to joining Microsoft, Tsilas practiced law at Willkie Farr & Gallagher in Washington, DC, where he specialized in telecommunications regulations and policy and in commercial media and Internet transactions. He was an electrical engineer at Westinghouse Corporation before becoming a lawyer. He was born in Athens, Greece, and now resides in Seattle.

Andrew Updegrove Andrew Updegrove, a cofounder and partner of the Boston law firm of Gesmer Updegrove LLP, has been structuring and representing technology consortia since 1988. During that time, he has worked with over a hundred such organizations, and has been retained by many of the largest technology companies in the world to assist them in forming standards setting and promotional consortia. He has written and spoken extensively on the topics of consortia and standards setting and given testimony to the U.S. Department of Justice and Federal Trade Commission on the same topics, and also filed "friend of the court" briefs on a pro bono basis with the Federal Circuit Court, Supreme Court, and Federal Trade Commission on leading standards litigation. In 2004, he was invited to become a member of the ANSI National Standards Strategy Committee. In the summer of 2002, he launched <http://www.consortiuminfo .org>, a Web site intended to be the most detailed and comprehensive Internet resource on the topics of consortia and standards setting. In

December 2002, he launched the *Consortium Standards Bulletin* (now *Standards Today*), a bimonthly eJournal of news, ideas, and analysis with a global audience of over 7,000 subscribers. He has also served on the boards of directors of the Free Standards Group, Linux Foundation, and ANSI. Besides working with consortia, he has a broad range of experience in representing both mature and emerging high-technology companies in all aspects of their legal affairs. He is a graduate of Yale University and the Cornell University Law School.

John S. Wilson John Wilson is a lead economist in the Development Economics Research Group of the World Bank. He joined the World Bank in 1999 and directs empirical and policy research on trade facilitation, standards, and regulatory reform issues, as they relate to economic development. Wilson also provides expertise in World Bank operations and spent two years in the Bank's infrastructure vice presidency. He has participated in World Bank projects under preparation and completed totaling over $1.3 billion. Wilson also provided leadership for the World Bank in the establishment of the interagency Standards and Trade Development Facility. He also developed the concept and provided expertise for the Bank's establishment of the Trade Facilitation Facility in 2009. Wilson is leading the Bank's Development Research Group in support of establishing a new public-private partnership on aid for trade facilitation at the World Bank Group. Wilson was previously vice president for technology policy at the Information Technology Industry Council in Washington, DC, and a visiting fellow at the Institute for International Economics. He was also a senior staff officer at the U.S. National Academy of Sciences and National Research Council and adjunct professor of international affairs at Georgetown University. He has degrees from Wooster College and Columbia University in New York.

Index